THE MILLENNIAL MOSAIC

THE MILLENNIAL MOSAIC

How Pluralism and Choice Are Shaping
Canadian Youth and the Future of Canada

Reginald W. Bibby
Joel Thiessen
Monetta Bailey

DUNDURN
TORONTO

Cover image: Sophie Paas-Lang
Printer: Webcom, a division of Marquis Book Printing Inc.

Library and Archives Canada Cataloguing in Publication

Title: The millennial mosaic : how pluralism and choice are shaping Canadian youth and the future of Canada / Reginald W. Bibby, Joel Thiessen, Monetta Bailey.
Names: Bibby, Reginald Wayne, author. | Thiessen, Joel, author. | Bailey, Monetta, author.
Description: Includes bibliographical references and index.
Identifiers: Canadiana (print) 20190100761 | Canadiana (ebook) 20190100850 | ISBN 9781459745605 (softcover) | ISBN 9781459745612 (PDF) | ISBN 9781459745629 (EPUB)
Subjects: LCSH: Generation Y—Canada.
Classification: LCC HQ799.8.C3 B53 2019 | DDC 305.2420971—dc23

1 2 3 4 5   23   22   21   20   19

We acknowledge the support of the **Canada Council for the Arts**, which last year invested $153 million to bring the arts to Canadians throughout the country, and the **Ontario Arts Council** for our publishing program. We also acknowledge the financial support of the Government of Ontario, through the **Ontario Book Publishing Tax Credit** and the **Ontario Creates**, and the **Government of Canada**.

Nous remercions le **Conseil des arts du Canada** de son soutien. L'an dernier, le Conseil a investi 153 millions de dollars pour mettre de l'art dans la vie des Canadiennes et des Canadiens de tout le pays.

Care has been taken to trace the ownership of copyright material used in this book. The author and the publisher welcome any information enabling them to rectify any references or credits in subsequent editions.

The publisher is not responsible for websites or their content unless they are owned by the publisher.

Printed and bound in Canada.

VISIT US AT

dundurn.com | @dundurnpress | dundurnpress | dundurnpress

Dundurn
3 Church Street, Suite 500
Toronto, Ontario, Canada
M5E 1M2

To Don Posterski
Colleague, friend, mentor,
Project Teen Canada survey series co-founder

CONTENTS

INTRODUCTION

The Worrying Continues ...
and Is Getting Worse

The phrase "What's the matter with kids today?" has become a cultural idiom, removed from its origins as a phrase in a popular movie many decades ago. In the four related books on youth that have preceded this one, a point that has been emphasized is that people seemingly have always worried about the latest youth cohort that has been making its way onto the social stage. So it was that Reg and Don Posterski, in the first of this youth book series, *The Emerging Generation* in 1985, cited educator Anthony Kerr's observation, "I have a pretty fair idea of history over the past twenty-five centuries and I cannot recall a time when the old were fully satisfied with the young."[1] To underline the point, a very old line from Socrates has frequently been recalled: "Children today are tyrants. They contradict their parents, gobble their food, and tyrannize their teachers."[2]

Lest the anxiety level about emerging generations be seen as subsiding as the twentieth century came to an end, Reg noted that a highly respected pollster, Alain Giguere, reflecting on his survey findings concerning the young people of the day, told an Ottawa gathering of the Canadian Conference of Catholic Bishops in 2000, "I tremble to see what kind of society they are going to produce in 20–25 years."[3]

We just never stop worrying about young people. Here we are on the eve of twenty-first century's version of the Roaring Twenties, worrying as much as ever about what the latest youth entry — the Millennials — are going to bring with them and the impact they are going to have on Canada, North America, and the rest of the world.

But there's a distinct difference in the nature of the anxiety this time around. People keep telling us that the impact is going to be unprecedented because of the revolution in technology that the Millennials have experienced from infancy. Pundits are reminding us that this is the first generation in history that has grown up with the Internet and social media; a generation whose genetic makeup has been affected by unlimited information and global communication.

The information and technological revolution of the late twentieth and twenty-first centuries has been of a magnitude that is extremely difficult to comprehend. Because of the way it has encompassed so much of life in tsunami-like fashion, it has taken on an incredible mystique. Most of us cannot begin to grasp the implications. If information and technology have altered how we meet and live and work and play, what kind of an impact is it having and going to have on life as a whole in the rest of the twenty-first century? All the new technology — texting, smartphones, social media, and online everything — has added new layers of mystery to what is going to happen next.

That's our way of saying that, yes, we have always worried about the newest, emerging generation, but Millennials in Canada are bringing with them a greatly magnified mystique. We've never seen anything like them before. As a result, lots of people have lots of anxiety. This anxiety over Millennials occurs at the very mention of the term. An article featured in *The Atlantic* in 2014 begins "We can all agree that Millennials are the worst." With that resolved, the article continues with an almost afterthought, by-the-way question: "But what *is* a Millennial?"[4] This book provides considerable information on who Millennials are, what's important to them, how they might turn out, and the impact they might have on everyone else. In the process, we intend to get past some of the mystique and myths about Millennials and also defuse a fair amount of the anxiety.

WHERE TO BEGIN

In its important study of Canadian Millennials released in February of 2017, Toronto-based research company Environics noted that "much of what passes for analysis of this generation of Canadian adults amounts to little more than anecdote and stereotype," with the Canadian conversation "remarkably devoid of solid evidence about how Millennials live, what they think, what they value, what they want, or what they hope to achieve." Environics made use of an online survey of 3,072 Canadians between the ages of 21 and 36 in July and August of 2016 to provide data on life goals, career aspirations, and political and civic engagement.[5] Similarly, Vision Critical, based in Vancouver with a considerable global reach, released a major overview on Millennials in 2016, drawing heavily on two national surveys with samples of some 800 young Americans early in the year. In introducing its report, it stated, "Companies can't rely on stereotypes about Millennials. They must become Millennial experts and tailor their brands to meet this generation's expectations."[6]

We solidly concur with the need to go beyond stereotypes and conjecture and obtain sound data on Millennials. That's why we have undertaken this project.

A prosaic but important point that we want to underline as we begin our examination of Millennials is that if we want to understand the ideas that people have in their heads, we have to ask them. Rather than standing a safe distance away from young people and pontificating from safe but poor sightlines about what they are thinking, planning, and doing, it's critically important to provide them with the opportunity to tell us what's going on in their lives.

That's what we have done. Through two major national surveys carried out in 2015 and 2016, we have had the opportunity to converse with more than 6,000 Canadians, including more than 1,000 young people between the ages of 18 and 29 who were born between approximately 1986 and 2000. These people under 30 have included the first teenagers in the new millennium — young adults who rightfully can be dubbed "Millennials." Close to 600 are 18 to 23. (For methodological details, see the Appendix.)

Generational Cohorts

Pre-Boomers	Pre-1946
Baby Boomers	1946–1965
Generation Xers	1966–1985
Millennials	1986–2005

What makes the examination of the younger Millennials in our surveys so fascinating is the fact that Reg — through his Project Teen Canada surveys dating back to the mid-1980s — has been looking at their slightly younger, 15- to 19-year-old counterparts over the past four decades. The 2015 and 2016 surveys have repeated many of the items from the earlier surveys, making trend examinations possible. For example, we can readily compare young people in 1984 with those in 2016.

But the ongoing surveys allow us to do much more. Individuals who were 15- to 19-year-olds in 1984 reappear in 2016 — 32 years later — as 47- to 51-year-olds in our latest large-scale national surveys. The same is true for teen cohorts in 1992, 2000, and 2008. By looking at them, respectively, 24, 16, and 8 years later, we can take a peek at how they have "turned out" … so far.

At the risk of making readers dizzy, we also can draw on Reg's Project Canada *adult* national surveys spanning from 1975 to now, which allow us to compare teenagers and adults over a considerable period of time. In short, we have access to a gold mine of youth and adult data that we can draw on, a body of trend data that simply cannot be matched.

From the outset, we want to remind readers that our primary interest does not lie with numbers but rather with ideas. Consequently, we don't want to simply throw numbers around so that this becomes a

A Clarifying Note on the Cut-Off Points for Millennials and Other Cohorts

A quick but important clarification on who Millennials actually are. Let's be clear from the outset: there is no such thing in an ultimate sense as "Millennials" — anymore than the gods have determined what exactly "Baby Boomers" and "Gen Xers" are. Those are simply cohort designations invented by observers who want to distinguish between age cohorts and "generations" that allegedly have unique experiences and collective identities. The precise cutting points are highly arbitrary. We, for example, see no value in coming up with uneven intervals — where Boomers are viewed as born in the 20-year period between 1946 and 1965, but Xers were born in the 15 years between 1966 and, say, 1980 — leaving Millennials to claim a 20-year interval between 1981 and 2000. For example, Environics uses 1981–2000; Pew (2018) has recently declared the span to be 1981–1996 after previously using 1981–2000; Vision Critical prefers 1980–1995; Gallup, 1980–1996; Strauss and Howe (who coined the term), 1982–2004; and Statistics Canada is not specific. These uneven intervals lead to unhelpful pronouncements, such as the Millennials' numbers — like the Boomers' — being "extremely large" — hardly shocking when the interval is 20 years versus 15 years for Xers.

Our starting point is to agree with most observers that the critically important Baby Boomer cohort was born between about 1946 and 1965. For simplicity, we prefer to proceed with similar 20-year intervals for the other cohorts, so that Gen Xers are seen as being born between 1966 and 1985 (rather than conventionally being truncated around 1980), and Millennials follow between about 1986 and 2005. We think our scheme is clearer, keeping in mind, after all, that the cut-off points are hardly precise, especially when we are working with the subjective concept of "generations." The generations "being created" by analysts should not be reified.

Despite the cut-off differences, we believe our statistically created Millennials are roughly comparable to the statically created Millennials of other observers and researchers. The same is true for our slightly larger cohort of Gen Xers.

tedious, statistical monograph. On the contrary, we want to look at the survey findings and attempt to interpret them in the context of everyday life. We will draw generously on relevant material from a wide range of academic and additional sources. In the end, we want the research to help us all to understand more clearly "how the world works."

A conscious goal is to make the material readily accessible. We want to write with clarity. What's more, we want this to be an enjoyable conversation, not a lifeless report written by dull clinicians. For worse, and we think for better, our personalities will be readily evident.

An Organizing Framework

A prominent sociologist from the past, C. Wright Mills, referred to the inclination to get lost in numbers as "abstract empiricism."[7] We can generate no end of data on no end of topics but be at a loss to grasp the "total picture" or context that enables us to make sense of all the empirical findings. The result is being strong on description but light on explanation. It's something like getting to an interesting place but having no idea where we are or how we got there — a playful observation that more than a few observers have directed at Columbus.

The other extreme, Mills noted, is the inclination to embrace "grand theory." Here we can climb so high up the idea mountain that we become out of touch with what is happening on the ground. The thoughts are "pretty" and make for stimulating discourse between a subculture of wine-sipping academics. But, parallel to the old critique of theologians, grand theorists can "be so heavenly minded that they are unable to do any earthly good."

We are well aware of the prominent and prevalent theoretical perspectives that sociologists can bring to the study of society, led by functionalism, symbolic interactionism, critical theory, feminism, and cultural studies.[8] That said, as we carry out our research, we see ourselves as theoretically eclectic, not selling our souls to one perspective over another, but variously drawing on perspectives that we find helpful as we try to "make sense" of what appears to be happening in the world.

For example, we think that the sources of a lot of things found in the lives of young people are fairly pedestrian, learned via well-intentioned parents, friends, and teachers. In other instances, racism, sexism, and exploitation clearly reflect power and privilege issues that call for critical analyses.

In looking at a large number of topics pertaining to Millennials, our approach is to be inductive, looking first at the data and then exploring theories and explanations that we think are helpful in accounting for the descriptive findings. We see the data-theory process as interactive: one informs the other. Some well-known and highly respected observers of youth culture, including Henry Giroux at McMaster University[9] and the duo of James Cote and Anton Allahar at Western University,[10] use critical theory in working deductively from the position that youth are a disadvantaged group relative to other age cohorts. We maintain that the specific appropriateness of such claims needs to be empirically verified. A major contribution to such debates, we believe, are the data that we are making available in this book.

Rather than taking a particular a priori theoretical position on Millennials, we want to begin by posing a fairly simple, structural framework that already has informed the data collection and has the potential to have considerable explanatory value. Our starting point is to recognize that life in Canada has come to be characterized by a central defining phenomenon: *pluralism*. In the face of diversity, there is a conscious effort to understand and accept differences, to interact and learn from one another.[11] Pluralism is a response to diversity.

Its roots are readily evident. Historically, the emergence of Canada has involved the attempt to create a country out of diverse parts — initially the founding Indigenous Peoples and later the arrivals from France and Britain. Over time, Canada's nation-building task has expanded in the course of it having to find ways of incorporating additional newcomers from other countries. It further has had to be cognizant of additional kinds of diversity as expressed in variables such as cultural background, gender, age, sexual orientation, and physical abilities. The country has launched a number of major initiatives to deal with its diversity. Among the most notable have been the Royal Commission on Bilingualism and Multiculturalism (1962–68), the Royal Commission on the Status of Women (1972–75), the establishment of the Charter of Rights and

Freedoms (1982), and the overdue Truth and Reconciliation Commission (2012–15). All such efforts have had a common goal: to facilitate equality and full participation for everyone.

Pluralism has been at the heart of Canadian life, symbolized by the enshrinement of the cherished mosaic metaphor. This is a country characterized by diversity, where people have the freedom to live out life however they want, within the parameters of the law and economic means. The mosaic is an idea that had its roots in the cultural and nationality realm. But over time, its application has expanded to virtually all spheres of Canadian life — including age, gender, sexual orientation, families, leisure, lifestyles, morality, religion, education, politics, law, and physical and mental attributes. Pluralism is Canada's response to diversity. And with diversity has come the freedom to choose from a virtually unlimited number of options.

Life in Canada is centrally defined by pluralism.

Along with pluralism, there are a number of other important sociological concepts that are helpful in better understanding Canadian Millennials. Individualism and choice are chief among them, as ways of thinking and behaving that parallel experiences of pluralism and heterogeneity that are common to nations such as Canada. Millennials, as we will see, place a high value on individual autonomy and authority. They don't want others to tell them how to think or behave. This outlook reflects a broad turn toward individualism in Western society over approximately the past five centuries. Further embedded and magnified in contexts where pluralism is alive and well is the value placed on choice. The trait permeates Canadian life from selecting a political leader through to choosing a school or a religion, picking one's romantic partner, deciding on consumer products in a shopping mall, or — more recently — the identity politics of gender, sexuality, and even race.

Without question, technological advances since the 1980s and the Internet specifically have amplified the "naturalness" that people give to pluralism, individualism, and choice as taken-for-granted plausibility structures to guide daily life. More than any other descriptor, Millennials believe that "digital literacy/social media/the Internet" sets their generation apart from other generations.[12] The convergence of pluralism, individualism, and choice — mediated in many ways with technological advances — in turn shapes how people see themselves and others. Our task in this book is to uncover many of these dynamics at work among Canadian Millennials.

But as we all know well, what happens in Canada is clearly influenced by a number of key determinants, some internal, some external. They include immigration, education, government, technology, the media, the economy, globalization and Americanization, religion, and changes in outlook and values.

Figure I.1 **Key Determinants of Life in a Pluralistic Canada**

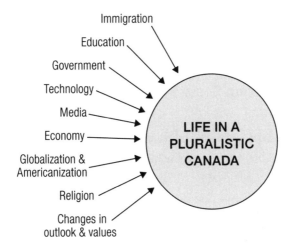

As we look at Millennials, we want to firmly root our examination in the centrally important pluralistic context. At the same time, we want to keep a close eye on the causal roles of these additional determinants and others as well. Understanding Millennials involves far more than seeing them as simply being members of a particular age cohort. As James Cairns has underlined, treating era of birth as the core determinant of ideas and behaviour is to ignore, for example, "inequalities running along lines of race, class, and gender that are far more powerful in shaping experiences and life chances than is shared generational membership."[13]

We also want to see to what extent Millennials themselves — as with previous youth cohorts that evolved into Gen Xers, Boomers, and Pre-Boomers — are showing signs of initiating change. After all, at our best, we as individuals like to see ourselves as more than simply "outcomes" of societal forces. We'd also like to think that we, or at least some of us, have agency, innovate, and bring something to culture and society that was not there before. Cairns puts things this way to Millennials: "Whether the future ends up being more of the same or whether new variations in the real entitlement framework are to come depends on your historical agency — your ability to make history."[14]

In addition to working with pluralism and key determinants of life as our guiding framework, we also will draw on the thinking and data of a wide range of academics and other thinkers as we look at our specific findings. Obviously, a large number of people have much to bring to our wide array of topics.

A Book Label Warning: Sociologists Are Seldom Surprised

As we begin, we need to admit that, as sociologists, we are going to find some things predictable. Sociologists work with the axiomatic assumption that we are shaped in large part by the social environments from which we have come. "New" generations do not get an exemption from that rule.

The things we value and enjoy and believe, for example, are far from random. On the contrary, the fact that we may value honesty or enjoy hockey or opt for atheism typically can be traced back to social sources, led by parents and other individuals whom we view as important. And while most of us like to think that we are free-thinking, creative individualists and, as just noted, we want to be on the lookout for creativity and innovation, the empirical fact of the matter is that most of the ideas in our heads can be fairly readily traced back to the social environments from which we have come. In the words of one prominent twentieth-century sociologist, Charles Horton Cooley, "In the give and take process, we typically take much more than we give."[15]

Consequently, for all the anxiety about the unpredictable nature of new generations of young people, sociologists would be surprised if the differences between emerging generations and existing generations was particularly pronounced. That's not to say that social change does not take place. But change is frequently exaggerated.

Highly respected social trends-watcher John Naisbitt has put things this way: "There is great hype about change and change is the currency of the media. Because we are bombarded with so much news about change, we think everything is changing." But, he says, "It's not true — most things don't change. Most things are constant." We are grounded in basic things like family and children, education, religion, and sports. Naisbitt even challenges the widespread assumption that the Internet, for example, is changing social life: "The Internet is a social phenomenon that by itself does absolutely nothing. We human beings use the Internet to do the things we've always done — to communicate, to be in touch with each other — only do [it] more efficiently and [have] a lot more fun." Naisbitt asks, "Is that change?" and responds, "It's change of a sort, but it's not really basic change."[16]

Given the explanatory framework we are positing, we would expect that Millennials — rooted as they are in a pluralistic milieu that is replete with choices — will be characterized by unprecedented levels of diversity in virtually all spheres of life. That diversity will be accompanied by a high level of official acceptance of people's choices. That's the way that pluralism works in Canada. And that's why we are dubbing them the *Mosaic*

What Makes Millennials Unique: Their Take

Some of the most valuable research on Canadian Millennials has been carried out by Environics and its founder, Michael Adams. Environics has its own sense of the cohort's uniqueness, in describing it as "the newest, biggest and most diverse target market" ever: 22 percent are members of visible minorities, compared to 10 percent of Pre-Boomers.

When Millennials were asked in open-ended fashion to identify at least one characteristic that defines their generation, there was surprisingly little agreement — and one-third could not identify anything. At the top — cited by 27 percent — was the theme of digital access, including the Internet and social media. No other characteristic was identified by as many as 1 in 10. For the record, open-mindedness came in second at 7 percent.

(Source: Environics 2017)

Millennials, and adding as the book's subtitle, *How Pluralism and Choice Are Shaping Canadian Youth and the Future of Canada.*

One final pertinent point about biographies as we begin: our efforts to identify and evaluate change, we think, benefit from the diversity that we three authors bring to the book. Reg is a borderline Boomer, Monetta and Joel are Gen Xers. Monetta is a woman of colour who knows the reality of immigration, having come to Canada from Barbados. Joel and Reg offer male and white perspectives. Reg has been able to monitor trends first-hand since the 1950s and professionally since the mid-1970s. Monetta and Joel are only a few years removed from Millennials and have grown up with Internet and computer-related technology, while Reg has been a later but extensive adopter.

All of this, we believe, has the potential to contribute to an informed and balanced take on the data and trends, not lacking for points and counter-points, correctives, and disagreements. The explicit tapping of our diversity will find expression in our frequent use of boxed inserts to clarify some of our varied interests, interpretations, and points of passion.

With that acknowledgement of our varied relationships to the data, let's turn to Millennials. Our starting place is to look at the things that matter most to them — and to other Canadians.

CHAPTER 1

What Matters: Values/Enjoyment

A s we begin a conversation with people we've just met, we typically start by taking care of basic biographical background details of the "where are you from" and "what do you do" variety. But fairly quickly after that, we consciously and unconsciously invariably zero in on the things that matter to them. "Are you flying to Vancouver on business or are you on a holiday?" "Do you enjoy teaching?" "Are you a Blue Jays fan?" "Are your kids still in school?" "How did you get into music?" Knowing what is important to people is one of the keys to understanding them.

That's where we want to begin our conversation with Millennials.

VALUES

Nickelback's lead singer, Chad Kroeger from Hanna, Alberta, says that when he was 13, he "got to know what it was like to be really broke.

I had to wear a ski suit to bed because we didn't have any heat in the winter. That wasn't a lot of fun." He says he has an IQ of 130 but didn't graduate from high school. "I was a few credits short of a diploma, and I just had no desire to go back to school, because I had a band waiting for me." His father left the family when Chad was two.[1] He now is said to be worth more than $60 million[2] and after having a long-time girlfriend, was married briefly to Avril Lavigne. Regarding the importance of relationships versus his career, Kroeger has had this to say: "Look, my band was everything even when it was nothing. And I will never put another human being in front of my band. Do you have any idea how hard it is to tell a woman you love that if it ever came down to her or the band, she'd be packing her suitcase?"[3]

Lots of values involved in Kroeger's biographical sketch. Lots of interesting choices.

A reminder that a basic starting point in learning about people is to gain an understanding of the things that are the most important to them. If we can get a sense of what they want out of life — *their goals* —we then can proceed to explore what we might refer to as *their means* — how they have chosen to go about pursuing their goals.

Valued Goals

For a number of years, the Project Canada surveys of young people and adults have asked Canadians about the importance they place on a number of goals. We have updated those readings with our extensive 2015 and 2016 national surveys.

From the beginning, Reg has drawn heavily on the pioneering work on values of social psychologist Milton Rokeach,[4] an American who taught for a while at what is now Western University in London and finished his career at Washington State University, where Reg met him as a graduate student. Rokeach differentiated between values that he called "terminal" (goal-like) and those that he referred to as "instrumental" (means-like). Many of his items have been retained over time, with Reg adding some new ones. The list of valued goals given to survey participants was not exhaustive but included many traits of considerable importance to many people.

Generational Comparisons

The surveys show that Millennials — adult Canadians under the age of 30 — place premier importance on *freedom* and *being loved*. Also among the top five valued traits are *family life*, *friendship*, and *self-reliance* (see Table 1.1). Here an age-old paradox is underlined: most of us want a high level of personal freedom to be who we want to be and live life the way that we want to live it. But, simultaneously, we place great importance on relationships — family, friends, and being loved.[5] It is an apparent contradiction that has not escaped the notice of academics.

Consistent with the freedom finding, veteran Environics pollster and values-tracker Michael Adams noted in his bestseller, *Sex in the Snow*, two decades ago, "My reading of Canadian values tells me that none has become more important in this country than autonomy."[6]

This focus on freedom is also evident in recent data from Statistics Canada's General Social Survey on what symbols people value most. The top three cited by individuals in the Millennial and GenX cohorts were the Charter of Rights and Freedoms, the flag, and the national anthem. Among Boomers and Pre-Boomers, the flag came in first, followed by the anthem, and then the charter.[7]

A quick note on friendships. As we all know well, technology has expedited social ties to an extent no one could have imagined. The transformation over just a few decades from letter writing and phone calls to instant audio, video, text, and face-to-face communication has been utterly mind-boggling. Little wonder we call it "social media."

Geographical boundaries to relationships have been erased. Canadians of all ages enjoy new friendships and enjoy established ties with people around the world. Reg recalls his Welsh relatives having to settle for letters and occasional, expensive phone calls to stay in touch. Monetta's family moved to Canada from the Barbados in the 1980s. At first staying in touch with the people left behind was tough. These days she is in daily contact with relatives and friends "back home" with the routine use of things like Skype, WhatsApp, and FaceTime. And it's all not only relatively new; it's also unbelievably inexpensive.

Researchers are documenting that reality. Reg, for example, found that 1 in 5 older Millennials in 2010 had at least one close friend who lived outside

The Dependency Paradox

Recent, widely cited research by psychologist Brooke Feeney of Carnegie Mellon University in Pittsburgh has provided support for the argument that accepting dependence actually promotes independence. Feeney maintains that her studies show that true independence and self-sufficiency emerge because of an individual's ability to depend on close relationship partners in times of need. Attachment theory, she says, suggests that "individuals function best when they have a secure base from which they can grow and explore as individuals," providing them with "the confidence and courage they need to make independent excursions."

(Source: Feeney 2007:284)

of Canada.[8] Two University of Waterloo researchers, Bronwen Valtchanov and Diana Parry, have similarly noted that younger immigrant girls to Canada are making substantial use of the Internet and social media in creating and expanding their social networks in both Canada and their home countries.[9] The same, of course, is true of younger males. Geographical barriers to social ties are a thing of the past.

While freedom and relationships are of foremost importance to 60–70 percent of Millennials, some 1 in 2 also view *a comfortable life* and *success* as "very important." Readers can readily identify with those emphases. We don't have to be social scientists to recognize that the emphasis on consumption and achievement is something we all experience on a daily basis. From the time we turn on our computers and iPhones, we are bombarded with emails and texts from any number of companies and individuals who are vying for our attention and our dollars, and that's before we go to sites where the advertising barrage continues. We can't watch a TV program without having to fend off innumerable commercials that these days even show up on any number of parts of the screen when the programs are running. And those of us who watch sports find that companies routinely are saturating the ice, fields, and uniforms with their names — further throwing in "virtual" ads that appear anywhere and everywhere in various venues.

Table 1.1 **Valued Goals of Millennials and Other Adults**

% Viewing as "Very Important"

	ALL	Millennials 1986–plus (18–29)	Xers 1966–1985 (30–49)	Boomers 1946–1965 (50–69)	Pre-Boomers Pre-1946 (70-plus)
Freedom	77	66	70	83	85
Family life	75	63	74	78	85
Being loved	63	63	59	65	70
Friendship	62	61	55	64	76
Self-reliance	61	59	58	62	73
A comfortable life	51	56	53	48	48
Success	46	52	43	44	50
Spirituality	29	28	25	32	33
Religion	18	17	14	18	29

Important note: In this and future tables, shading indicates differences in the cohorts or other variables involved of 10 percentage points or more, a difference we view as substantively significant.

What's more, let's be honest: many of us like a lot of it. That's why companies spend millions to do it. Thanks to their ads and brand placement, we discover new things that we would like to have and believe we need to have. Visits to the malls and the specialty stores are enjoyable, offering us additional forms of entertainment, food, and drink.

These days, of course, Millennials and many of the rest of us are also enjoying shopping from the comfort of home.

- More than 80 percent of Canadians, led by Millennials, shop online, with more than $6 billion in sales in 2012 and close to $20 billion in 2016. Almost 50 percent of us are buying from foreign sites. Projections see online spending doubling to about $40 billion around 2020 at which point purchases will represent about 10 percent of total retail transactions.[10]
- In the U.S., a similar 80-plus percent of Americans shop online with sales topping $370 billion in 2017. For the record, in 2000, just 22 percent of Americans had made a purchase online. The major criterion for shopping online or in stores? Price.[11]

- Major companies have become well aware that consumers are increasingly blending the physical and the digital when it comes to shopping, payment, and delivery. Millennials and the rest of us variously explore, buy, and order items online but sometimes pick them up in stores. And have you noticed how many people are on their smartphones these days while they are shopping? They're not just talking to friends. Many are accessing their shopping lists, going to product websites, comparing prices, retrieving coupons, and making payments. The dividing line between the digital and physical has been erased.[12]

An annual snapshot of our endless indulgence in consumption? The pre-Christmas sales followed by the Boxing Day sales followed by the New Year's sales. And the parking lots are always jammed. By the way, where did those Black Friday sales come from?

Highly regarded American sociologist Christian Smith documents a series of concerns among the younger cohort (18 to 23 years old) of emerging adults in his book *Lost in Transition* that seem applicable to Canada. Among those fears are the perils of consumerism. He writes, "The American economy's survival and thriving depends upon consumerist addiction to an endless stream of stimulating goods and services that the economy churns out, most of which consumers do not actually need yet cannot do without."[13] But lest we blame young adults for this reality, says Smith, "The fault is not primarily that of emerging adults. They are simply mirroring back to the older adult world, to mainstream society and culture, what has been modeled for them and what they have been taught."[14] Here we have a sociological reminder that Millennials do not grow up in a vacuum. In large measure, they are products of the social environment in which they are raised.

As for *success*, Millennials join other Canadians in placing a high value on achievement. What is one of the most disparaging words that can be said of someone? How about "Loser!"? We don't typically want to be mediocre; we want to be "winners." We want to be successful.

There's not much more that needs to be said.

Of considerably less salience for most Millennials and others are *spirituality* and *religion*. Yet, when we look at religious behaviour, beliefs, and practices, large numbers of Canadians, including Millennials, continue to identify with a religion — although a growing number do not. Belief in things like life after death, angels, and the ability to get in touch with the spirit world continue to be surprisingly prevalent. In addition, in recent years, large numbers of people have indicated that they see themselves as "spiritual but not religious."

The apparent paradox of the persistence of religion and the increase in the abandonment of religion is, we think, something that warrants a closer look. The topic has been one of interest to both Reg and Joel for some time. We'll turn to it in some detail in Chapter 6.

It is interesting to see how pervasive many of these values are across generational cohorts. Gen Xers, Boomers, and Pre-Boomers all see freedom, family, friendship, being loved, and self-reliance as their primary valued goals. However, with age — or possibly reflecting different generational experiences — all but a comfortable life and success are viewed as increasingly important.

Millennials differ very little from other age cohorts in the importance that they collectively give to a comfortable life and success. The 3 in 10 Millennials who highly value spiritualty is close to the same level as everyone else. The 2 in 10 who say they view religion as "very important" is similar to levels of Xers and Boomers. The level rises to 3 in 10 for Pre-Boomers.

In short, Millennials look very much like older Canadians when it comes to what they view as important in life. Relationships are supreme, and material comfort and success know a high but secondary level of importance. Spirituality and religion are important for smaller numbers of people. On the surface, however, it appears that younger adults are placing considerably less value on family life than older adults. Then again, perhaps things have always been that way. Perhaps it's "just a stage" that many younger people go through. After all, who didn't know times of disenchantment with parents, for example, when they were in their late teens-plus?

The Importance of Freedom, a Comfortable Life, and Family Life Over Time

Between the mid-1980s and today, a decline has taken place in the importance young people have placed on freedom and a comfortable life, with the lower levels in each case resembling the levels of Gen Xers. However, there actually has been little change over time in the importance that younger people have given to family life.

Figure 1.1 **Select Valued Goals of Youth: 1984–2016**

% Indicating "Very Important"

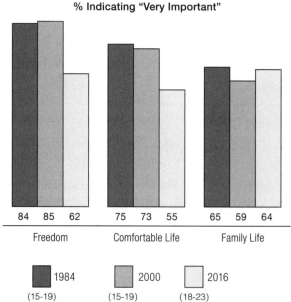

84	85	62	75	73	55	65	59	64

Freedom   Comfortable Life   Family Life

■ 1984   ▨ 2000   □ 2016
(15-19)   (15-19)   (18-23)

Maybe young people today know the reality of both greater personal freedom and more comfortable lives than their youth counterparts in 1984 and 2000. Consequently, these themes don't carry the levels of priority that they did in earlier decades. The teens of the 1980s and '90s were the children of the Baby Boomers and Gen Xers who had lived through the freedom movements. Younger people today have known increased levels of individual freedom. It is largely a given, virtually a right. There are fewer battles to fight.

Changes in What's Important
as Young People Get Older

Because the Project Canada surveys have repeated many items over time, it's possible to carry out "cohort analyses" that allow us to look at the extent to which young people have changed over time — thereby tapping so-called life cycle effects.

Figure 1.2 **Select Valued Goals: Teens 15–19 in 1984**
as Adults 47–51 in 2016

% Indicating "Very Important"

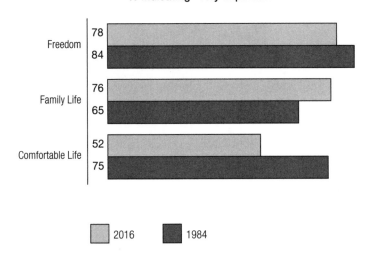

In 1984, 84 percent of 15- to 19-year-olds placed a high level of importance on freedom. As of 2016, the figure for those teens — now 47 to 51-years-old — was only slightly lower at 78 percent. However, the importance they were giving to a comfortable life was shared by far fewer (52 percent) than in 1984 (75 percent). Conversely, family life had become slightly more important overall (76 percent versus 65 percent then). These patterns are consistent with what we have just seen with the survey trend data, suggesting the trends are associated with both changing times and life cycle.

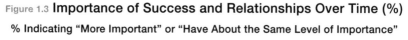

Figure 1.3 **Importance of Success and Relationships Over Time (%)**

% Indicating "More Important" or "Have About the Same Level of Importance"

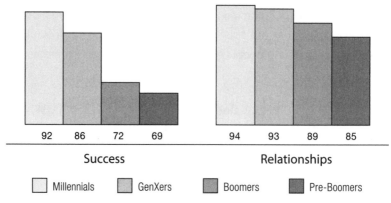

| 92 | 86 | 72 | 69 | | 94 | 93 | 89 | 85 |

Success   Relationships

☐ Millennials   ☐ GenXers   ☐ Boomers   ■ Pre-Boomers

Our findings so far suggest that the "terminal," goal-like values of Canadians have remained fairly consistent over time and across generations, including the declining importance of success with age and the stable-to-growing importance of relationships.

These patterns are corroborated with some additional survey findings. We asked our survey participants directly about the relative importance of a number of things over time, including "being successful" and their "marriage or relationships." What we found is that solid majorities of people in all four generational cohorts, led by Millennials and Gen Xers, say that success has continued to be important (Figure 1.3). But with time, even larger numbers in all four cohorts say that relationships have come to be more highly valued.

Variations in Valued Goals

About two decades ago, sociologist Susan McDaniel, currently the director of the Prentice Institute at the University of Lethbridge, wrote a stimulating article drawing attention to the importance of seeing gender through the lens of generation, using the term "gendered generations."[15] Our surveys show that, in general, women and men — whether Millennials or older Canadians — tend to rank valued goals very much the same. But beyond rankings, there are some noteworthy gender differences.

- What stands out is the inclination for more women than men, regardless of age, to place high levels of importance on relational values — *family life, friendship,* and *being loved.* These gender differences were apparent in our first youth survey in 1984 and have persisted through all of the Project Canada surveys of teens and adults over the years.[16]
- The fact that gender differences have continued through to the present time is fascinating, giving even more prominence to the question of why. Whether the answers lie with "nurture" or "nature" factors — biological and neurological versus socialization and learning — are academic questions. The reality is that the differences continue to exist.
- In contrast, differences by both gender and age are relatively small for traits such as *freedom, intelligence, a comfortable life,* and *success.* But they exist to some extent for both *spirituality* and *religion.*

The persistence of these gender differences with relationships is very important. Why? Because of the significant implications for interpersonal life. Beyond family and friendships, think of the implications for everyday contact in schools and universities, workplaces, in the media, on the Internet, with government, and for life at local, national, and global levels.

We'll return to this important topic shortly.

THE MAGNIFIED MOSAIC
Valued Goals and Gender

	Millennials		Other Canadians	
	Women	Men	Women	Men
Family life	74%	50	83	73
Freedom	70	63	79	76
Being loved	68	59	73	54
Friendship	68	54	69	55
Self-reliance	61	57	65	58
Intelligence	54	63	51	51
A comfortable life	54	58	52	48
Success	52	53	45	44
Spirituality	30	26	35	23
Religion	19	15	21	15

Valued Means

All one has to do to get an animated response from a listener over the age of 40 is to pass on the news that one is writing a book on youth. Invariably and without any invitation, an innocent author is informed that young people today aren't what they used to be — that this is a tough time to be a parent or grandparent. "Kids today are so self-indulgent," one of us was informed recently. "They don't think about anyone but themselves, have no loyalty to their employers, are all about entitlement, and are always on those damn phones."

When people worry about "the next generation," they are not typically troubled about changing goals — what young people want out of life. The likelihood of good relationships and success continuing to be highly valued is not in doubt. Their angst has to do with the persistence of values that make for good interpersonal life.

Dating back to the early 1980s, Reg — with the help of Milton Rokeach — has been asking Canadians young and old about the importance they give to a variety of such interpersonal traits.[17]

Generational Comparisons

It's clear from our most recent surveys that two values that are essential to positive interpersonal life — *honesty* and *politeness* — are highly valued by Millennials. Some 75 percent tell us that honesty is "very important" to them, while about 60 percent say the same thing about politeness. For those readers who are having to suppress some cynicism, remember, of course, that we are looking here at values and not behaviour — a distinction that we will be conscious of throughout this book. But also keep in mind that these values and others are typically selectively applied. Put bluntly, "we pick our spots." We aren't necessarily always honest or polite with everyone. That's not to say we don't value those traits. Some one-half or more also say that characteristics such as *intelligence, hard work, humour, concern for others*, and *forgiveness* are "very important" to them.

For all the uniformity, there is a consistent increase by age in the valuing of all of these traits, with the sole exceptions of intelligence and hard work, where levels are similar to older Canadians. These two exceptions may be due in part to the heightened emphasis across our society on the importance of a good education in order to "succeed." Here Millennials are encouraged and frequently pressured to value intelligence and hard work by parents, extended family, teachers, the media, and politicians. Even humour tends to be highly valued by slightly more Boomers and Pre-Boomers than Gen Xers and Millennials. The latter finding on humour may reflect, in part, the fact that political correctness has meant that topics and targets of humour have been decreasing over time. Bygone days saw many jokes being told about women and Ukrainians and gays and Newfoundlanders. Not anymore.

In putting these findings together, it seems clear that the importance of honesty is down a bit for Millennials relative to other adults. But it remains solidly valued by some 75 percent of young adults and should not decrease significantly in the future. Interpersonal courtesy can be expected to increase, while the importance of working hard — emphasized by many parents and teachers through high school — slips to some extent; it already seems to be on par with older adults. In short, contrary to widespread alarm, there doesn't seem to be much to fear when it comes to interpersonal values.... Well, at least in the case of women.

Interpersonal Values: Period Effects or Life-Cycle Effects?

Do some of the interpersonal value differences between age cohorts reflect different eras or simply people getting older? Maybe, for example, people become increasingly civil as they get older — or maybe times have been changing.

Our trend and cohort analyses, focusing on three interpersonal values — the kinds of values that older generations seem to have in mind when they express concern about today's young people — honesty, politeness, and working hard — show that honesty and hard work were viewed as "very important" by more young people in 1984 than in 2000 or 2016. However, after some slippage in 2000, the level of importance accorded politeness was even slightly above its 1984 endorsement level as of 2016.

Figure 1.4 **Select Interpersonal Values of Youth: 1984–2016**

% Indicating "Very Important"

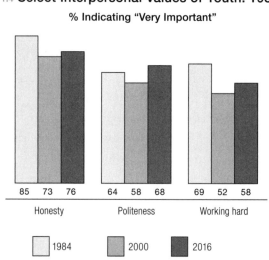

85	73	76		64	58	68		69	52	58
Honesty				Politeness				Working hard		

☐ 1984   ▨ 2000   ■ 2016

Our cohort analysis allows us to look, for example, at the values of 15- to 19-year-olds in 1984 and compare what the same cohort was saying as of 2016, as people now 47 to 51. We find that the importance of honesty has not changed over time, whereas the value placed on politeness has increased and the importance placed on working hard has decreased, consistent with our argument that it wanes as teens "age away" from the admonitions of teachers and parents.

Figure 1.5 **Select Interpersonal Values: Teens 15–19 in 1984 as Adults 47–51 in 2016**

% Indicating "Very Important"

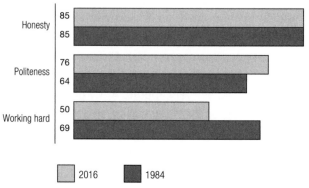

☐ 2016   ■ 1984

Paper Route Anyone?

When I (Joel) was a kid, my parents modelled and stressed hard work for my sister and me. At about 10 years old, I had my first paper route. I was up before sunrise every Sunday morning to deliver flyers, and again after school twice a week. I recall one day when I threw myself over my red wagon with my papers, shouting to the neighbourhood, "I quit," because it was rainy, windy, and cold. My parents would not allow me to quit, teaching me at an early age the importance of hard work and perseverance. These lessons remain with me today. When we think of Millennials and hard work, sociology reminds us of the powerful impact that parents have to influence their kids' narratives on working hard — for better or for worse. In this, affluence, technology, individualism and choice, education, and a comfortable life — narratives and experiences that many parents seek to provide their children — directly impact Millennials' perceptions and behaviours toward working hard.

Table 1.2 **Valued Interpersonal Characteristics of Millennials and Other Adults**

% Viewing as "Very Important"

	ALL	Millennials 1986–plus (18–29)	Xers 1966–1985 (30–49)	Boomers 1946–1965 (50–69)	Pre-Boomers Pre-1946 (70-plus)
Honesty	84	75	80	90	93
Politeness	68	62	65	74	77
Cleanliness	58	47	54	63	73
Forgiveness	56	49	52	60	63
Humour	57	54	53	60	63
Concern for others	55	49	49	61	66
Intelligence	53	59	52	48	57
Working hard	51	55	49	52	53

Variations in Valued Means

At a press conference in Australia in June of 2013, the Dalai Lama called for more leaders with compassion and added, "In that respect, biologically, females have more potential. Females have more sensitivity about others' well-being."[18]

Such an assertion is certainly contested by many academics, who offer an array of explanations for why women are more likely than men to explicitly say that they value social compassion.[19] Monetta, for example, reminds us of the important causal roles of both socialization and marginalization. Young women are taught to be caring; they also can empathize and sympathize with those who are marginalized. While the precise sources are debated, our Project Canada surveys dating back to the 1970s have consistently found females to be more inclined than males to place a high value on virtually any traits of a personal and relational nature. In addition, the same pattern holds for any number of interpersonal values, and for Millennials as well as older age groups.

- Those traits include honesty, politeness, working hard, cleanliness, forgiveness, humour, and concern for others.
- The levels of Millennial women tend to be lower than older women so far, but nonetheless are consistently higher than the levels of Millennial men.

As we just mentioned in our reflections on gender differences and valued goals, we think that these findings are extremely important. They have far-reaching implications for the potential impact on Canadian life as women continue to have increasing influence and power.

Increasingly since the 1960s, women have moved from the margins to the centre of Canadian life. Their potential for influence in all spheres of Canadian society has increased dramatically as they have flooded spheres such as education, commerce, the media, politics, the civil service, health, entertainment, and religion. To an unprecedented extent, people across the country have become aware of issues championed, in particular, by women — such as sexual assault, harassment, child abuse, gender inequities, daycare, minimum wages, parental leave, and children with special needs. In the past few years, the #MeToo movement, for example, has had a dramatic global impact on the awareness of sexual misconduct and violence. Much work still remains in many of these areas, yet significant strides have been taken in recent Canadian history.

Women, with their heightened inclination to value relationships and social compassion more than men, have been playing and will continue to play a pivotal role in bringing out some of the most valued features of pluralism — equality and safety, interpersonal tolerance and respect, cultural acceptance and adoption.

On the heels of the 1992 Project Teen Canada national survey, Reg and his co-author Don Posterski drew extensive attention at the time to similar differences in civility and compassion levels between young women and young men in their best-selling book, *Teen Trends: A Nation in Motion.*[20] "One of the striking findings of the surveys," they wrote, "is the consistent tendency of young women to outdistance males in the positive attitudes they have toward others. Regardless of whether we are talking about interpersonal values, social concerns, or resolving problems, the findings remain the same," they pointed out. "Young females are far more caring, sympathetic, and responsive toward people in general and the d$privileged in particular."

Reg and Don added this concluding observation to underline their point: "This is one instance of a gender gap that most of us would like to

THE MAGNIFIED MOSAIC
Valued Means and Gender

	Millennials		Other Canadians	
	Women	Men	Women	Men
Honesty	82%	67	90	82
Politeness	68	56	78	64
Working hard	58	51	54	48
Cleanliness	51	43	64	57
Forgiveness	54	42	67	47
Humour	58	50	63	52
Concern for others	54	43	68	46

see closed, not by having women match men, but by having men match women — where the level of male concern for others is raised to that exhibited by females."[21]

We likewise think that these days, beyond merely debating why it exists, high priority needs to be given to closing "the compassion gap."

ENJOYMENT

Everyone wants to be happy — at least in Canada, the United States, and much of the world. But before we begin to focus on how happiness is being experienced in Canada, we want to throw in a caveat: happiness may not be the goal of everyone.

Recently, two Americans teamed up to pen an article for *Scientific American* in which they argued that not everyone wants to be happy. Jennifer Aaker, a social psychologist at Stanford, and Emily Esfahani Smith, a Connecticut-based journalist who specializes in culture and relationships, wrote that Americans are obsessed with happiness, but many other cultures see things differently. In some parts of the world, they maintain, people are suspicious of individual happiness, giving greater emphasis to social harmony. In East Asia, for example, pleasure is associated with fulfilling relational obligations. "Personal happiness," they write, "can become aversive, particularly when it comes at cost to the social harmony or moral obligations held in high esteem." They conclude that perhaps American culture needs a more balanced approach to happiness: "In some moments, we may need and benefit from feeling good, but in other moments, we might be better served anchoring on balanced, meaningful life focused on others."

Okay. But allowing for cultural and personal variations, the empirical fact of the matter is that, for better or worse, most Canadians want to be happy, regardless of the importance that they place on other people likewise being happy.

What's more, the vast majority claim to be experiencing it. Some 83 percent of Millennials say they are either "very happy" or "pretty happy" — close to the same level as that of Gen Xers (86 percent) and Baby Boomers (89 percent). Pre-Boomers, born before 1946 and now over 70, are a particularly buoyant bunch, readily exceeding everyone else at 97 percent. So much for the stereotype that our oldest Canadians, beset with health and financial problems, are a disgruntled crowd!

Yet, as we are reminded in the Environics report on Millennials, life satisfaction more generally tends to increase with income and education, as well as stability of employment and relationships (e.g., marriage).[22] In fact, as we note in several places in our analysis — consistent with thousands of sociological studies across time and space — these variables go a long way to accounting for people's attitudes and behaviours.

Generational Comparisons

So, what's the secret of happiness? In five words, *good ties with other people*. Reflecting the importance that they give to relationships, Millennials and everyone else report that their primary sources of enjoyment tend to be *family* and *friends*. *Siblings* specifically are important to Canadians of all ages. *Marriage* and *children* are not yet as important to Millennials as they are to older individuals. *Parents* and *grandparents* are especially important to younger adults — who typically still have them. And don't underestimate the importance of *pets*. According to the most recent data, about 4 in 10 Canadian households — some 7.5 million — have pets, led by around 9 million cats and 8 million dogs.[23] Contrary to stereotypes, *pets* are not as significant in the lives of people over 70 as people who are younger, in large part because older people are no longer able to have them. We'll come back to the importance of relationships, including pets, when we look at families in more detail in Chapter 5.

Jobs, a topic we say more about in Chapter 7, are seen by only about 40 percent of Millennials and other Canadians as a noteworthy enjoyment source — perhaps a bit surprising given the central place jobs have in most people's everyday lives. Presumably jobs are viewed as a means to a financial end for large numbers of people, where the high points are the end of the week or the end of shifts, along with days off and summer holidays.

An important asterisk: when we isolate people who have jobs — versus asking the question of everyone — the enjoyment figure increases to 57 percent. Here enjoyment increases by age: 52 percent for Millennials, 53

Table 1.3 **Social Sources of Enjoyment for
Millennials and Other Adults**

% Indicating Receive "A Great Deal" or "Quite a Bit" of Enjoyment

	ALL	Millennials 1986–plus (18–29)	Xers 1966–1985 (30–49)	Boomers 1946–1965 (50–69)	Pre-Boomers Pre-1946 (70-plus)
Family life generally	87	80	87	88	94
Friends	81	82	77	82	89
Marriage/ relationship	65	46	67	69	71
Your child/children	59	20	59	70	86
Your mother	52	74	58	43	23
Brother(s) or sister(s)	52	56	46	53	54
Your pets	48	47	51	49	33
Your father	41	61	48	31	20
Your job	39	39	46	38	22
Your grandparents	28	48	31	18	18

percent for Gen Xers, 63 percent for Boomers, and no less than 77 percent for the small number of Pre-Boomers over 70 (5 percent of the workforce). Pre-Boomers and Boomers — the oldest people in the paid workforce — are also the people who, overall, enjoy their jobs the most and seemingly carry them out with high levels of enthusiasm, experience, and expertise. It's a Canadian labour force illustration of the axiomatic law of the survival of the fittest. Not wise from the standpoint of optimum human resources to call for their ejection from the paid workforce.... (Obviously Bibby, the self-described "borderline Boomer," wrote the first draft of those lines, but Thiessen and Bailey signed off on them.)

Apart from relationships, Millennials say they receive considerable enjoyment from four things in particular — their *leisure activities, music,* the *Internet,* and *being by themselves.* Older adults give similar importance to those sources, except for ranking enjoyment from their *houses and*

Millennials and the YOLO Outlook

Canadian rapper Drake popularized these words in his 2011 song "The Motto": "You only live once — that's the motto ... YOLO." And with that, Millennials had a marching call to happiness. The hashtag YOLO appeared on Twitter, Instagram, and on other social media outlets. YOLO encouraged young people to live their lives to the fullest whether through travelling, working hard, pursing their goals, or fighting for social change.

For an age group that seemingly gives limited thought to dying, the acronym underlined the idea that life is short and should be enjoyed to the fullest. Recent research published in the *Journal of Positive Psychology* suggests there is merit to such an outlook. Researchers asked a sample of American university students to imagine that they only had 30 days left in their current location, and to engage in activities and associate with people they would miss. When compared to the control group facing no such impending move, students in the experimental group reported higher levels of well-being.

Maybe there is something to the YOLO outlook after all.

(Source: Layous et al., 2017)

apartments higher and enjoyment from the Internet a bit lower (see Table 1.4). There's little doubt Millennials are making use of technology to enjoy relationships. Vision Critical makes the observation that "Where previous generations typically found community through religion, workplace and neighborhood, Millennials find it online" in ways that are "as rich and rewarding as any local pub or church basement."[24] Statistics Canada tells us that "nearly 100 percent of youth aged 15 to 24 use the Internet on a daily basis" with usage very similar regardless of geographical location or income levels.[25] Still, maybe all that time spent on phones and the Internet is resulting in Millennials gaining renewed appreciation for also having the chance to spend some time alone.

Reading is a significant source of enjoyment for about 65 percent of Millennials. Contrary to common allegations, Millennials *are* still reading and on a level that exceeds other adults. Neil Howe, a prominent American youth trend-watcher, drawing on recent Pew research, claims that in the

U.S. "Millennials lead other generations in reading and still generally prefer print books to e-books." Howe says that younger Millennials, 18 to 29, are the age group most likely to have read a book in any format over the past year, usually for a specific purpose such as work, school, or research but also for pleasure or to keep up with events. Millennials are far more likely than older adults to read digital books. But only about 6 percent read digital books exclusively. Howe concludes, "Millennials are not giving up traditional books, but they are trending more toward phones and tablets."[26]

Pew's research has further found that Millennials under 35 are more likely than other cohorts to use libraries. The research centre notes that the high library use in part seems to reflect important changes in public libraries over the past 20 years or so, where young people are now able to make extensive use of computers and the Internet in libraries.[27]

And, for all the talk about cable-cutting tied to the Internet alternative, *television* is hardly being totally abandoned. Close to 60 percent of Millennials and other Canadians say they receive a high level of enjoyment from television. What's more, 62 percent of Millennials who are enjoying the Internet are also enjoying TV, while 85 percent who enjoy TV also enjoy the Internet. There is a lot of overlap between the two platforms. Cables might be getting cut, but TV sets are still being turned on. Still, U.S. Millennials are more likely to watch cable TV on devices other than a television set and also more likely to subscribe to Netflix than cable TV.[28]

As for *sports*, journalists and others who cover sports are inclined to think that most Canadians are avid sports fans. Two out of the three of us are — but surveys over the years have found that most Canadians are not! Our 2015–16 surveys show that only about 1 in 3 Millennials and other adults say that they receive a high level of enjoyment from sports, a level well below that of leisure activities more generally (85 percent).

When it comes to *email* and *cell phones*, generational differences are dramatic: a simple rule of thumb is that younger Canadians enjoy their cells, older Canadians their email. We see this with our students. We are hard pressed to reach them or receive timely responses via email. But we know, because they tell us, that life would be much easier for them, and in turn us, if we could communicate with them by texting.

What is important to keep in mind as we look at any number of enjoyment areas and life in general is the central role that the Internet and social media are playing in the lives of young people. Let's be clear: Canadians of all ages are using the Internet. Statistics Canada says, as of 2016, usage levels had reached 90 percent for people 15 to 44 but also had passed 80 percent for individuals 65 to 74, and 50 percent for people 75 and older. [29]

That said, Millennials are fairly distinct in their approach to technology and social media. A Pew study on American Millennials shows that they are far more likely than older cohorts to do any of the following: create social networking profiles, use social networking sites, post messages to an online profile, post videos of themselves online, access news online, play video games online, and text. Millennials also view technology more positively than other adults in terms of it making life easier and tasks more efficient, as well as strengthening social ties. Such views increase with education.[30]

Table 1.4 **Other Sources of Enjoyment for Millennials and Other Adults**

% Indicating Receive "A Great Deal" or "Quite a Bit" of Enjoyment

	ALL	Millennials 1986–plus (18–29)	Xers 1966–1985 (30–49)	Boomers 1946–1965 (50–69)	Pre-Boomers Pre-1946 (70-plus)
Your leisure activities	85	86	85	84	87
Your house/ apartment	76	63	74	81	90
Music	74	82	72	71	71
Being by yourself	68	73	70	64	66
Reading	67	62	63	70	74
Internet generally	65	79	66	57	66
Television	59	54	61	60	62
Email	40	30	36	42	63
Your car	39	34	36	40	55
Sports	36	40	40	32	33
Your cell phone	31	54	37	18	17

Figure 1.6 **Youth Enjoyment from Internet, Email, Cell Phone, and Being by Oneself: 2000–2016* (%)**

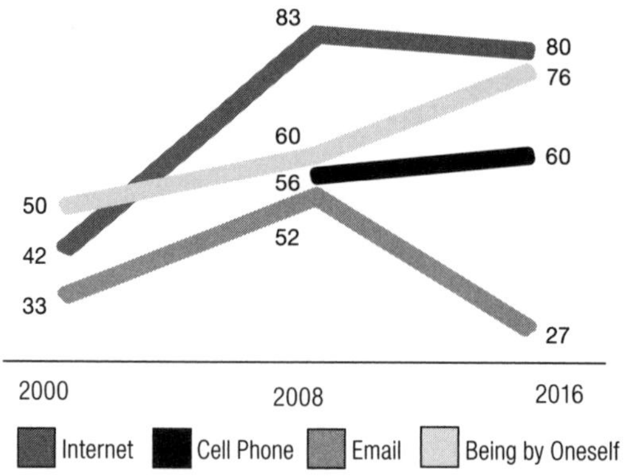

*2000 & 2008: ages 15–19; 2016: ages 18–23

But the benefits and drawbacks of technology, particularly the smartphone, are increasingly being debated. Jean Twenge, a psychologist at San Diego State University, notes in *The Atlantic* that the "iGen" — the group after Millennials — are hanging out with friends less, in no rush to get their driver's licences, dating less, and getting less sleep, all the while feeling more lonely.

We will pick up this theme and more of Twenge's research in the next chapter. But this comment from one of the individuals she interviewed is telling as we begin to grapple with the impact of technology and smartphones on younger generations: "Like her peers, Athena is an expert at tuning out her parents so she can focus on her phone. She spent much of her summer keeping up with friends, but nearly all of it was over text or Snapchat. 'I've been on my phone more than I've been with actual people,' she said. 'My bed has, like, an imprint of my body.'"[31]

The Trend and Cohort Findings

Trend-wise, since 2000, enjoyment from the *Internet* and *cell phones* is up for young people while enjoyment from *email* is down. The proportion of youth indicating they receive a high level of enjoyment from *being alone* has increased from 50 percent in 2000 to 76 percent today.

We want to keep an eye on at least a couple of these patterns. One would think that greater use of the Internet and involvement in social networks would lead to more social interaction and lower levels of loneliness, for example.

But here we see the seemingly paradoxical pattern of young people enjoying the Internet and cell phones, yet also — in greater numbers — enjoying being alone. Part of the equation, we think, is the fact that people have larger homes and fewer children than ever before. More square footage opens up the possibility for more alone time in rooms and places that constitute one's "own spaces." Add today's technology and an individual obviously can be "alone without being lonely." A young person who was alone in a room with a book in days gone by is a far cry from the young person of today who is alone in a room with an iPhone, complete with phone, text, FaceTime, Skype, Facebook, iTunes, YouTube, and unlimited website possibilities. While those choices hardly require solitude, they can make "being alone" an attractive option to anything else. Maybe nothing to worry about — as we all know, being alone is hardly the same as being lonely. Still, at minimum the findings are a cause for pause.

Monetta reminds us that another factor to consider in the loneliness of Millennials is their immigrant status or ethnic origin. Research shows that those who move to Canada, particularly women, express higher levels of loneliness than others due to loss of networks.[32]

We'll come back to this topic in more detail shortly when we look at the kinds of things that trouble young people.

Compared to the mid-1980s, young people today — perhaps reflecting the greater number of choices, including the option of spending more time alone — are less likely to report that they are receiving high levels of enjoyment from friends, music, and television. Enjoyment from moms, dads, siblings, grandparents, and pets, however, has changed little. There are not as many options in those areas.

The significant drop in the enjoyment of sports is worth looking at in a bit more detail. The Project Teen Canada surveys of 15- to 19-year-olds through 2008, and extended with the current examination of the roughly comparable 18- to 23-year-old cohort, have found that the interest in pro

Table 1.5 **Youth Enjoyment Sources: 1984 and 2016**

% Indicating Receive "A Great Deal" or "Quite a Bit" of Enjoyment

	1984 (15–19)	2016 (18–23)
Friends	96	85
Music	94	81
Your mother	79	79
Reading	41*	67
Your father	74	66
Brother(s) or sister(s)	54	59
Your grandparents	56	54
Television	69	54
Your pets	48*	46
Sports	73	38

*1992; not in 1984 survey

Millennials: The Multi-Screen Generation

Vision Critical has done considerable research on Millennials and the media. VC notes that the media and entertainment industries in North America are currently at a disruptive peak. "All the traditional measures of success are in decline," including newspaper and magazine readership, radio and television audiences, and movie theatre attendance. "Millennials, with their preference for technologies that give them greater control, have fuelled the emergence of digital content and on-demand streaming. They're cord-cutters, file sharers and avid streamers." Millennials in the U.S. spend twice as much time in a week on computers and smartphones (30 hours) as they do watching TV (15 hours).

Millennials, says Vision Critical, "can't stand it when advertising gets in the way of their content." Advertising is effective to the extent that it draws their attention to products, but "they'd rather turn to their personal and online social networks, or even to Google searches, for advice and information" as "part of their own streaming when it suits them."

(Source: Vision Critical 2016:17, 19)

sports among Canadian young people has decreased over the past 25 years (see Table 1.6). Apart from "period effects," the cohort analysis — where teens who were 15 to 19 in 1992 and offered updated responses as 39- to 43-year-olds in 2016 — suggests that, as people have aged, their interest in the NHL and professional football has remained essentially the same. However, they "have grown out" of their teenage intrigue with the NBA. Baseball interest has gone up and down, primarily in keeping with the ups-and-downs of the Blue Jays and their heavy following in southern Ontario.

In recent years, the sports fraternity has been increasingly concerned about the decline in television ratings. Even the seemingly invincible National Football League experienced a significant drop in ratings over the 2016 and 2017 seasons.[33]

However, in Canada, buttressed by extensive corporate support and powerful ownership of teams in Toronto in particular, the image is that sports interest is on the rise. Leagues such as the NHL and MLS, in particular, seem to be thriving. The number of TSN and Sportsnet specialty channels has been multiplying. The level of sports interest in the country seems to be unprecedented. These survey data, however, say otherwise. The key reason, we think: the explosion of entertainment choices.

Table 1.6 **Youth Interest in Pro Sports 1992–2016: Period and Cohort Effects**

% Indicating Follow "Very Closely" or "Fairly Closely"

	1992 (15–19)	2000 (15–19)	2008 (15–19)	2016 (18–23*)	2016 (39–43*)
NHL	45	34	35	37	46
MLB	33	17	10	15	22
NBA	27	30	21	17	13
NFL	26	21	19	14	22
CFL	22	16	14	14	20
MLS	—	—	—	11	9

*Special Project Canada survey, April 2016: N, 18–23 = 96, 39–43 = 93. Averaged with Vision Critical survey, April 2015: N, 18–23 = 276 (total 372), 39–43 = 255 (total 348)

Variations in Enjoyment

We want to continue to keep a close eye on gender and generations.

- *Millennial women* exceed their male counterparts in the levels of enjoyment they say they receive from family and pets.
- On the technological front, *Millennial men* are more inclined than Millennial women to receive a "great deal" or "quite a bit" of enjoyment from the Internet and sports. That said, young women outdistance young men in the levels of enjoyment they receive from their cell phones and music.
- *Millennial women and men* are equally inclined to say that they receive high levels of enjoyment from friends, being by themselves, and watching television.
- *Boomers, Gen Xers, and Pre-Boomers* know few gender differences when it comes to areas of enjoyment, with the exception of women being more inclined to enjoy reading, pets, email, and cell phones and considerably less likely to enjoy sports.

ASSESSMENT

We don't have much to worry about when we look at Millennials and what they want out of life. They are looking like their parents and grandparents in wanting to experience both a high level of personal freedom and good relationships. Beyond that, they also want to live well — to be successful and have comfortable lives. Environics has documented the same emphases: "What Millennials most want to have in their lifetime is positive family or partner relationships, followed by financial security and a meaningful career or work."[34] Gallup says that similarly, Millennials in the U.S. "want to have high levels of well-being"; purposeful lives; social ties; steady; engaging jobs; and financial stability.[35]

On the interpersonal front, they continue to value core traits such as honesty and politeness. Other characteristics important to social civility, such as concern for others and politeness, working hard and humour, also continue to be highly valued by large numbers of Millennials and other Canadians.

Those values are reflected in what Millennials and others enjoy. John Naisbitt seems to be right: technology, led by the Internet, is altering how we relate to each other. Yet what we enjoy has not changed very much, at least not in recent decades.

That said, the ability to go online via any number of devices, communicate with others, and be entertained by enumerable sites in keeping with interests and tastes is having one important consequence: more young people today are choosing to spend time by themselves and less time with friends. The wide range of activity choices also means that they are less inclined than young people in the past to rely so heavily on music as a source of enjoyment. The same is true of television and, in particular, sports. In the past, sports were particularly important to males; now they, like their female counterparts, have any number of alternatives.

In many ways, "what matters" to young people hasn't changed a great deal; however, the ways that they can engage with the things that matter have been changing, in large part because of the new possibilities that technology has brought into being. So it is that the ways in which Millennials can enjoy the things they enjoy the most — relationships, music, reading, the Internet, cell phones, television, leisure time — have been becoming increasingly varied.

This brings us back to the central interpretive framework that we are using. As we pointed out in the Introduction, life in Canada has come to be characterized by accelerated diversity as a result of immigration, education, technology, globalization, changes in outlook, and more. At the same time that greater diversity is associated with unprecedented choices and a rise in individualism, considerable societal effort — led by governments and educational institutions — has been expended on finding ways for diversity to contribute to positive collective life. Centrally important has been the promotion of pluralism — the highly conscious effort to understand and accept differences and to interact and learn from one another.[36] The ideal of pluralism is the Canadian response to diversity. So when we look at values and sources of enjoyment, we see a mixture of importance given both to individual and interpersonal life.

There we have it — lots of things being enjoyed by Millennials and others. But like every generation before them, Millennials do not lack for concerns, personally and socially. That's the topic we want to turn to next.

THE MAGNIFIED MOSAIC
Enjoyment and Gender

	Millennials		Other Canadians	
	Women	Men	Women	Men
Family	85%	73	90	87
Friends	82	82	83	79
Music	87	78	74	70
Being by yourself	75	72	69	65
Internet	74	85	62	62
Reading	71	54	79	56
Cell phone	59	49	30	22
Pets	56	37	53	42
Email	29	32	47	37
Sports	31	49	24	46
Television	59	50	61	60
Your car	33	34	41	40

CHAPTER 2

Their Concerns: Personal/Social

As we all know well, a fundamental reality of life is that sources of enjoyment co-exist with sources of strain. After all, in the words of the well-worn Buddhist proverb, "Life is difficult." Dartmouth history professor and best-selling author Darrin McMahon, who specializes in the study of happiness, has recently put things this way: "A life of happiness will necessarily involve considerable pain. Flourishing involves knowing how to deal with and respond to setbacks. If you think about it, happiness would lose its meaning without its opposite."[1]

Canadians of all ages have dreams. But we also have our personal and social concerns. We can spin them as "challenges" and "opportunities." Regardless, they get in the way of good things and call for a response.

PERSONAL CONCERNS

In order to get a sense of what kinds of things trouble Millennials and other Canadians, we provided our survey participants with a list of 30 common areas of concern — many of which have appeared in Reg's previous surveys. Here is what they say troubles them the most.

Generational Comparisons

Major Concerns. The four items at the top of the concern list of Canada's Millennials, cited by 60 percent or more, are the *future*, *lack of money*, *lack of time*, and the feeling that they *should be getting more out of life* (see Table 2.1).[2]

It's interesting to see that those four concerns — while primary for Millennials — are not shared to the same extent by older Canadians. In fact, the future troubles fewer Gen Xers, Boomers, and Pre-Boomers, while concerns about money, time, and getting more out of life decrease progressively with age. Presumably, as people get older, they have more money and time and have reached a point where they are feeling satisfied with life. Then again, for many, it may be a case of their having lowered their expectations and become more content with what they have and what they can accomplish.

More specifically, the fact that the *future* troubles more Millennials than others could be related to at least three possibilities. First, it may simply reflect the fact that most of them have the prospect of having more years ahead of them than everyone else and aren't at all sure how things are going to turn out — what we might call an *"unknown times"* argument. Second, as many observers these days adamantly emphasize, it could be because, objectively, they are facing conditions that are making life extremely difficult and are not sure things are going to get much better — a *"tough times"* view of what is happening. Third, maybe much of the apparent consternation about personal matters is largely because our information-laden society is drawing an unprecedented amount of attention to personal issues of every kind, in the process resulting in young people believing they personally are being affected. We might dub this an *"informed times"* explanation. In the rest of this chapter and the rest of the book, we will be keeping all three possibilities in mind.

Illustrative of the "tough times" take on things, a senior editor at *The Atlantic*, Derek Thompson, has described American Millennials — and we do think that Millennials in Canada and the United States have much in common — as "the unluckiest generation." He points out that they have had to live through "the economic sledgehammer" that followed the collapse of the U.S. housing market in 2007–2008. He writes that "the aftereffects, economists fear, may dog them for the rest of their working lives." Large numbers have had to postpone things like buying a house and even a car, getting married, and having children. Many have moved back in with their parents. "Millennials," he writes, "have been scorned as perma-children, forever postponing adulthood, or labeled with that most un-American of character flaws: helplessness." Thompson thinks that "Millennials may well outgrow their miserable circumstances" but echoes experts in concluding, "Despite their relative youth, they may not be able to make up the lost ground."[3]

Maybe, in part, because the American housing tsunami seems to have had only a marginal effect on Canada, this country's Millennials have a more positive view of what lies ahead — although all that bleak talk about the future spilling into Canada from the U.S. undoubtedly has them blinking as they look ahead. In addition, while they may have escaped the American economic "sledgehammer" tied to housing, Canadian Millennials hardly have known an exemption from spiraling housing costs. We will return to their views of the future in some detail in Chapter 7.

Concern about *health* increases somewhat as people get into their 30s and 40s. However, it remains at a fairly steady level after that, rather than increasing with age as many of us might think. In fact, health is a concern for about 45 to 50 percent of adults *in every age cohort* — including Millennials. Large numbers of people do not take health for granted, regardless of their age.

In some ways, the health finding may come as a surprise, given modern advances in science, medicine, technology, the Canadian social health care safety net, and the fact that large numbers of Canadians have the resources or are assisted in having the resources to live healthy lives.

Table 2.1 **Major Personal Concerns of Millennials and Other Adults**

% Indicating Areas Concern Them Personally "A Great Deal" or "Quite a Bit"

	ALL	Millennials 1986–plus (18–29)	Xers 1966–1985 (30–49)	Boomers 1946–1965 (50–69)	Pre-Boomers Pre-1946 (70-plus)
The future	55	71	54	49	53
Health	48	43	49	49	47
Lack of money	47	64	54	40	28
Never seem to have enough time	44	63	53	31	25
Feeling that they should be getting more out of life	44	62	49	36	24

Important note: In this and other tables, shading indicates differences in the cohorts or other variables involved of 10 percentage points or more, a difference we view as substantively significant.

That said, in keeping with our "informed times" argument, the importance of health is something that is heavily promoted in Canada. Extensive government and private sector initiatives have been supplemented, for example, by the voices of parents, teachers, politicians, media, and celebrities who call on people to live well and live long. Examples abound.

- Health Canada's role "is to help Canadians maintain and improve their health," including informing "Canadians to make healthy choices."[4]
- In 2019, a new Canadian Food Guide was released, packaged as a significant update reflecting the country's demographic diversity — and diverse takes on healthy eating.[5]
- The federal government has been a global leader in reducing smoking with impressive results: since the early 1960s, the adult smoking level in Canada has dropped from 50 percent to 18 percent (men from 61 percent to 20 percent, women from 38 percent to 15 percent).[6]
- ParticipACTION asserts that "Canadians of all ages need to move their bodies more at work, school, and play" and offers an array of programs with partners.[7]

- Food & Consumer Products of Canada, representing food, beverage, and consumer products, maintains it is "Supporting Canadians' Health and Wellness."[8]
- The Heart and Stroke Foundation tells Canadians to "Make healthy lifestyle choices."[9]
- Even the always controversial Don Cherry admonishes young kids not to do drugs, saying that hockey is a breath of fresh air when it comes to drugs — unlike the NBA, MLB, and NFL.[10]

Throw in groups that warn us about such wide-ranging things as the perils of alcohol, careless driving, safety on the job, the importance of getting enough sleep, early disease detection, and making regular trips to the doctor and the net result is obvious: Canadians of all ages are not presumptuous about their health. On the contrary, most are acutely aware of their vulnerabilities.

Oh, and then there's what Vision Critical refers to as the "Millennial Diet." Based in large part on their own information gathering, Millennials "are more likely than any other generation to read ingredient listing and nutritional information, to look for organic and fair-trade certifications, and to find out where a product was manufactured and where it was shipped from." They also love food diversity: "They want a variety of experiences," says VC, "from epicurean feasts to the fastest food. And they have different expectations for each." The combination of wanting to try new things and thriftiness has also spurred the growth of "fast casual" restaurants that offer affordable meals with fresh ingredients and more complex flavours in a nicer environment.[11]

Moderate Concerns. An array of other issues trouble around 4 in 10 Millennials and, with only a few exceptions, are issues for fewer Canadians in the three older age cohorts.

- Concern about *getting older* is fairly uniform from Millennials onward. Surprise! Few people want to see life going by (see Table 2.2).
- Many issues are a concern for more Millennials than others: some are change-related (*so many things changing: looks, height, and weight*), some philosophical (*the purpose of life*), some emotional (*loneliness,*

depression, inferiority feelings, boredom), as well as *sexual.* Seemingly many personal concerns decrease with time, while others such as concern about one's children, once one has them, increase.

It seems clear that most of these personal concerns are life-cycle related — consistent with our "unknown times" argument. However, the sociologist in us reminds readers that some issues may also be tied to social developments ("period effects"), some of which are fairly unique to a given cohort ("cohort effects"). This would especially seem to be true of four concerns that appear to be somewhat anomalous, given the emergence and explosion of social media in the twenty-first century: *loneliness, depression, boredom,* and *inferiority feelings.* They are of the "informed times" variety.

Table 2.2 **Moderate Personal Concerns of Millennials and Other Adults**

% Indicating Areas Concern Them Personally "A Great Deal" or "Quite a Bit"

	ALL	Millennials 1986–plus (18–29)	Xers 1966–1985 (30–49)	Boomers 1946–1965 (50–69)	Pre-Boomers Pre-1946 (70-plus)
Getting older	36	37	35	37	31
Your height or weight	35	40	37	32	29
The purpose of life	33	44	35	27	28
Concerns your children	33	12	35	37	47
Your looks	32	46	33	25	25
So many things changing	32	42	34	27	29
Loneliness	28	45	28	23	19
Depression	28	36	34	24	15
Your sexual life	28	31	36	23	16
Boredom	25	35	25	21	20
Inferiority feelings	24	37	28	18	10
Your marriage/ relationship	19	18	22	17	16

As we discussed earlier, social media seemingly are contributing significantly to the decline of isolation that should result in reduced levels of depression, loneliness, and boredom. In keeping with axiomatic ideas concerning the social construction of self — going back to theorists such as Charles Horton Cooley ("the looking glass self") and George Herbert Mead ("role-taking") — increased interaction with friends, relatives, and other like-minded individuals via social media should collectively have a positive impact on individuals. Yet, Statistics Canada reports that, as of 2016, about 50 percent of adults under 35 admitted that they were engaging in at least one unhealthy practice such as smoking, illicit drug use, or heavy drinking.[12] In the United States, recent research has found that loneliness is increasing across all age groups, with young adults leading the way.[13] In Britain, Prime Minister Theresa May went so far as to appoint a Minister for Loneliness after the recommendations of the Loneliness Commission.[14]

So what's happening? A number of possible factors are worth considering. Among them? Divorce and single parent families, school and career pressures, comparing oneself to ideal people and ideal bodies, being inundated with a myriad of choices that lead to the questioning of one's decisions, two parents being employed outside the home, and parents in general simply being too preoccupied with other matters to give sufficient time to their children who are still at home or are now out on their own.

Then, too, let's not forget that some of the increase in these concerns may lie with a fairly obvious source: increased awareness. In recent decades, the consciousness of all four of these issues has been raised, and the stigma toward each decreased. Accordingly, growing numbers of individuals believe they are experiencing such personal problems. Still, many observers insist that Millennials may be struggling more than other generations. A 2017 Ipsos report claimed that as many as 63 percent of Millennials are at "high risk" for mental health issues — up from 56 percent in 2016 and 53 percent in 2015 — compared to only 41 percent of Canadians as a whole. The upside to the story, if there is one, is that these concerns are also being diagnosed earlier.[15]

Why Millennials Are Lonely

In a recent article for *Forbes* magazine, Caroline Beaton has taken on the question of Millennial loneliness. She notes that the number of Americans with no close friends has tripled since 1985. The average number of people they feel they can talk to about important matters has dropped from three to two. "Mysteriously," she notes, "loneliness appears most prevalent among Millennials."

She offers two explanations. First, lonely people tend to become lonelier if they're around people who also are lonely. They can destabilize an entire network like a single thread unraveling a sweater, she writes. Loneliness is contagious. Second, the Internet makes it viral. While it provides "happy touch points," superficial Internet connections can get in the way of genuine offline connections.

In a follow-up article, Beaton picked up on the idea that technologies provide the illusion of companionship without the demands of relationships. "Just meeting people," she says, "isn't enough. We also need to sacrifice for them." That component of friendship, she suggests, is largely foreign to Internet "friendships."

Sources: Beaton, 2007a, 2007b

We won't leave all these potential factors dangling. On the contrary, we will return to many of them as we move through additional findings relating to "the origin" of social problems, as well as our examination of families in Chapter 5.

Youth Survey Trends

Apart from generational differences that can be explained in terms of life cycle, has there actually been an increase over time in the inclination of young people to feel that they are experiencing a number of these personal problems?

The short answer is "Yes." Concerns about lack of time and money, loneliness, and feelings of inferiority have all increased significantly among young people since 1984 (see Figure 2.1). Those findings point the causal finger at social and cultural change, not life cycle.

Figure 2.1 **Select Personal Concerns: 1984, 2000, 2016 (%)**

% Indicating Concerned "A Great Deal" or "Quite a Bit"

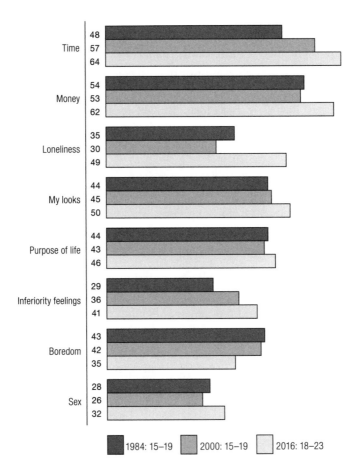

Keep in mind that, as of 2016, most 15- to 19-year-olds in 1984 and 2000 had become Gen Xers (47 to 51 and 31 to 35). What the trend data show is that those Xers typically were exhibiting lower levels of concern than today's young Millennials when they were approximately the same age.

The *time* finding is somewhat unexpected. Surely technology should have a time-saving function for just about everybody, shouldn't it? A possible hint in the case of time shortages for Millennials is offered by trend research carried out by Cathleen Zick of the University of Utah. In comparing adolescents in 1977–78 with their young Millennial counterparts in 2003–2005, she found a decrease in paid employment and an increase in leisure time. The time problem was not associated with school work or house work but with time spent with technology.[16] Hmm. Maybe the old folk wisdom applies: we have time for the things we define as priorities. The question is what Millennials are seeing as their priorities. Then again, many experts say this is no laughing matter — that they are extremely "squeezed" when it comes to time. We'll return to this question in Chapter 7, where we focus on the future.

As we've been noting, what is also surprising is the increase in *loneliness*. No less than 86 percent of Millennials say they text at least once a week, 66 percent daily and, as we saw in the previous chapter, many claim to receive high levels of enjoyment from being alone. Throw in visual interaction possibilities such as FaceTime and Skype and one is hard-pressed to account for why there has not been a significant reduction in loneliness over time. The seemingly obvious conclusion: while online links have many functions, they often — by themselves — do not alleviate loneliness. Millennials and everyone else seem to need more than online links to alleviate loneliness.

Charlton Heston — the veteran actor best known for his role as Moses in *The Ten Commandments* — once said that "The Internet is for lonely people."[17] And a current take offered by highly respected author and screenwriter Allison Burnett is fairly similar. In his novel, *Undiscovered Gyrl*, Burnett's lead character, Katie, sums up things this way: "Only on the Internet can a person be lonely and popular simultaneously."[18]

Those kinds of assertions, however, are irritating to those who find that social media and the Internet more broadly have immeasurably enhanced ties with friends and relatives and enabled them to make connections with many new friends and acquaintances. In addition, those negative generalizations about the Internet and interpersonal ties can readily be refuted by some basic data.

- As we have seen, our latest surveys show that 28 percent of Canadians say that they are troubled by loneliness, including 45 percent of Millennials.

- However, 65 percent of Canadians, including 79 percent of Millennials, are saying that they are receiving high levels of enjoyment from the Internet. It obviously is not only "for lonely people."

Clearly there are many different takes on the pluses and minuses of the use of social media and the Internet. Its assessment requires our ongoing attention and analyses.

Changes as Young People Get Older

So far we are finding that Millennials are far more concerned with a number of personal issues than older age cohorts. What's more, the data generated from looking at things over time show that the concern levels of young people have been increasing from 1984 through 2000 to 2016. These trend data point to changes that are taking place, societally and culturally, versus changes that merely reflect the life cycle as Canadians move from youth to early and middle adulthood.

What still is not clear from our data, however, is the extent to which young Canadians actually change as they get older — potentially reflecting *both* life cycle and socio-cultural factors.

Our cohort analysis provides us with a glimpse of such change. We are able to look at the extent to which 15- to 19-year-olds were concerned about a number of personal issues in 1984 and then, by identifying 47- to 51-year-olds in our 2016 survey, ask them about the extent to which they are troubled about the same issues today.

The news is extremely good (see Figure 2.2). In every instance, their levels of concern now are down from what they were some 30 years ago.

Such "progress" is consistent with sociological thinking that goes back to at least the late 1960s and Travis Hirschi, who taught at the University of California Berkeley. According to his "social bond" theory, as people age they tend to develop a range of social attachments and involvements that typically neutralize a variety of negative traits, ranging from loneliness to deviant behaviour. In the case of the latter, young people typically "grow out of deviance."[19]

They also undoubtedly learn how to live life. By that we mean that all of us have to learn how to cope with many things — money, time, aging,

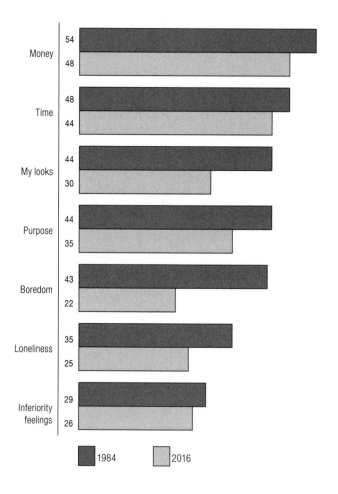

Figure 2.2 **Select Personal Concerns: Teens 15–19 in 1984 as Adults 47–51 in 2016 (%)**
% Indicating Concerned "A Great Deal" or "Quite a Bit"

purpose. Our society readily recognizes the need for us to learn and grow, from the preschool years through our final years. A considerable range of resources are made available to all of us along the way. With the help of those resources, family, friends, and others — not to mention sheer experience — we improve as we get older. As a result, life, for most of us, gets a bit easier.

Hey, the Times *Are* Definitely Tougher: One Expert's Take

Psychologist Jean Twenge, a professor at San Diego State University, has written a provocative book, *Generation Me: Why Today's Young Americans Are More Confident, Assertive, Entitled — and More Miserable Than Ever Before.*

Millennials, she maintains, have been socialized and coddled by schools, parents, religious groups, and the media to feel special. They receive participation ribbons for last place finishes, undivided attention as the only child in the home, inflated grades by teachers, "likes" on social media, and so on. But then "adulthood shock" strikes and Millennials realize that they are not that special after all: they cannot necessarily do everything they dreamed of, they lacked honest feedback in their earlier years, and life is not actually fair.

This leads to a second observation by Twenge regarding resources. As Millennials confront adult life, they do so as a cohort more likely than previous generations to have divorced parents, have numerous failed attempts at love as the average age of marriage rises, live on their own, move several times for school or career, experience school pressures and competition, confront depressing economic and employment realities, and live excessively busy lives that isolate them from others.

These limitations are only magnified in the age of the Internet and social media where individuals are encouraged to express themselves virtually, all the while comparing themselves to the perfect and beautiful lives that others seemingly have based on their Facebook status or Instagram images. In part, these resource shortages are the price of individualism and choice. In Twenge's words, "The sadness of being alone is often the flip side of freedom and putting ourselves first. When we pursue our own dreams and make our own choices, that pursuit often takes us away from our friends and family."

In short, argues Twenge, many Millennials simply are ill-equipped for adulthood and frequently lack the resources of strong and healthy ties with individuals and institutions.

(Source: Twenge 2014:63–64, 156)

Still, allowing for all that, our current survey findings indicate that the levels of concern about virtually all these issues are higher for Millennials than they were for their youthful predecessors, dating back to at least the early 1980s.

That's not to say that with time, today's Millennials "will not catch up" in having their concerns alleviated. But collectively, they have further to come than any other generation that we have been tracking now for more than three decades.

Ironically, the heightened level of concerns among young people appears to be accompanied by solutions. Further to our "informed times" thesis, the very societal sources that have been raising awareness of the existence of personal "challenges" often are also the same entities that pose alleged solutions. They may be starting lots of the fires, but they also claim to know how to put most of them out. Having made young people more aware than ever before of issues such as body image, self-esteem, loneliness, and depression, public and private market entries invariably also pose remedies to the very problems they have been identifying.

Experts, for example, who tell us in workshops about the prevalence of eating disorders also suggest ways in which they can be addressed. The same is true of a seminar leader who talks about illicit drug use but proceeds to offer ideas about how such problems can be neutralized. The people "in the know" are strong on diagnosis, but they also come equipped with possible ameliorative responses. Maybe there is more hope that we first thought.

Variations in Personal Concerns

Millennials' personal concerns are highly pervasive across many key characteristics. Consistent differences are surprisingly few by variables such as urban and rural residence, birthplace, ethnicity, and sexual orientation. That said, there are noteworthy variations.

- Millennial *women* are more likely than their male counterparts to express a number of concerns, notably with respect to looks, depression, and inferiority. These kind of gender differences have persisted over the years, since the first Project Teen Canada in 1984.[20] What's troubling is that, despite Canada's strong emphasis on gender equality, presumably reinforced in recent years by social media, higher levels of concern on the part of women about looks, depression, and feelings of inferiority are not going away. Who said that ideas entrenched in the 1980s are a thing of the past?

- *Urban–rural* variations are typically small — with the sole exception of concern about money: Millennials in communities with a population under 1,000 are somewhat more likely than their counterparts elsewhere to say they are troubled by the lack of money. Interestingly, similar urban–rural differences are also found for Gen Xers but not for Boomers or Pre-Boomers.

- *Income differences,* to document the fairly obvious, are strongly related to concerns about money. But they also are associated with higher levels of loneliness, depression, and inferiority feelings. The folk wisdom that emphasizes that "money is power" also extends to the belief that money facilitates social acceptance, happiness, and positive self-esteem.

- *Religious involvement* is associated with being less concerned with the purpose of life. But Millennials who are religiously involved are also less concerned about money and depression.

- An increasingly important variable in understanding Millennials is *immigration.* Since the early 1990s, the annual number of landed immigrants has averaged some 235,000, up markedly from the 1980s. Currently some 50 percent are Millennials; the median age is 31.7. The proportion of the foreign-born population has increased from about 14 percent in 1951 to over 20 percent today. After previously coming primarily from European countries, the main source of immigrants is now Asia.[21] In 2016, 76 percent of Toronto youth between the ages of 15 and 34 had at least one parent who is an immigrant.[22] Differences in personal concerns between Millennials born in Canada and those born elsewhere are most pronounced when it comes to purpose. Some concerns related to social belonging — looks, loneliness, and feeling inferior — are also slightly higher among young adults born outside of Canada than those born here. However, depression levels are not any higher for those foreign-born. And concern about money is, if anything, slightly lower.

• Statistics Canada tells us Millennials are the most culturally diverse of our current generational cohorts, with 27 percent of those under 35 identifying as what StatsCan refers to as *visible minorities,* along with the older term *Aboriginal* and the newer term *Indigenous* — up from 13 percent in 1996 — compared to about 10 percent of Pre-Boomers, for example. In Toronto and Vancouver, more than 50 percent of youth between the ages of 15 and 34 identify as belonging to visible minority groups; in Calgary, the figure is about 35 percent.[23] Despite their growing numbers, visible minority youth are more likely than others to express concern about loneliness, purpose, and feeling inferior, seemingly reflecting their marginalized status. A positive finding: such feelings do not appear to translate into higher levels of depression.

An important note: we emphasize that, in drawing on Statistics Canada surveys, along with surveys of other prominent pollsters such as Angus Reid and Environics, we frequently are faced with the difficulty of making use of items that vary considerably when it comes to speaking of "race," "cultural group," and "visible minorities." Sociologists increasingly use the term "racialized" in acknowledging that individual and group categories are neither fixed nor predetermined. Rather, they are the result of a social construction whereby individuals are defined as being in physical categories based on characteristics that members of a society deem as important. As Vic Satzewich and Augie Fleras, for example, note, we tend to use physical markers, such as skin colour, to denote membership in a racial group and assign members to an ethnic group based on their cultural heritage. While aware of considerable variation in terms, it is our intent to be both accurate in our use of data and respectful of the individuals and groups involved.

According to the 2016 census, *Indigenous Peoples* now make up 4.9 percent of the Canadian population, up from 3.8 percent in 2006 and 2.8 percent in 1996.[24] Between 2006 and 2016, the number of Indigenous youth ages 15 to 34 increased by 39 percent. Our two pivotal surveys in 2015 and 2016 included 143 and 159 Indigenous Canadians respectively

— about 5 percent of both of the survey samples. The total for Millennials and Gen Xers for each survey is 94 and 98 respectively. However, about 8 in 10 Indigenous persons live in urban areas (over 1,000 people). We are using these survey results to provide some very preliminary, heuristic data on young Indigenous adults. Findings reported in the Magnified Mosaic on page 61 show that Indigenous young people are slightly more likely than others to express concern about loneliness and depression, along with sex. Beyond what is reported by this limited sample, a significant increase in suicide has been reported among Indigenous Canadians in recent years. Health Canada, for example, says that suicide rates are 5 to 7 times higher for First Nations and Inuit youth than for non-Indigenous youth, with rates among Inuit youth now among the highest in the world.[25]

- Statistics Canada estimates that, as of 2016, anywhere from 4 percent to 10 percent of Canadian youth 15 to 34 are either homosexual or bisexual.[26] Our surveys have found that about 8 percent of Canadians identify themselves as *LGBTQ*. Perhaps in part reflecting the greater freedom to be open about one's sexual orientation, they include 16 percent of Millennials compared to 7 percent of Gen Xers and Boomers and 6 percent of Pre-Boomers. While the sample sizes are small, we include some findings for heuristic, reflective purposes.* These results suggest that younger people who identify as LGBTQ tend to be slightly more likely than their heterosexual counterparts to express concern about a number of issues, including money, looks, depression, feelings of inferiority, and sex.
- These findings are consistent with a UBC analysis of the Canadian Community Health Survey data, published in the *American Journal of Public Health* in 2016.[27] The study found that gay, lesbian, and bisexual Canadians experience about twice the rates of anxiety and mood disorders of heterosexuals. Rates for bisexual Canadians are particularly high. Basia Pakula, who headed up the study, noted that "an extensive body of research suggests gay, lesbian and bisexual people

---

* The sample sizes for all the independent variables used in the Magnified Mosaic capsules are found in the Appendix.

experience chronic stress related to prejudice and stigma" that takes the form of "daily slurs or prejudiced comments [that] can be psychologically damaging."[28]

One further note on the importance of recognizing the complexity of these individual variables that we are isolating. The differences by *gender and race combined*, for example, are noteworthy and the findings mixed. Millennial women who are members of racialized groups are somewhat more likely than Caucasian Millennial women to express concern about a number of areas, notably their looks, loneliness, depression, and feelings of inferiority (see Figure 2.3). However, they do not exhibit a greater level of concern about lack of money — in part, it would seem, because the levels of income they report are very similar to that of Caucasian women. A key reason is that racialized, second-generation women tend to have comparable educational levels to white women — levels that in both instances are higher than males.

Figure 2.3 **Personal Concerns of Visible Minority and White Millennial Women (%)**

% Indicating Concerned "A Great Deal" or "Quite a Bit"

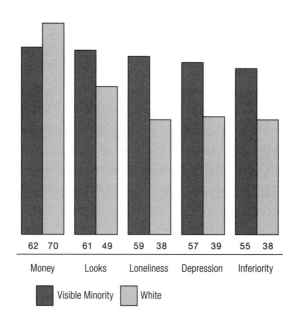

62	70	61	49	59	38	57	39	55	38
Money		Looks		Loneliness		Depression		Inferiority	

■ Visible Minority ▢ White

This overview of variations in the levels of personal concerns serves to remind us that Millennials — contrary to popular stereotypes — are not a homogenous group. They obviously have age in common. But the things that concern them the most vary by any number of important variables, including the ones we have looked at here: gender, ethnicity, income,

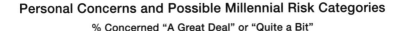

THE MAGNIFIED MOSAIC

Personal Concerns and Possible Millennial Risk Categories

% Concerned "A Great Deal" or "Quite a Bit"

	Money	Looks	Loneliness	Purpose	Depression	Inferiority	Sex
NATIONAL	64	46	45	44	36	37	31
Female	68	52	44	45	43	42	29
Male	59	41	46	43	29	33	32
Urban	63	46	45	45	35	36	31
Rural	76	49	38	34	39	45	28
<$50,000	74	43	54	44	42	42	27
$50–99,000	65	54	35	54	42	39	39
$100,000+	40	49	33	43	21	23	42
Services: Monthly*	48	41	48	42	30	38	30
<Monthly	70	49	43	44	38	37	31
Born elsewhere	56	47	50	54	34	40	28
Born in Canada	65	44	44	41	36	36	31
Visible minority	63	50	57	58	38	43	37
Caucasian	65	44	39	36	39	35	29
Indigenous**	60	38	41	38	40	26	43
Non-Indigenous**	57	35	33	38	34	32	33
LGBTQ**	61	42	24	44	39	41	39
Heterosexual**	52	38	28	38	34	30	33

*Weekly and monthly levels combined because of small sample sizes.
**Millennials and Gen Xers combined because of small sample sizes.

religiosity, birthplace, and sexual orientation. Environics, in its important study of Millennials released in early 2017, emphasized the same point. "Canadian Millennials are a diverse group," sharing a common age bracket but having "a range of experiences, perspectives, attitudes and activity when it comes to how they approach life."[29]

An adequate understanding of the personal concerns of Millennials requires our recognizing that they constitute a highly varied mosaic with highly varied personal preoccupations.

SOCIAL CONCERNS

So far we have seen that Millennials and other Canadians do not lack for joy. There are many things — led by relationships — that add much to their lives. We also have seen what we all know well: that life is sometimes difficult, resulting in Millennials and the rest of us giving much of our time and energy to problem-solving.

Beyond what is happening in our individual lives, of course, there are societal and global issues — perceived and real — that also have the potential to have an important impact on our levels of happiness and well-being. We asked Millennials and other Canadians "how serious" they see some 20 frequently cited issues. Obviously, the perceived severity of these issues will be influenced in large measure by media attention, simply because most have limited direct exposure to them. They carry essentially two tiers of importance — viewed as "very serious" by more than 30 percent of Millennials and other adults and as serious concerns for less than 30 percent.

Generational Comparisons

Some 45 percent of Millennials say that they see *global warming* and the *environment*, along with *sexual assault*, as "very serious problems" (see Table 2.3).

Around 40 percent of Gen Xers, Boomers, and Pre-Boomers share those same three concerns, while also emphasizing the *economy*. Boomers express particular concern about *child abuse* and *poverty*. Pre-Boomers also emphasize

Table 2.3 **Major Social Concerns of Millennials and Other Adults**

% Viewing as "Very Serious"

	ALL	Millennials 1986–plus (18–29)	Xers 1966–1985 (30–49)	Boomers 1946–1965 (50–69)	Pre-Boomers Pre-1946 (70-plus)
The economy	41	33	39	42	47
Child abuse	39	32	34	45	53
Poverty	38	37	36	43	38
Sexual assault	37	43	36	38	42
Drugs	36	24	25	39	57
Teenage suicide	36	35	34	39	44
The environment	35	44	33	35	34
Global warming	33	45	32	33	36
Cyberbullying	33	34	31	32	36
Unemployment	32	31	31	32	34

Table 2.4 **Moderate Social Concerns of Millennials and Other Adults**

% Viewing as "Very Serious"

	ALL	Millennials 1986–plus (18–29)	Xers 1966–1985 (30–49)	Boomers 1946–1965 (50–69)	Pre-Boomers Pre-1946 (70-plus)
Crime	29	21	24	33	39
Terrorism	26	17	22	32	36
Aboriginal and non-Aboriginal relations	24	37	22	23	26
Unequal treatment of women	23	23	22	26	31
Racial discrimination	21	25	21	22	23
Juvenile delinquency	20	15	19	23	26
Lack of Canadian unity	16	13	14	16	22
American influence	15	16	15	15	16
Threat of nuclear war	13	14	14	13	12
French–English relations	10	10	10	10	13

Some Notes and Data on Marijuana

As of October of 2018, Canada's Cannabis Act made it legal for adults 18 and over to legally possess and share up to 30 grams of legal cannabis, to purchase cannabis from a provincially licensed retailer, or to purchase cannabis online from a federally licensed producer. Adults are also allowed to grow up to four cannabis plants and make cannabis products; some restrictions apply. Federal, provincial, and territorial governments share the responsibility for overseeing production, distribution, and use, including imposing criminal penalties where necessary.

Our surveys found that 60 percent of Canadians agreed that "the use of marijuana should be legalized," led by Millennials (65 percent) and Gen Xers (64 percent), followed by Boomers (59 percent) and then Pre-Boomers (41 percent). The agreement figure among adults stood at only 26 percent in 1975 and 31 percent in 1995, before rising to 44 percent in 2005. Among 15- to 19-year-olds, approval increased from 28 percent in 1984 to 50 percent in 2000, climbing further to 62 percent in 2016 for roughly comparable 18- to 23-year-olds. Reflecting period effects, the 28 percent level for teens in 1984 jumped to 58 percent for those teens — now 47- to 51-year-olds in 2016 — strongly pointing to period effects. In the U.S., the adult approval figures were similar — 30 percent in 1980 and 57 percent in 2016.

Sources: Government of Canada 2017a; Geiger 2016)

child abuse but are more inclined than other adults to be concerned about *drugs* and *teenage suicide*. Here their concern seems to be directed specifically at Millennials and teenagers, variously reflecting negative perceptions, concern, and even a measure of disdain toward young people.

The relatively low ranking that Millennials give to the seriousness of drugs is perhaps somewhat surprising in light of the extensive media attention that has been given in recent years to opioids generally and fentanyl specifically. For example, *Maclean's* has written about "Canada's opioid crisis"[30] while the *Globe and Mail* has addressed the question of "How Canada

Indigenous Canadians

As of the last census in 2016, 1.7 million people reported an Aboriginal identity. Some 58 percent identified as First Nations, another 35 percent as Métis, 4 percent as Inuit, and 3 percent other. They accounted for 5 percent of the total population, up from 4 percent in 2006 and 3 percent in 1996. Significantly, the average age of the Indigenous population was 32, compared with 41 for the non-Indigenous population. More than 70 Aboriginal languages were reported.

Indigenous children were more likely than others to live in a variety of family settings. Some 60 percent of those under the age of five lived with both parents, compared to 86 percent of non-Indigenous children. The respective figures for children under four living with one parent were 34 percent and 13 percent. Statistics Canada indicated that the interplay of cultural and economic factors contributed to 18 percent of Indigenous children zero to four sharing a household with at least one grandparent; the comparable non-Indigenous figure was about 9 percent. Some 3 percent of Indigenous children under four were in foster care, compared to 0.2 percent of other children; they comprised 51 percent of all foster children in this age group, similar to 2011.

Health-wise, the most recent Statistics Canada data reveal that 52 percent of Indigenous people indicated they were in "excellent" or "very good" health — versus 61 percent of non-Indigenous individuals. The figures dropped to 41 percent and 53 percent respectively for people 45 and over.

(Sources: Statistics Canada 2017i, j, k)

got addicted to fentanyl."[31] As readers may know, opioids are narcotics that are primarily prescribed as painkillers but also are used simply to get high. They are extremely addictive.

According to the United Nations, Canadians are the second highest per-capita consumers of prescription opioids in the world, behind only Americans. And, unlike in the U.S., the numbers are rising.[32] What has escalated the opioid problem is the arrival of illicit fentanyl pills from China that have flooded the black market. Deadly in even small doses, fentanyl is said to be 100 times more potent than morphine and up to 50 times stronger

Changes in the Perception of Serious Social Problems
with Time and as Young People Get Older

Fluctuations in the perception of issues as problems is readily evident when we look at how young people have viewed things over time (see Figure 2.4). Since 1984, concern about the seriousness of the environment has gone up, and concern about drugs and nuclear war has gone down. During the same period, the percentages of youth troubled about Indigenous–white relations and the economy have fallen and then risen; in the case of the unequal treatment of women, it has risen and then fallen.

Those fluctuations are further evident when we look at the 15- to 19-year-old cohort in 1984 and fast-forward to 2016 and their views as 47- to 51-year-olds (see Figure 2.5).

Figure 2.4 **Select Social Concerns of Youth: 1984, 2000, 2016 (%)***

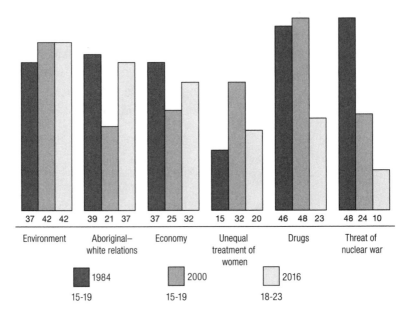

% Indicating "Very Serious"

Environment	Aboriginal–white relations	Economy	Unequal treatment of women	Drugs	Threat of nuclear war
37 42 42	39 21 37	37 25 32	15 32 20	46 48 23	48 24 10

■ 1984   ■ 2000   □ 2016

15-19   15-19   18-23

*Environment: 1984: "pollution" used. Aboriginal–white relations: 40% = 1992; 1984 not asked.

Many issues that they viewed as very serious in 1984 — unemployment, child abuse, nuclear war, and even sexual assault — are no longer seen that way by as large a number. Given the extensive competition for public attention, it is difficult for any given social issue to stay "on top of the charts" for a very long time.

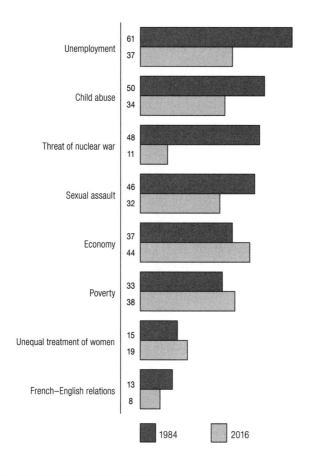

Figure 2.5 **Select Social Concerns: Teens 15–19 in 1984 as Adults 47–51 in 2016 (%)**

% Indicating See as "Very Serious"

Concern	1984	2016
Unemployment	61	37
Child abuse	50	34
Threat of nuclear war	48	11
Sexual assault	46	32
Economy	37	44
Poverty	33	38
Unequal treatment of women	15	19
French–English relations	13	8

than heroin. An amount the size of two grains of salt can kill a healthy adult.[33] Dealers mix it into drugs like heroin to stretch their supplies. The result, says Dr. David Juurlink, the head of clinical pharmacology and toxicology at Sunnybrook Heath Sciences Centre in Toronto, is that "the illicit drug supply has never been more dangerous because of the profusion of fentanyl-related compounds." According to Health Canada, 2,978 people died of apparent opioid-related causes in 2016 and 3,987 in 2017. Another 2,066 died between January and June of 2018. Fentanyl-linked deaths in 2017 were highest in British Columbia (1,399), Ontario (1,125), and Alberta (714). Some 20 percent of those who died were 20 to 29 years old, and another 27 percent were 30 to 39. Close to 80 percent were males.[34] Indigenous youth in southern Alberta have been among the most vulnerable victims.[35]

A number of other highly publicized areas of Canadian life are major concerns for less than 30 percent of Millennials and other adults. They include *crime, terrorism, the unequal treatment of women, racial discrimination, lack of unity,* and *the threat of nuclear war* (see Table 2.4).

However, an important exception in the case of Millennials is *Aboriginal–white relations* (the survey phrase used through about 2015), which 37 percent of Millennials view as a "very serious" problem. The profile of Indigenous people was raised dramatically by the historic Truth and Reconciliation Commission, which tabled the results and recommendations from its five-year work in 2015. The Commission's executive summary included 94 Calls to Action aimed at redressing the legacy of residential schools and advancing reconciliation in Canada. The federal government committed itself to fully implementing the recommendations.[36]

- *Boomers* and *Pre-Boomers* express somewhat higher levels of concern than others about *crime, terrorism*, and *delinquency* — seemingly tied in large part to anxiety for many about personal safety as they get older. Otherwise differences are fairly minor.
- Issues that were "big" in previous decades such as *American influence, the lack of unity, the threat of nuclear war*, and *French–English relations* are now a source of consternation for relatively few Millennials and others. But they could rise again "on the social concern charts."

The Impact of the #MeToo Movement

In its year-end issue for 2017, *Time* magazine declared the "Person of the Year" to be the many women who it described as "The Silence Breakers: The Voices That Launched a Movement." The magazine pointed out that movie stars who "are supposedly nothing like you and me" are in fact "more like you and me than we ever knew." In October of 2017, Ashley Judd and others broke the silence about the sexual advances of Harvey Weinstein, the head of the prominent studio Miramax, in the *New York Times*. Subsequently, the hashtag #MeToo provided a portal for millions of people around the world to offer their stories.

Time notes that, while the explosion of disclosures appears to have occurred overnight, it has been simmering for years: "Women have had it with bosses and co-workers who not only cross boundaries but don't even seem to know that boundaries exist ... with fear of retaliation ... of being fired from a job they can't afford to lose ... with the code of going along to get along." The results have been dramatic with CEOs being fired, icons disgraced, and criminal charges being brought forward. "The women and men who have broken their silence span all races, all income classes, all occupations and virtually all corners of the globe." Those "corners" have included Canada.

(Source: Zacharek, Dockterman, and Edwards 2017)

Why do we say that? Because, when it comes to social concerns, we need to keep the camera running. So-called social problems literally compete for public attention. Something like terrorism, that is a primary concern in one month or one year, invariably slips as other issues — such as the economy or violence — ascend in the public eye. As sociologist Armand Mauss once put it, "There's only so much room on the front page of the newspaper."[37] And as the late Anglican Archbishop of Toronto, Lewis Garnsworthy, reminded people, "The paper that carries today's headline will carry out tomorrow's garbage."[38] With respect to American influence, for example, the 2016 survey was conducted about two weeks before the election of Donald Trump as U.S. president. Initially, there allegedly was a fair amount of

Millennials and Sexual Assault ... Are Things Changing?

Sexual assault continues to receive considerable attention, because it isn't going away. In recent years, the topic has moved to the headlines, in large part, because of the #MeToo movement.

However, for all the consternation about sexual assault, greater awareness is not translating into Millennials leading the way in reporting incidents and sexual assault being addressed. Statistics Canada pointed out in a 2017 release that "the rate of self-reported sexual assault in 2014 remained unchanged from 2004." Only 1 in 20 sexual assaults were reported to the police, compared to 1 in 3 other types of crime.

Offenders were most often men, acting alone, and under 35. Just over half of the victims knew the person who sexually assaulted them. Those at higher risk included individuals who were women, young, single, Indigenous, gay or bisexual, and sometimes in poorer mental health.

This means that victims are very often Millennials — who seldom report the assault.

(Source: Conroy and Cotter 2017)

concern in Canada. By the time you read this, we suspect the concern level re: American influence will have gone up and gone down ... several times.

Social scientists have emphasized that, apart from objective conditions, social problems are largely created by social movements that have "life cycles." There initially has to be a conscious push for a given issue by advocates, who receive major assistance when the issue is brought to the public eye through a related, high-profile event. The event or events provide the public and politicians with "evidence" that the issue requires a problem-solving response.

For example, when Marc Lépine killed 14 women in a shooting rampage at Montreal's École Polytechnique in 1989, the tragedy became a major catalyst for feminists and others to call for the end of hatred and mistreatment toward women in Canada. The tragic events that unfolded in New York and Washington on September 11, 2001, summed up by the poignant image of the World Trade Center's Twin Towers crumbling, led to a dramatic increase in concern about terrorism and an acceleration of security initiatives in airports and many other public places.

More recently, the #MeToo movement has raised awareness and women's voices around the world.

In short, social movements create social problems. Indicative of the importance of the social component of social problems, they rarely, if ever, really "solved." Rather, the movement gradually dissipates and, without support, the issue slips from the public eye.[39]

Why the extensive concern about the threat of nuclear war among young people in 1984? It was largely the result of the highly publicized ABC television movie *The Day After* that aired on November 20, 1983. It is described as "a graphic, disturbing film about the effects of a devastating nuclear holocaust on small-town residents of eastern Kansas."[40] The show was given extensive American and Canadian media attention both before and after the broadcast. Its viewing audience in the U.S. was record-setting at the time, with its audience in Canada also very high. The two-hour film received 12 Emmy nominations and won two awards.

In Canada, one indicator of the movie's impact was the fact that our 1984 national survey of teens found that 48 percent felt the threat of nuclear war was a "very serious" problem — the same level accorded crime and surpassed only by unemployment (61 percent) and child abuse (50 percent). Today the possibility of nuclear war is seen as a severe problem by only 10 percent of young people.

However, all it would take is for people to be convinced, for example, that North Korea is serious about directing a nuclear attack on North America for the issue to readily return to "the top of the social problems charts." Like the rest of us, Millennials are not immune to the creation of a "moral panic," which, as Stanley Cohen recognized in his classic 1971 book, *Folk Devils and Moral Panics*, is initiated by the media's creation of a group or issue as a threat to larger social safety.[41] Clearly, what we feel "panicked" about changes over the generations.

Variations in Social Concerns

We would expect that the perceptions of the seriousness of social issues would vary across the Canadian population in other ways besides age. Presumably two key predictable factors would be involved: (1) personal experience and (2) media attention. Such an expectation is fairly readily borne out when we look at six illustrative variables — *region, community size, gender, education, race,* and *sexual orientation.* Some select highlights, with the detailed Magnified Mosaic table below:

- Not surprising in light of the recent economic downturn in Alberta, Millennials there are considerably more likely than their counterparts elsewhere to see the economy as a "very serious problem." But nationally, *community size* makes little difference, except in the case of teenage suicide and sexual assault — where concern is higher in rural communities.
- Millennials who are university graduates generally are less likely than others to view social concerns as "very serious" — with the sole exception of Indigenous issues. This finding would suggest that higher education tends to bring a more critical attitude to highly publicized issues that are portrayed by the media and interest groups as "severe."
- Young women are more likely than young men to view almost all social problems "with an explicit human face" — such as sexual assault, suicide, Indigenous relations, and the unequal treatment of women — as severe problems. Something like the economy is not seen in the same light.
- *Visible minority Millennials* are consistently more inclined than *Caucasian Millennials* to view almost all issues as serious problems; the differences, however, are marginal.
- *Indigenous* individuals are also consistently more inclined than others to express concern about most issues, led by sexual assault, teenage suicide, crime, and Indigenous and non-Indigenous relations.
- Canadians who identify as *LGBTQ* are somewhat more likely than others to see a number of equity issues — racial discrimination, the unequal treatment of women, and Indigenous issues — as primary social concerns.

ASSESSMENT

We have been emphasizing a reality which all of us know well: joys and concerns are both inevitable components of everyday life.

Such a basic fact helps us to understand how so much of what takes place in our society involves two elements: helping us to enjoy life and helping us to problem-solve. And the realization of one is dependent on the realization of the other. The result is that our institutions typically emphasize both themes — be they families, schools, the media, health care, governments, leisure industries, religious groups, and any other groups. Over the years, Reg has frequently cited the wise synthesis offered by former University of Alberta sociologist Gwynn Nettler, who pointed out decades ago, that the universal goals of people across the planet are (1) to stay alive and (2) to live well.[42] Everyone wants to be able to cope with life in order to enjoy life.

Millennials obviously are no exception to the rule. Like the rest of us, they want to enjoy life. But they also have an array of personal and social concerns. Are they therefore any different from earlier young adults and today's Gen Xers, Boomers, and Pre-Boomers? Well, the decisive, short answer is "No and Yes." They too face personal and social issues.

Yes, objectively, these are "tough times." However, it also is clear that one of the reasons why today's Millennials are more likely than their 1980s and 1990s predecessors to express so many personal concerns is the "information times" factor. We are living in a period in history when unprecedented "space" can be given to everything — unlimited digital TV channels, the Internet, social media. There have never been so many people claiming expertise about so many things and — as we have pointed out — just by coincidence, packaging themselves and their teams as precisely the people who can offer the most effective responses. In recent decades, the number of "syndromes" for just about everything has expanded exponentially — as has the number of possible remedies. Such are the wonders of an information society.

This is not at all to minimize significant personal problems that have a debilitating impact on individuals. And the good news is that we are directing more resources than ever before to identifying personal difficulties and attempting to respond well to them. Indeed, the proliferation of diagnoses and prognoses may be putting us in a position to respond more effectively to personal problems than in any time in history.

Therefore, the fact that Millennials are more inclined than earlier generations to report personal problems may reflect in large part the activity of "the diagnostic industry." But it also means they may be in a better position than any generation before them to have their personal concerns addressed — and eventually resolved.

As for Millennials' social concerns, we know well by now that social issues have always existed and will always exist. "Only the names and faces change" in keeping with personal experiences and the emphases that the media, governments, interest groups, and entrepreneurs give to specific issues. One problem will slip from public view, only to be replaced by other problems that clamour for attention.

To the extent that social issues have a serious impact on personal life, their priority levels will rise. But, unlike personal issues, they seldom will actually be resolved — just addressed, and then, as energies wane and new concerns arise, slip quietly from public view. That "life cycle" of a social problem is not a cause for concern. It's just the way things work with social problems.

That doesn't mean for a moment that we don't take social concerns seriously. Of course we do. But it is important to recognize both their transient nature and elusive resolution. In our highly diverse Canada, we expect that the ever-expanding mosaic will also function to expand the ever-growing number of social issues that compete for attention.

If Millennials and others find that their concerns don't receive the attention they believe they should, it's because "there's only so much room on the front page of the newspaper." In an increasingly diverse Canada what we can expect is ever-increasing competition not only for attention but also for the resources groups feel are needed to respond to the concerns they are expressing. Diversity will contribute to the proliferation of both specific personal concerns as well specific social concerns.

Getting the attention of individuals and institutions is the topic we turn to next.

THE MAGNIFIED MOSAIC

Millennial Social Concerns by Select Variables

% Who See as "Very Serious"

	Sexual assault	Economy	Teenage suicide	Indige-nous & non-In-digenous	Drugs	Crime	Racial discrim.	Unequal treatment of women
NATIONAL	40	36	34	34	27	21	21	21
British Columbia	40	38	37	36	29	26	19	25
Alberta	44	68	29	29	27	22	18	27
Manitoba-Sask.	43	25	43	34	35	26	24	17
Ontario	36	36	29	31	20	18	20	17
Quebec	41	23	37	40	25	22	24	19
Atlantic	52	26	49	39	50	20	24	34
Urban	38	37	31	34	26	22	23	22
Rural	52	31	52	37	31	17	12	18
Women	53	34	44	40	28	28	24	26
Men	27	38	25	28	25	15	18	16
Degree-plus	31	28	26	40	16	12	20	18
Some post-secondary	43	45	38	27	36	23	15	20
HS or less	51	38	42	33	31	32	28	27
Visible minority	44	39	39	40	31	26	26	25
Caucasian	39	35	33	32	25	20	19	20
Indigenous*	52	43	43	45	32	35	27	29
Non-Indigenous*	36	38	33	24	27	23	21	21
LGBTQ*	41	36	35	41	17	20	28	28
Hetero-sexual*	36	38	33	24	29	24	21	20

*Millennials and Gen Xers combined because of small sample sizes.

CHAPTER 3

How They See Life:
Individuals/Institutions

As we all know well, life is inherently social. It's one thing to have per-
sonal values and personal concerns, but life is experienced socially.
Classic thinking going back to the origins of sociology and people like
Auguste Comte and Émile Durkheim grounds the individual in the social.
How we emerge, develop an identity, come to think, and how we act invariably have social sources. John Donne's oft-cited line from around 1600,
to the effect that "no man is an island," is vintage sociology before its birth.
But, for the record, even more poignant thoughts on the topic predated
Donne by about 2,000 years. Around 350 BC, Aristotle put things this
way: "Man is by nature a social animal. Anyone who either cannot lead the
common life or is so self-sufficient as not to need to, and therefore does not
partake of society, is either a beast or a god."[1]

What transpires for Millennials and the rest of us is highly dependent
— and typically almost totally dependent — on other people and the

institutions they have created. Let's take a close look at how Millennials view the two key components of their social settings — other Canadians and Canadian institutions.

INDIVIDUALS

In our surveys, we've attempted to get a reading on how Canadians view each other, particularly in light of our growing diversity. A sneak preview of the big picture: we are pretty positive about one another. But there are a few asterisks.

Generational Comparisons

Civility and Compassion

About 75 percent of Millennials and even larger numbers of Gen Xers, Boomers, and Pre-Boomers feel that "most of the time people try to be helpful." Nine in 10 adults of all ages agree that "overall, we continue to be a highly compassionate country" and reaffirm the basic rights of all people to have both medical care and incomes adequate to live on.

Maybe Queen Elizabeth II wasn't exaggerating after all when she issued a special statement to Canadians as the 150th anniversary year of Confederation began. She said that Canada has "earned a reputation as a welcoming, respectful, and compassionate country."[2] These data are consistent with such an appraisal.

Beyond attitudes, we probed behaviour, using three items that Gallup has used in worldwide surveys.[3] We asked our survey respondents, "In the last month, have you... (1) donated money to a charity, (2) volunteered time to an organization, and (3) helped a stranger who needed help?"

Some 53 percent told us that in the last month they had *donated money to a charity* while 34 percent indicated they had *volunteered time to an organization*. No less than 55 percent said that they had done something to *help a stranger* (see Table 3.1). The corresponding global figures as of 2016 were all lower: 27 percent for donating money, 20 percent for volunteering time, and 44 percent for helping a stranger.[4]

As might be expected, given that extra money and extra time are frequently scarce for Millennials, their level for donating money falls well below that of older adults, and their level of volunteering below that of Pre-Boomers. Research carried out by Environics adds an interesting qualifier: although lack of time is an issue, many haven't volunteered because "no one has ever asked them."[5] We think that lower levels of giving and volunteering simply are tied to life stage, rather than reflecting a significant generational shift in "helping behaviour."

Then again, as we saw in Chapter 1, only 49 percent of Millennials and Gen Xers say they place a "very high" level of importance on "concern for others," compared to 61 percent of Boomers and 66 percent of Pre-Boomers. Before we let Millennials off the hook, we need to keep our eye out for further information on "generosity and generation." It's an important question.

Table 3.1 **General Views of Canadians: Millennials and Other Adults**

% "Yes"

	ALL	Millennials 1986–plus (18–29)	Xers 1966–1985 (30–49)	Boomers 1946–1965 (50–69)	Pre-Boomers Pre-1946 (70-plus)
Most of the time people try to be helpful	82	74	77	86	93
I think that, overall, we continue to be a highly compassionate country	91	89	89	93	90
People who cannot afford it have a right to medical care	95	92	95	95	97
People who are poor have a right to an income adequate to live on	86	81	85	89	90
Helped a stranger who needed help in previous year	55	57	57	56	43
Donated money to a charity in previous year	53	41	48	57	72
Volunteered time to an organization in previous year	34	36	30	33	48

Important note: In this and other tables, shading indicates differences in the cohorts or other variables involved of 10 percentage points or more, a difference we view as substantively significant.

Anxiety and Suspicion

We can take it for granted. But perhaps one of the most fundamental build-ing blocks of personal well-being is feeling safe. Research in Canada and around the world has documented the obvious: feeling safe is a key compo-nent to success in such diverse situations as children at school, employees in the workplace, travelling abroad, or being an immigrant in a new country.[6] Come to think of it, feeling safe is also a prerequisite for our peace of mind when we are alone — relaxing at home, walking, driving, flying, sleeping, and so on. We've gotta feel safe! Otherwise, life is stripped of joy.

In 2008, the Project Teen Canada national survey asked 15- to 19-year-olds across the country to respond to two simple, blunt state-ments: "I feel safe at home" and "I feel safe at school." About 94 percent of teens said they felt safe at home — impressively high until one realizes that means that approximately 1 in 20 young people does not feel safe at home … conjuring up images of pain and strain in places where they should not be experienced. As for school, the "feel safe" figure dropped to 84 percent — meaning about 1 in 7 teens feels unsafe at school. And there were no significant differences either at home or school between females and males.[7] That's a lot of lives. We've got to do better.

Monetta reminds us that safety at school is a particular problem for LGBTQ students. National research by Catherine Taylor and Tracey Peter of the University of Winnipeg has found that they are far more likely than other students to feel unsafe at school.[8] What's more, Taylor has further found that LGBTQ teachers are reluctant to come out for fear of being harassed.[9] We'll come back to these issues when we look at sexualities in Chapter 4.

Our cities, towns, and other communities hopefully are safe places. Vancouver, for example, sees safety as essential to well-being and has a goal of becoming "the safest major city in Canada."[10] It doesn't lack for compe-tition: all of our cities place a high value on safety.

The fact of the matter, however, is that, for all the civility and valuing of safety in Canada, large numbers of Millennials and others express fear and suspicion in the course of living out their everyday lives (see Figure 3.1). Millennials (43 percent) lead the way in saying that there is an area

Figure 3.1 **Fear and Apprehension: Millennials and Other Adults (%)**

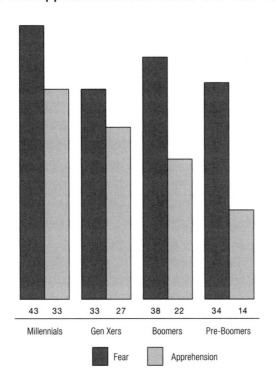

| 43 | 33 | 33 | 27 | 38 | 22 | 34 | 14 |

| Millennials | Gen Xers | Boomers | Pre-Boomers |

■ Fear   ▢ Apprehension

within a kilometre of their homes where they "would be afraid to walk alone at night" with the level for women (60 percent) more than double that of males (24 percent). Further, 33 percent of Millennials think that "a stranger who shows a person attention is probably up to something" — an apprehension level that exceeds those of Gen Xers, Boomers, and, especially, Pre-Boomers (14 percent).

Suspicion levels, however, are no higher for Millennial women than men (33 percent each). For the record, wariness of strangers may be even higher among American Millennials: just 19 percent say that most people can be trusted, compared to 31 percent of Gen Xers and 40 percent of Boomers.[11] The fear finding may reflect Millennials having greater exposure to media portrayals of crime and therefore being more anxious about their safety. Another factor may be sheer experience: older cohorts have had more time

Table 3.2 **Canada's Top 10 Safest and Unsafest Cities**

Based on Index of Crime & Crime Severity

	Top 10 Safest Cities		Top 10 Unsafest Cities	
1.	Quebec City	41.8	Saskatoon	112.5
2.	Barrie	43.3	Regina	107.6
3.	Toronto	45.7	Edmonton	101.6
4.	Ottawa	46.5	Kelowna	98.0
5.	Guelph	48.4	Abbotsford	96.6
6.	Sherbrooke	49.2	Vancouver	96.2
7.	Hamilton	50.5	Winnipeg	87.2
8.	St. Catharines	52.2	Thunder Bay	80.1
9.	Gatineau	53.6	Moncton	78.5
10.	Saguenay	53.8	Calgary	78.3

(Source: Statistics Canada 2016)

to have some of that apprehension negated. The anxiety about talking to a stranger may be tied to the same two factors — media portrayals and experience. It also undoubtedly reflects the age-old parental advice that children have received about not talking to strangers.

In reality, Statistics Canada tells us, less than half of violent attacks — excluding spousal abuse — involve a stranger. Robbery is the crime most likely to be committed by a stranger (63 percent of robberies), while sexual assault is the least likely (44 percent).[12] That's no reason for all of us to stop keeping an eye on people we don't know. But it does suggest that many of us may be giving strangers excessive attention.

Intergroup Attitudes

As we have been emphasizing from the beginning of the book, Millennials have been raised in a Canada that, since the 1960s, has given premier importance to pluralism, enshrined in the twin policies of bilingualism and multiculturalism, and expanded in scope in 1982 when the Canadian Charter of Rights and Freedoms became part of the Canadian Constitution. They also are the most ethnically diverse generation in the country's history.[13]

Worst Advice Ever: "Don't Talk to Strangers"

The idea that children should follow the advice, "Don't talk to strangers," is questioned by Sherry Hamby, a research professor in psychology at the University of the South in Sewanee, Tennessee. In a *Psychology Today* blog, Professor Hamby has written that "if it was ever good advice, it is not now." While the warning reflects good intentions about the safety of children, "avoiding strangers and avoiding social interaction ends up sending the wrong message."

Hamby reminds readers that "criminals prey on vulnerable and weak people." She maintains that children today therefore need what she calls "assertiveness training," where they "are taught how to identify safe adults such as police officers and staff members to whom they can turn." That includes familiarity with dialing 911. "They should not be afraid to talk to any stranger," she says, but "should know who to ask for help."

(Source: Hamby 2015)

It therefore is not surprising to see that Millennials lead the way in maintaining that "racial and cultural diversity is a good thing for Canada" and seeing *immigration* as a plus for the country (see Table 3.3). Incidentally, in 1950 Gallup found that 66 percent of Canadians felt immigration was a good thing, just slightly below the 68 percent figure today.[14] Millennials (71 percent) are also somewhat less inclined than adults in the three older cohorts to maintain that "immigrants to Canada have an obligation to learn Canadian ways."

That's not to say we are equally open to every kind of immigrant. In 1955, Gallup asked Canadians if they would approve or disapprove of having "a few families from Europe come to this neighborhood to live." Some 56 percent said they would approve.[15] In 1995, Reg updated the item to read, "I'd approve of having families from Asian countries come to live in my neighborhood." The approval figure was 85 percent. Our latest surveys have found that, even with an accelerated level of immigration, the figure for Asian families continues to be very similar (83 percent). But we added another possibility — how people would feel about Muslim families coming to live in their neighbourhoods. In this case, the approval figure dropped to 70 percent. The good news is that the approval level was highest among Millennials (76 percent), and above that of Gen Xers (72 percent), Boomers (66 percent), and Pre-Boomers (65 percent). We'll return to the Muslim question shortly.

Table 3.3 **Diversity Issues: Views of Millennials and Other Adults**

% "Yes"

	ALL	Millennials 1986–plus (18–29)	Xers 1966–1985 (30–49)	Boomers 1946–1965 (50–69)	Pre-Boomers Pre-1946 (70-plus)
Racial & cultural diversity is a good thing for Canada	76	83	78	73	69
Immigration					
On the whole, immigration is a good thing for Canada	68	74	66	67	73
Immigrants to Canada have an obligation to learn Canadian ways	89	71	89	93	94
Bilingualism and Multiculturalism					
Canada should have two official languages – English and French	63	71	64	58	61
Favour the "melting pot" model	41	21	38	49	54
Favour the "mosaic" model	39	53	42	33	31
No preference/other	20	26	20	18	15
Gender, Age, Sexual Orientation					
Homosexuals are entitled to the same rights as other Canadians	90	91	90	88	90
Women in this country now encounter very little discrimination	44	48	45	39	47
A person should retire at 65, regardless of health	29	31	31	28	24

The pluralistic mindset of Millennials extends to their greater inclination to endorse official *bilingualism* and favour the *mosaic* intergroup ideal over the *melting pot* model. It also can be seen in other areas, such as *sexual orientation* and *gender equality*. Millennials lead the way as some 9 in 10 adults agree that people who identify as gay or lesbians are entitled to the same rights as everyone else. A slight majority of Millennials and other adults disagree that Canadian *women* "now encounter very little discrimination." Only about 3 in 10 Millennials endorse mandatory retirement — very similar to the proportion of people in the other three age cohort categories.

In short, against our pluralistic ideals, things are looking fairly good on the interpersonal front in Canada, particularly among Millennials. Diversity is being applauded, the official linguistic and cultural policies endorsed, discrimination on the basis of variables, including sexual orientation, gender, and age, are deplored. In fact, this increasing acceptance among Millennials is so prominent that it has been coined "cognitive diversity," whereby Millennials value organizations that are inclusive and support "engagement, empowerment and authenticity." [16] Is the golden goal of a society where everyone can pursue the best in life without concern for social barriers within our reach?

Well, unfortunately — as we just saw with the reception given Muslims — not quite. While considerable progress on the intergroup acceptance front is evident, we still have a distance to go, particularly in the area of race and ethnicity. We'll see later when we look at families in Canada that one important indicator of group acceptance — intermarriage— is being realized.

However, sizable numbers of Canadians continue to hold negative attitudes toward some specific categories and groups, with the latter including Muslims, Sikhs, and Hindus. Moreover, while there is considerable traction on the heels of the Truth and Reconciliation Commission to respond to the difficulties experienced by Indigenous Peoples, a 2016 survey report by Environics shows the country is far from unanimous in exhibiting sympathy and a will to turn things around.[17]

But hope for better interpersonal relations may be on the horizon: in each instance, the negative views decline with each age cohort

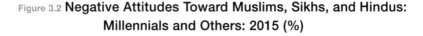

Figure 3.2 **Negative Attitudes Toward Muslims, Sikhs, and Hindus: Millennials and Others: 2015 (%)**

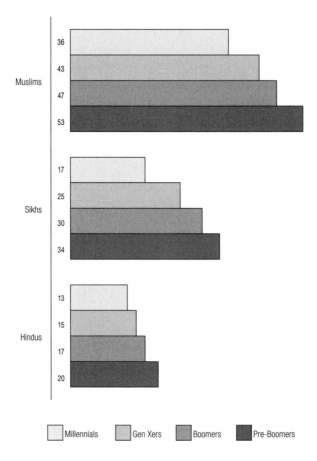

and are lowest among Millennials. Still, even here, a segment of our youngest adults clearly continues to hold negative views of some Canadians — notably Muslims (see Figure 3.2).

Accelerated immigration from Pacific Rim and African countries in recent decades has also seen an increase in concern about racist attitudes and behaviour toward Asians and black people. People from China and particularly from Hong Kong have been widely viewed as responsible for inflating housing prices in markets like Vancouver.[18] A prominent magazine

Colonialism's Effects Behind Us? Not So Fast

In the spring of 2018, an important report was released by the First Nations Information Governance Centre (FNIGC). The report was based on survey responses from more than 20,000 First Nations children, youth, and adults living on reserves and in northern communities. The survey, carried out between March 2015 and December 2016, was unique in that it was created, conducted, and carried out by First Nations people for First Nations people.

In the concluding chapter, the authors note that it is often incorrectly assumed that residential schools were a problem in the distant past. That's not the case. The report maintained the direct negative health effects of residential schools are still commonly being felt among the 15 percent who attended the schools and are still alive. Moreover, the intergenerational negative effects on health — including suicidal thoughts and substance abuse — are evident among an additional 60 percent of adults and some 65 percent of youth and children whose parents or grandparents attended such schools — and are particularly severe among those who had a parent who attended the schools.

(Source: First Nations Information Governance Centre 2018:140)

like *Maclean's* created a firestorm of controversy a few years ago by raising the possibility that Asians are overwhelming Canadian universities to the detriment of other students.[19] Black feminist activist and author Robyn Maynard claims in her 2017 book, *Policing Black Lives*, that anti-black racism has been present through to the present day, hidden under what she refers to as "white benevolence" — an official embracing "of racial diversity and tolerance that has never been the case."[20]

In addition, organizations like B'nai Brith Canada say that anti-Semitism is on the rise, with the 1,728 incidents in 2016 being the highest the group has ever recorded.[21] In addressing the United Nations in September of 2017, Prime Minister Justin Trudeau acknowledged the need for Canada to respond to the "humiliation, neglect, and abuse" that has been suffered by Indigenous people in Canada.[22]

This illustrative short list of ongoing intergroup concerns hardly attests to a Canada where pluralism, in practice, is on the verge of being

Compassion, Comfort, and Acceptance Over Time

Over time, younger Canadians have been exhibiting higher levels of tolerance and compassion.

- The right to medical care has been endorsed by 9 in 10 young adults spanning the 1980s through today (Figure 3.3).
- Suspicion levels — where one thinks "a stranger who shows a person attention is probably up to something" — has remained at about the same 1 in 3 level. It may never get much lower, given the widespread perception that we all can potentially be victims.
- The acceptance of official bilingualism has increased modestly over time. Given the policy has been instilled in young people from the first days of school, it's not surprising that it has continued "to take" in Canadians' early years.
- The perception women are now experiencing little discrimination has not declined in a consistent, linear fashion. Rather, it has increased and dropped. Those currently maintaining little sex discrimination exists include 44 percent of males and 62 percent of females.
- The belief that homosexuals are entitled to the same rights as other Canadians has jumped significantly — from 67 percent in 1984 to 93 percent today.

realized. Waterloo sociologist Augie Fleras reminds us that while most people endorse multiculturalism and pluralism as an ideology or policy, the practice of multiculturalism is much more difficult to realize. So it is that Millennials and others endorse pluralism, yet maintain that immigrants should, for example, accept Canadian values. Fleras argues that "official multiculturalism is prone to paradoxes" based on "the balancing act between unity (commonality) and difference. Put bluntly," he says, "too much multiculturalism (differences) and not enough monoculturalism (unity) may destabilize a society to the point of dismemberment."[23]

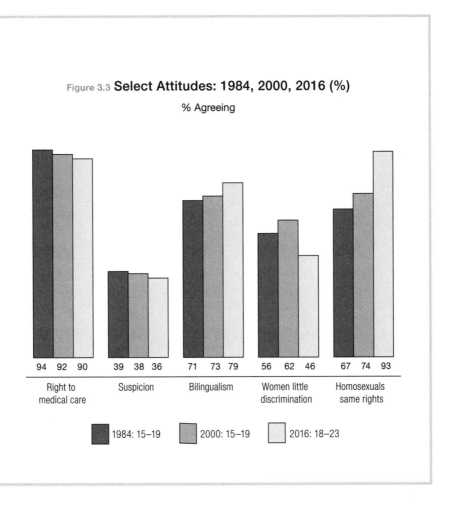

Figure 3.3 **Select Attitudes: 1984, 2000, 2016 (%)**

% Agreeing

| 94 | 92 | 90 | 39 | 38 | 36 | 71 | 73 | 79 | 56 | 62 | 46 | 67 | 74 | 93 |

| Right to medical care | Suspicion | Bilingualism | Women little discrimination | Homosexuals same rights |

■ 1984: 15–19   ■ 2000: 15–19   □ 2016: 18–23

We will also see this play out when we discuss multiculturalism among various groups, including Muslims and Indigenous Peoples.

Pluralism in practice is clearly the proverbial "work in progress."

These overall trend findings suggest that social and cultural factors have played a limited role in influencing a number of social attitudes. They simply haven't changed very much over time. The sole exception for the illustrative items we have looked at is, as noted, the increase in the endorsement of gay rights. Here, there is little doubt that a consistent, significant emphasis on equality for gays and lesbians over time has contributed to changes in attitudes.

On the Dangers of Exaggerating Racism: One Observer's Take

Recently, award-winning journalist Douglas Todd, who has been assessing intergroup relations from Vancouver for some four decades, offered this take on things.

There is little doubt that some degree of discrimination and racism exists in B.C. and Canada. Media frequently report on racist graffiti, online comments, or remarks. And any racism is too much. It's just that we have to keep the extent of it in proportion. And we have to define it. If we don't, well-intentioned activists will create unnecessary suspicion, mistrust, and division among us. Behaving ethically requires accuracy, especially over an infamous wrong like racism. A Gallup poll conducted in more than 50 countries discovered 84 percent believe Canadians are "tolerant of others who are different," the highest ranking of any country. Could the world really be so wrong about Canada?

(Source: Todd 2017)

If social and cultural factors (period effects) have not significantly altered many social attitudes — apart from equality — we would expect that the attitudes of 15- to 19-year-old teens in 1984 would not have changed very much as they evolved into 47- to 51-year-olds in 2016.

The cohort analysis bears out such thinking (Figure 3.4). The levels of support for an adequate income and medical care, and concern about racial discrimination and the unequal treatment of women have remained similar over time for the 1984 cohort.[*] However, seemingly reflecting societal shifts, support for bilingualism for this group that is now part of the GenX cohort is down from what it was in 1984, as is the endorsement of the mosaic over the melting pot. In sharp contrast, the endorsement of gay rights is up substantially. Here period effects seem readily apparent.

While the tide of global support for gay lifestyles since at least the 1980s readily explains the large increase in support in Canada for same sex rights, the sources of the lack of support for bilingualism and the mosaic versus melting pot model are not clear.

---

[*] The differences are particularly small, especially allowing for the relatively small sample size of the cohort in 2016. The error range is about 6% points either way, 18 times in 20.

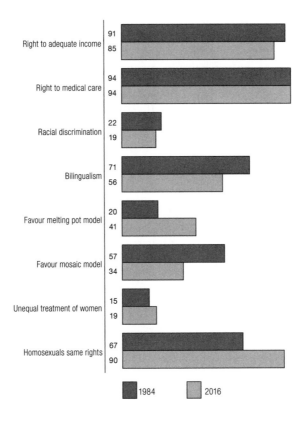

Figure 3.4 **Select Attitudes: Teens 15–19 in 1984 as Adults 47–51 in 2016 (%)**

% Agreeing

Perhaps improved French–English relations in recent years have, ironically, reduced the sense that there is a need for two official languages. It also may be that growing numbers of Canadians, bolstered by large numbers of immigrants with a limited understanding of the rationale for bilingualism, are once more feeling that preference should not be shown for any one second language, besides English.

In the case of declining support for the multicultural model, it may be a case of Canadians, as they age, developing increasing skepticism about the concept. Experience and ongoing tension, particularly across the globe, may be contributing to growing numbers leaning toward integration as the policy of choice. Let's be clear: Millennials and others solidly endorse pluralism. But they increasingly want to know that the mosaic tiles come together into an integrated whole.

Variations in Social Attitudes

The fact that Millennials are anything but a homogenous group is readily apparent when we look at attitudes across eight illustrative variables: *region, community size, gender, education, birthplace, race, Indigenous/non-Indigenous*, and *sexual orientation*. The full data that follow in the Magnified Mosaic table can make any reader a shade dizzy; the details are being made available for the taking. Here are a few highlights.

- The idea that *diversity is good for Canada* (85 percent) is highly pervasive with noteworthy variations limited to community size and education.
- The belief that people have a *right to an income* adequate to live on is held by slightly more people in B.C. than elsewhere and also increases with education.
- Somewhat paradoxically, 40 percent of Millennials say that their *suspicion of people* has increased in recent years — almost the same proportion as those who indicate that their *concern for people* has increased. Suspicion is slightly higher in B.C. and Alberta, in rural communities, and among women; concern is higher in B.C. and among Millennials born outside Canada.
- Negative views of *Muslims* are highest among Millennials in Alberta, Quebec, and the Atlantic region, in rural areas, among individuals who are not university graduates, among those born outside of Canada, and Caucasians.

In sum, overall, Millennials and other Canadian are displaying very positive attitudes toward each other, complete with expressions of social compassion. At the same time, as they live out life, many express a measure of fear and apprehension. They want to be safe and they don't want to feel anxious.

 THE MAGNIFIED MOSAIC

Millennial Social Attitudes by Select Variables

	Diversity good for canada	People's right to income	Suspicion of people: has increased	Concern for people: has increased	Negative toward Muslims
NATIONAL	83%	81	41	45	36
British Columbia	83	92	50	63	25
Alberta	83	80	50	43	42
Manitoba-Saskatchewan	78	83	41	43	32
Ontario	86	81	36	45	27
Quebec	82	78	39	37	49
Atlantic	80	78	44	46	53
Urban	87	82	39	47	35
Rural	64	76	53	38	44
Women	86	82	47	50	35
Men	81	80	36	41	36
Degree-plus	90	90	37	48	26
Some post-secondary	79	81	47	44	43
HS or less	80	78	42	44	37
Born elsewhere	88	89	45	56	46
Born in Canada	82	80	40	43	34
Visible minority	84	85	39	48	25
Caucasian	83	80	42	44	41
Indigenous*	82	84	45	44	32
Non-Indigenous*	80	83	38	36	41
LGBTQ*	83	84	39	40	38
Heterosexual*	79	84	30	36	42

*Millennials and Gen Xers combined because of small sample sizes.

Millennials are comfortable with diversity. They have grown up with it or, as immigrants, discovered it. A 7 in 10 majority of Millennials lead Canadians in maintaining that immigration is good for the country, with the same proportion favouring the current two official languages policy. They currently endorse the mosaic model for accommodating differences but, as they get older, may well follow GenX, Boomer, and Pre-Boomer cohorts in being attracted in greater numbers to the melting pot model.

We said in the opening pages of the book that the key to understanding our emerging Canada lies in our national emphases on diversity and pluralism. Canadians frequently differ from one another. Hopefully, they are trying to understand, accept, and appreciate their differences. Pluralism is the affirmation of diversity that ideally contributes to an enhanced life for everyone.

These findings suggest that the majority of Millennials are embracing both diversity and pluralism. That bodes well for the future of interpersonal life in Canada.

INSTITUTIONS

"Millennials put very little confidence in established institutions, perhaps because established institutions have yet to deliver for them." Such was the take of a bi-partisan, U.S. think tank as it released the findings of a major survey of 1,200 American Millennials in 2016.[24]

The Economic Innovation Group (EIG) found that only 2 of the 13 institutions polled received confidence levels above 50 percent — the military (55 percent) and colleges and universities (51 percent). The endorsement levels of the rest were all very low, ranging from 32 percent for professional sports to a mere 20 percent for corporate America. In between, at around 25–30 percent, were labour, banks, Silicon Valley, the justice system, religion, the news media, and local, federal, and state governments.

As we will see shortly, our results for Canada are close to a photocopy.

Institutions are a central part of our social environment. They historically have been seen as responses to five areas of life — family, education, economy, religion, and government. Many other areas of life, including media, leisure, and technology, have seen the emergence of additional organizational responses.

What's important is to recognize that the lives of Millennials and everyone else are lived out in the context of a large number of such institutions. How they feel about life, including the possibility of realizing their hopes and expectations today and in the future, can be expected to be closely tied to their views of key institutions and how they are being run.

Millennials and Health

The changing posture that Millennials have toward health and the health profession has been noted by Canadian global research and "insight community" provider Vision Critical. In a comprehensive overview, Vision Critical refers to Millennials as "the ultimate empowered patients." They are a health-conscious generation, as seen in their preference for organically grown foods, emphasis on fitness, and overall lifestyles that make them "more proactive about their health than any generation before them."

As Millennials enter their 30s, medical resources are taking on greater importance. While most trust health care professionals, they report that their primary source for information on health and nutrition is Google searches, followed by family and friends, and then medical people, such as doctors, nurses, and pharmacists. They do their homework on health professionals and candidly ask questions about procedures and costs. In many respects, these actions typify the themes of individualism and choice that are prevalent throughout our read of Millennials and Canadian society at large.

Vision Critical offers this radical thought: "The health care sector will need to learn fast from the experience of other consumer sections and quickly get accustomed to treating patients like customers."

(Source: Vision Critical 2016)

Our most recent 2015–16 national surveys examined the confidence that Millennials and other adults have in our major institutions, repeating a number of questions that Reg has put to young people in earlier surveys to make tracking possible. An array of additional items were included that explored more specifically how institutions are functioning.

A central overview item asked respondents how much confidence they have "in the people in charge" of 14 institutions, with the four response options being "a great deal," "quite a bit," "some," and "little or none."

What is immediately apparent is the fact that we Canadians have high expectations of our primary institutions and the people who run them. Only one area — *the police* — receives the positive endorsement of more than 50 percent of Millennials and adults as a whole.

Changes in Confidence in Institutions:
Life Cycle and Period Effects

When we look at the confidence levels of 15- to 19-year-olds in 1984 and compare them to what the group is saying now as 47- to 51-year-olds, we find a significant, consistent drop in confidence in every institutional instance (see Figure 3.5). In some cases, the declines are dramatic — schools, the court system, television, and newspapers. It would be easy

Figure 3.5 **Select Areas of Institutional Confidence:
Teens 15–19 in 1984 as Adults 47–51 in 2016 (%)**

% Indicating "A Great Deal" or "Quite a Bit"

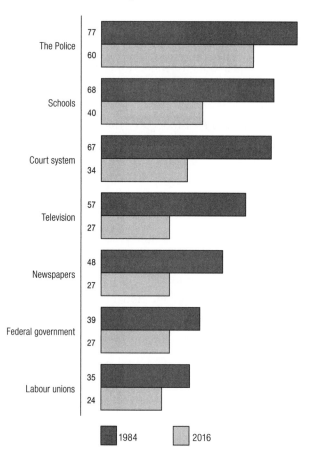

to explain the drop-offs in terms of life cycle: as young people get older, experience also allows them to get wiser. They start off naive; with the passage of time they encounter the realities of life and become more critical — and jaded — about leadership.

However, the trend data suggest that there might also be some important "period effects" involved that have had an important impact on younger people and older adults alike. A comparison of confidence levels in 1984, 2000, and 2016 shows a consistent decline in confidence among youth cohorts over time — plateauing only in the case of the federal government (Figure 3.6). The rank order of confidence has remained similar, with the police and schools accorded the highest levels of confidence. But the levels have dropped significantly.

Figure 3.6 **Confidence in Select Institutions: 1984, 2000, 2016 (%)**

% Indicating "A Great Deal" or "Quite a Bit"

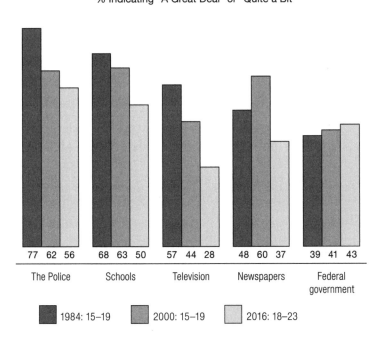

77 62 56	68 63 50	57 44 28	48 60 37	39 41 43
The Police	Schools	Television	Newspapers	Federal government

■ 1984: 15–19 ■ 2000: 15–19 □ 2016: 18–23

Table 3.4 Views of Institutions and Institutional Leadership

"How much confidence do you have in the people in charge of...?"

% Indicating "A Great Deal" or "Quite a Bit"

	ALL	Millennials 1986–plus (18–29)	Xers 1966–1985 (30–49)	Boomers 1946–1965 (50–69)	Pre-Boomers Pre-1946 (70-plus)
The police	58	52	52	64	68
Schools	43	43	41	44	49
Court system	38	42	36	35	42
Computer industry	36	40	37	33	35
Financial institutions	35	30	30	38	46
Federal government	34	40	32	32	36
Newspapers	31	36	28	31	30
Television	29	30	27	29	30
Major business	29	27	27	27	38
Music industry	28	30	28	29	22
Labour unions	26	29	26	25	24
Your provincial government	26	29	24	24	32
Movie industry	25	28	26	26	13
Religious organizations	24	26	24	21	26

- The confidence levels that Millennials accord institutions are very similar to those of Gen Xers and Boomers, which in turn are frequently slightly lower than the levels of confidence expressed by Pre-Boomers.

- Some 30 percent to 40 percent of Millennials and others express high levels of confidence in the *court system, computer industry, financial institutions*, the *federal government*, and *newspapers* (see Table 3.4).

- The levels of confidence drop from just under 30 percent to about 25 percent in the case of *television, major business*, the *music industry, labour unions, provincial governments*, the *movie industry*, and *religious organizations*.

Table 3.5 **Some Specific Views of Institutions
and Institutional Leadership**

% Agreeing

	Millennials	Other Adults
Police		
Law enforcement is applied evenly to those who break the law	33	30
Teachers		
Overall, public school teachers are very competent	73	76
Courts		
In general, the courts do not deal harshly enough with criminals	67	82
The death penalty should sometimes be used to punish criminals	46	64
Media		
The CBC is important to Canada	81	75
Government		
The political and economic system we have in this country is about the best there is	40	53
People like me don't have any say about what the government does	58	55
So far Justin Trudeau is doing a pretty good job as prime minister	77	68
Movies		
On the whole, movies have a good influence on young people	44	32

The main takeaway from all these numbers is this: Millennials and other Canadians are not exactly deferential when it comes to institutions and institutional personnel. They hopefully are reasonably respectful and courteous — in keeping with the interpersonal ideals that they profess to have. But they also are extremely demanding. These are not easy days to be involved in virtually any kind of institutional leadership. They also are not easy days for people who are "the face" of institutions and their infrastructures, who have to relate to their publics.

The surveys offer an array of illustrative findings about how Millennials and other adults view their performances (see Table 3.5).

The Paradox of Unattachment and Connection

In summing up the characteristics of American Millennials, Gallup maintains that, more so than the generations before them, they are "a group without attachments. They do not feel close ties to their jobs or the brands to which they give their money. Millennials are waiting longer to get married, and they are less likely than other generations to feel pride in their communities or to identification with particular religious affiliations or traditional political parties." Gallup says this doesn't mean that Millennials will take a pass on marriage and groups. But it does suggest Millennials view many institutions differently than their predecessors.

Yet, despite their apparent lack of attachments, Gallup points out that its surveys find that Millennials are highly connected to the world around them. "The introduction and evolution of the Internet, Wi-Fi, laptops and smart-phones," says Gallup, have made it possible for Millennials "to instantly and constantly access entertainment, news, friends, strangers, and nearly any-thing else." Gallup maintains that their "hyper-connectedness has helped them gain a unique global perspective and has transformed the way they interact, consume content, browse, buy, and work."

Such a paradox, we think, also appears to characterize their Canadian counterparts.

(Source: Adkins 2016)

- *The police* may be accorded a relatively high level of confidence. Yet only a one-third minority of Millennials and others think they are enforcing the law evenly. Monetta suggests that this finding is not surprising, given the diversity of Millennials and the experiences that racialized individuals, for example, have with the police and the crim-inal justice system. The perception that racialized youth have of the police and justice system in Canada has always been a cause for con-cern.[25] With increasing discourse around the interactions with racial-ized youth and the justice system, Millennials are losing confidence in the justice system, particularly the police.

- A resounding 3 in 4 Millennials and older Canadians say that, overall, *public teachers* are very competent. That's identical to what Reg found in his 1995 Project Canada Survey, with both results very close to the 80 percent figure Gallup found in 1950.[26]
- *The courts* have been criticized for years for not dealing harshly enough with criminals. That's still pretty much the case. The finding that fewer Millennials than older adults think the courts are not harsh enough shouldn't hide the fact that a solid majority of 2 in 3 (67 percent) *do* feel the courts are too lenient. Fewer Millennials than Gen Xers, Boomers, and Pre-Boomers are in favour of capital punishment — yet almost 1 in 2 (47 percent) favour the death penalty being used on some occasions.
- Perhaps surprisingly, in an era of unprecedented television and radio options and cynicism about media, *the CBC* continues to be highly valued by Millennials and others. The current support level of 76 percent who think the CBC is important to Canada is solidly above the levels of 64 percent for CBC TV and 55 percent for CBC Radio that Reg found in 1995.[27] Who said people think it's time to mothball the CBC?
- Politically, Millennials are less inclined than older adults to endorse our political and economic system, with a 6 in 10 majority joining with Xers, Boomers, and Pre-Boomers in maintaining they "don't have any say about what the government does." A large majority, however, do applaud the performance of Prime Minister Justin Trudeau.
- Some 1 in 2 Millennials are positive about the influence of today's *movies* on young people, compared to just 1 in 3 older Canadians. In 1945, Gallup found that very similar levels of 50 percent of adults under 30 agreed with the statement, as did 38 percent of older adults.[28]

One "period" explanation is that, since the turn of the twenty-first century, teens — equipped with the Internet and an increasingly large number of additional platforms — have had unprecedented access to information.

Moreover, social media is used to circulate videos of those in positions of authority who abuse their authority (e.g., white police officers beating/

killing African-American citizens). Such events are on display in "real time" for the world to see. Further, Millennials especially respond to and engage with these stories and with one another on various online platforms. For example, they see and dialogue about the police as unfair and prejudiced, political and economic leaders as corrupt, the school system as ill-preparing students to obtain jobs later in life, the elite few controlling and shaping the messages on television, and newspapers as biased and partisan.

They consequently have become much better informed and far less deferential. They also have been accustomed to having a say in just about every sphere of life. Greater awareness and opportunities for input, mainly via the Internet, have contributed to elevated expectations and a significantly increased level of criticism of everyone and everything. Many now see themselves as experts on almost any topic.[29]

One of the consequences of these social changes is found in social and civic engagement activities among Millennials. Reminiscent of our discussion on social problems in the previous chapter, the current issues that Millennials do or do not take an interest in, and the ways that they get engaged, are intricately tied up with how problems are portrayed online.

Research on civic participation among university students, for example, suggests there is no one-size-fits-all approach,[30] a finding verified in research on Canadian Millennials who participate in a range of online and in-person activities.[31] Millennials initially tend to gravitate toward online communities as passive followers, followed by actively contributing to those communities. In-person involvements are a distant third and fourth. More often than not, online involvement rises quickly and fades away just as fast.

By way of illustration, for all the hysteria in our classrooms for a couple of weeks in 2012, does anyone remember KONY 2012 now? That said, there are some movements that gain momentum for longer periods of time. Ruth Milkman, in her 2016 presidential address at the American Sociological Association annual meeting, outlined a series of social movements recently led by college-educated Millennials. The Occupy Wall Street movement in 2011 and the Black Lives Matter uprising more recently, among other movements, arose because of a widespread and shared Millennial critique of injustices committed against marginalized people by society's elite — based on any combination of race, gender, sexuality, and class.

As we will see in the coming chapters, Millennials have strong and increasingly liberal views on these topics. They believe in equality, tolerance, and respect in a pluralistic Canada. Some can be expected to leverage social media with in-person protests to get their messages out and try to bring about social change.

That information transformation has, of course, been shared by all generations. Two trends seem noteworthy. First, young people are better informed and more critical of leadership than previous generations. Second, those levels of information and reservation about leadership now characterize all ages, so that the overall confidence levels of Millennials differ little from others.

So it is that among Millennials and just about everyone else, confidence in leadership in the police and schools only reaches 50–60 percent and confidence in leadership in other places trails well behind. It's not so much a matter of our various institutions being under attack. But they are viewed with caution and their leaders are seen as fallible. Confidence and respect have to be earned. Further, lack of confidence among Millennials that often has been relatively latent and unexpressed among other age cohorts can be expected to become increasingly overt, assisted by the technological resources that can give expression to discontent.

Some valuable additional information on the political involvement inclinations of Canadian Millennials has been generated recently by Environics. Generally speaking, interest in politics is slightly lower for Millennials than Gen Xers, with the gap increasing relative to Boomers and Pre-Boomers.[32] Still, many Millennials follow national and world news fairly closely and do not lack for social concerns. Depending on the specific topic, between 50–75 percent of Millennials say that they are interested in politics and follow current news events regularly,[33] despite feeling less informed on political matters or less likely to be personally contacted by politicians than older Canadians.[34] Millennials are less likely than other adults to turn to television, newspapers, or the radio to obtain election information. However, just over one-third turn to social media, websites, and word of mouth, more than the double the level of their parents or grandparents.[35] Leading up to the 2015 federal election, adults under 30 were more likely than older cohorts to talk about politics with their family and friends.[36] That's not to say every Millennial is interested in what is taking place around them. Despite almost unlimited access to seemingly unlimited information, Statistics Canada tells us that the proportion of young people, 15 to 34, who acknowledge they "rarely" or "never" follow the news almost doubled from 11 percent in 2003 to 21 percent in 2013.[37]

Online–offline comparisons shift when we expand to account for active Millennial involvement in social causes or issues. Around one-quarter of Millennials indicated they were actively involved in the past year, usually in areas involving social justice, the environment, politics, or health care. Like those older than them, most Millennials tended to passively get involved via online channels (e.g., "liking" a post or sharing a post), though some participated in person too (e.g., attended a political meeting, rally, or protest).[38] For the most part, Millennials are not that different than older generations in this respect.[39]

As for voting, it's no secret that national voting rates have declined over the past two elections, especially among Canada's youth. An anomaly took place with 2015 federal election — when Justin Trudeau was elected prime minister. Just under 70 percent of eligible Canadian voters cast a ballot in that election, the highest since 1993. This included around 70 percent of Canadians under 35 years old (up about 10 percent from the previous federal election).[40] Incidentally, the three main reasons young adults cited for not voting were disinterest in politics, the belief their vote could not make a difference, or the fact they didn't have the time.[41]

What remains to be seen is whether the voting uptick in 2015 among Canadians overall, and Millennials in particular, was a blip on the radar or a sign of things to come. Statistics Canada offers the interesting footnote that political interest and involvement is more common among Millennials and others who feel a strong sense of belonging and social inclusion. Significantly, with those sentiments among immigrants increasing with the time they have been in Canada, it may be that the reduction in marginalization will contribute to higher levels of political participation.[42]

Variations in Institutional Confidence

The relatively low levels of confidence that Millennials have in virtually all areas of leadership are very consistent across a range of demographic characteristics. Here again we provide considerable data and a few highlights, so that the information is available for those who wish to pursue it in detail.

- Differences by *gender, income, education, birth place, race, Indigenous/ non-Indigenous identity*, and *sexual orientation* are relatively minor, although females are consistently slightly less likely than males to express confidence in leaders. This may in part reflect fewer females in positions of institutional leadership.
- *Visible minorities* (43 percent) are somewhat less inclined than others (56 percent) to express confidence in the police, undoubtedly reflecting both the experiences some have had with the police and the increasing scrutiny the police have faced in both Canada and the United States.
- *Indigenous* individuals express lower confidence in religious leaders (16 percent) than others (25 percent), seemingly reflecting the churches' involvement with residential schools. This predominantly urban sample does not, however, exhibit lower levels of confidence in the police or the courts.
- Millennials who identify as *LGBTQ* express somewhat lower levels of confidence than other Canadians in both the police and religious leaders — suggesting there is still a distance to go for some members of the community to feel they are accepted in both society as a whole and in religious environments specifically.

ASSESSMENT

Millennials — like Gen Xers, Boomers, and Pre-Boomers — for the most part are highly positive about interpersonal life in Canada. They see most people as civil and decent and our society as compassionate. They donate their money and time as they are able, and they are adamant that people, regardless of income, receive medical care and have incomes adequate to live on.

That is not to say that younger and older Canadians alike do not have a measure of trepidation and even fear as they live out life. We all typically "proceed with a measure of caution" in dealing with strangers and venturing into certain places, especially at night.

But Millennials and the rest of us value and enjoy interpersonal life. Most are also willing to expand their social boundaries. The vast majority maintain that racial and cultural diversity is a good thing for the country. They recognize and accept the reality of immigration, hardly surprising in light of the fact that almost all of us are descendants of immigrants ourselves. Canadians young and old also endorse the idea of all people being able to share equally in Canadian life, regardless of characteristics such as gender, sexual orientation, and age.

Those things said, the heralded mosaic is still a goal rather than a reality, as seen, for example, in the persistence of negative views and behaviour toward groups like Muslims and renewed concern about the discriminatory treatment of women.

If Millennials are relatively positive with respect to individuals, the same cannot be said of their attitudes toward institutions and their leaders. Primarily reflecting, we think, trends related to the information explosion and the desire for input, Canadians have become increasingly reflective about life and leaders. As a recent Angus Reid Institute–CBC examination of views toward institutions noted, Millennials' access to wider sources of information via technology leads them to understand more clearly the impact of Canadian policies and question our institutions. "Distrust of Canadian institutions therefore is fuelled by the tool that drives Millennials … technology."[43] The days of uninformed acquiescence are over.

To an unprecedented extent, Millennials and others are becoming increasingly armed with information about what is happening around them. Equipped in particular with the Internet, they are becoming more aware than their predecessors of what is taking place in such diverse areas as law enforcement, schools, finance, medicine, law, government, and entertainment. And that's just the short list. Deference has been replaced by discernment, truth claims by perusals of the Internet and any number of additional platforms to obtain information and "second, third, and fourth opinions" on just about everything. It all is having a revolutionary impact on information authority.

What is important to keep in mind is that Millennials and others do not simply have a passive relationship to institutions. They interact with them and make it necessary for institutions and their players to make adjustments. Otherwise, organizations associated with various institutional spheres can readily become irrelevant, wither up, and die. Vision Critical notes that in the U.S., for example, Millennials with their large numbers and growing resources can "transform entire economic sectors and even hobble the balance sheets of industry behemoths." By way of illustration, it notes that "dominant beer brands such as Budweiser and Coors Light have been suffering declining sales since the first Millennials were old enough to drink, while the rise of craft breweries has occurred in lockstep with their passing into the age of majority."[44] Vision Critical says that, in the future, Millennials are going to transform industries and by the time they reach middle age "will have already remade the world in their image."[45]

To sum up in terms of the Millennial mosaic framework we have been posing: Canada's emerging young adults have a pervasive mindset characterized by themes such as diversity and pluralism, individualism and choice. They are generally positive toward individuals but highly critical of institutions and — as necessary — are willing to take them on. The Millennial mosaic is comprised of a large number of moving parts.

Lots of changes, lots of adjustments in the face of emerging Millennials. One area of Canadian life that has been profoundly affected by all this is sexuality, the topic to which we now turn.

 THE MAGNIFIED MOSAIC

Millennial Institutional Confidence by Select Variables

	The Police	Schools	Courts	Computer industry	Financial institutions	Television	Religious leaders
NATIONAL	52%	43	42	40	30	30	26
Women	53	41	37	38	27	29	24
Men	51	45	47	43	34	31	28
<$50,000	51	44	43	45	30	33	28
$50–99,000	59	50	49	34	33	28	28
$100,000+	53	38	36	33	33	30	19
Degree-plus	49	44	47	43	31	25	24
Some post-secondary	56	40	42	38	32	31	30
HS or less	51	45	36	39	29	36	25
Born elsewhere	52	48	49	42	36	33	39
Born in Canada	52	42	41	39	29	30	23
Visible minority	44	47	44	36	33	29	31
Caucasian	54	42	42	40	30	30	24
Indigenous*	54	59	38	43	33	27	16
Non-Indigenous*	52	58	38	38	30	28	25
LGBTQ*	46	46	42	37	30	26	17
Heterosexual*	53	41	38	39	30	29	25

*Millennials and Gen Xers combined because of small sample sizes.

CHAPTER 4

Sexualities: Sex/Equality Issues

In November of 1967, comedian Pat Paulsen, known for his wry and provocative editorials on the highly controversial *Smothers Brothers Comedy Hour* on CBS, started one editorial this way:

> The time has come to stop whispering ... THE TIME HAS COME TO STOP WHISPERING about the biggest issue facing our educational system today ... an issue which must be discussed boldly ... courageously and in an adult manner. I am referring, of course, to the whole subject of S.E.X.[1]

It all seems so long ago. Social historians tell us that, through the 1950s, sex was largely a taboo topic. Sex outside of marriage was widely viewed as inappropriate, strongly enforced in Canada by religious bodies led by the Catholic Church. Most people and most institutions did not speak openly about sex. In some places, the very term was replaced with euphemistic phrases such as "you know what" and "going all the way." Sex education was frequently left to chance, sometimes to family members, often to friends. In one Canadian national survey conducted as the twenty-first century began, 17 percent of Pre-Boomers recalled that school had been a major source of their information about sex, compared to 29 percent of Boomers and 50 percent of Gen Xers.[2] Given the lack of good information about birth control, for example, what was believed was neither sound nor particularly effective. In the 1950s and '60s, even the pollsters weren't asking. One looks in vain for early public opinion items on sexual attitudes, let alone sexual behaviour.

A telling bit of unobtrusive data? Social scientists claim that topics of humour often involve things that we don't speak openly about. In the past they have included immigration, race, women, and, of course, sex. The latter was among the most popular topics for jokes and humour generally.

And then came the 1960s and "the rights revolutions." Starting with the American civil rights movement, the emphasis on freedom expanded to touch much of life, including race, ethnicity, women, lifestyles, religion, families, sex, and sexual orientation. A poignant and timely symbol of the Sexual Revolution was the appearance of "the pill" in 1960.

These days, what we are experiencing is the normalization of sex. In contrast to life in the Pre-Boomer era, sex is now simply part of life for most people. University students, for example, typically see sex as "no big deal" — something to engage in or not engage in, depending on one's values and inclinations. For some, it is still restricted to marriage. For most, there are no such restrictions. Oh, and jokes about sex have largely disappeared from the humour landscape — except in settings where it continues to be taboo.

If anything, the focus of sexual attention in recent years has moved from sexual behaviour to sexual orientation and gender issues. In 2014, *Time* magazine, for example, proclaimed that transgender rights will be "the next civil rights frontier."[3]

We will first look at sex and then look more closely at orientation and identities. In doing so we draw attention, once more, to the recurring place that pluralism plays in Canadian society. This focus includes the centrality of both individualism and choice among Millennials when expressing their attitudes regarding sexuality.

SEX

Sexual Attitudes

Social scientists have found that a precarious relationship exists between attitudes and behaviour.[4] Attitudes typically reflect values, but neither necessarily translates into behaviour. One of the areas of social life where these differences are readily apparent is sex. We want to first look at attitudes and then examine behaviour.

Generational and Trend Data

The demise in the mystique surrounding sex can readily be documented using trend data. The first survey items on views about the topic appeared in 1975, some 15 years into the Sexual Revolution.[5] Reg's first Project Canada national survey of adults found that 32 percent of Canadians felt premarital sex was "always wrong" or "almost always wrong." A Gallup poll early the same year pegged the "wrong" figure at a similar 36 percent.[6] The Project Canada survey, using an item drawn from the National Opinion Research Center (NORC) in Chicago for both accuracy and comparison purposes, found that 29 percent of Canadians maintained that premarital sex was "sometimes wrong." The "not wrong at all" figure in Canada was 39 percent and, NORC found, 33 percent in the U.S.

Acceptance of premarital sex increased steadily from the 1970s onward. Today that "not wrong at all" figure for Canada stands at 69 percent. NORC tells us that, south of the border, the number has also risen from 33 percent in 1975 to a current 59 percent. Incidentally, for those asking why the Canadian–U.S. difference, one major reason has been the larger number of Americans who have been aligned with conservative Protestants groups — some 30-plus percent versus under 10 percent in Canada — that have tended to frown on premarital sex.

Figure 4.1 **Belief that Premarital Sex Is "Not Wrong at All":**
1975–2016 (%)

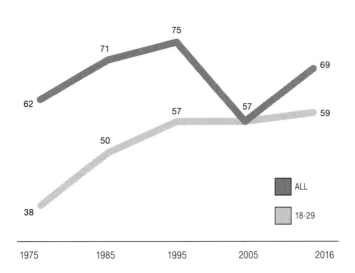

However, in the twenty-first century, an interesting development is evident among Canadian Millennials. In the 1970s, '80s, and '90s, younger adults had led the nation in their approval of premarital sex, with their endorsement level peaking at 75 percent around 1995.

But, over the past two decades or so, the approval numbers for people under 30 *have declined* to just under 60 percent. That level is lower than that of Gen Xers and Boomers and only slightly above that of Pre-Boomers (see Figure 4.1). More specifically, 59 percent of Millennials say that premarital sex is "not wrong at all," 18 percent think it is "sometimes wrong," 8 percent maintain that it's "almost always wrong," and 15 percent feel it is "always wrong." We must confess these figures are a little surprising. While it is important to keep the camera rolling to gain clarity about these changes, we do want to offer some tentative thoughts as to what may be happening here.

Accounting for the Millennial Attitudinal Anomaly

The big breakthrough with the Sexual Revolution was the freedom for people to do what they wanted sexually, which seemingly included greater sexual involvement outside of marriage. It also meant better sex education, where some 95 percent of Canadians young and old, for example, were maintaining since at least the 1970s and '80s that birth control information should be available to teenagers who wanted it.[7] But in recent decades, growing numbers of young people appear to have come to realize that true sexual freedom means having the freedom *to engage* in sex *or not* engage in sex. In short, in an era of personal freedom, premarital sex has come to be viewed as sometimes appropriate and sometimes not. As one American sex educator has bluntly put it, being sexually liberated and sexually empowered means that sometimes "You can keep your clothes on."[8]

Those thoughts are supported by data on sexual attitudes and religious service attendance (see Figure 4.2). As would be expected, given the teachings of the Catholic Church and other religious groups, such as evangelicals and Islam, only 23 percent of weekly service attenders maintain that sex before marriage is "not wrong at all." However, without the influence of religious group pressures, 15 percent of Canadians who "never" attend services and some 30 percent who seldom attend services also *do not* give an unqualified green light to premarital sex. Those two figures are 16 percent and 33 percent respectively in the case of Millennials.

Figure 4.2 **Premarital Sexual Attitudes by Service Attendance (%)**
% Indicating "Not Wrong at All"

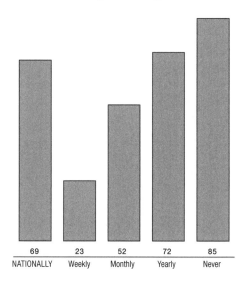

69	23	52	72	85
NATIONALLY	Weekly	Monthly	Yearly	Never

In the post-1960s, younger Canadians in particular were basking in the idea of sexual freedom. Now, five decades later, they show signs of having a more thoughtful sense of what sexual freedom means. In the case of premarital sexual activity, it means having the choice of being sexually involved and sometimes not.

Such patterns are further reflected in the trend data. In 1984, 80 percent of 15- to 19-year-olds agreed that "sex before marriage is alright when people love each other." That figure remained at close to the same level through 2000 but dropped to 72 percent in 2008. From the early '90s through 2008, approval of sex involving people "who like each other" declined from 64 percent to 38 percent. The 2016 survey, using the "right–wrong" NORC item we looked at earlier, has found that 59 percent of 18- to 23-year-olds maintain that premarital sex in general is "not wrong at all." But another 17 percent say it is "sometimes wrong," 7 percent that it is "almost always wrong," and 17 percent that it is "always wrong" (see Figure 4.3).

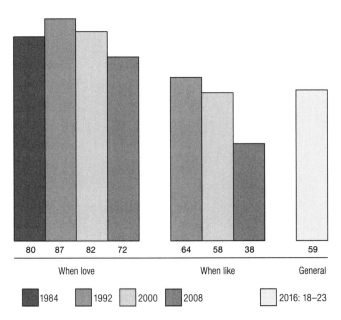

Figure 4.3 **Sexual Attitudes of Youth: 1984–2016 (%)**

(% Approving)

80	87	82	72	64	58	38	59

When love · When like · General

■ 1984 ■ 1992 □ 2000 ■ 2008 □ 2016: 18–23

In the meantime, the cohort analysis shows that the downward pattern among younger adults did not take place among Gen Xers. The 80 percent figure for 15- to 19-year-old teens in 1984 was virtually the same for the cohort as 47- to 51-year-olds in 2016 — 78 percent.

Taken together, it is clear that considerable sexual freedom exists. But, as we are emphasizing, that sexual freedom involves the freedom for people to engage or not engage in premarital sex. Millennials may have a better grasp of what sexual freedom actually means than many of their freedom-minded GenX, Boomer, and Pre-Boomer predecessors. This, in part, could be a reflection of the many sources of information they have about sex, including the Internet, school, the media, and home. Such information often comes with the pros and cons associated with sexual activity.

It's interesting to note that, for the overwhelming number of Canadians younger and older, post-'60s sexual freedom has not been extended to *extramarital sex*. Currently only 5 percent of Millennials and similar percentages of older adults feel that "a married person having sexual relations with someone other than their marriage partner" is "not wrong at all" (see Table 4.1). The figure in 1975? Also 5 percent. In 1984, 12 percent of 15- to 19-year-olds said they approved of extramarital sex; as of 2016, as 47- to 51-year-olds, the figure had slipped to 7 percent.

In the 1970s, many observers were unsure where sex and marriage were going. Some people advocated open marriages, where partners could be free to have sexual relations with any number of individuals besides their wives or husbands. Affairs notwithstanding, extramarital sexual liaisons is an idea that has never taken hold in Canada. In 1984, 12 percent of teenagers agreed that it is sometimes alright for a married person to have sexual relations with someone other than their marriage partner. By 2000, the figure had fallen to 9 percent. Today it stands at 5 percent among young people in the closely comparable 18- to 23-year-old category. In acknowledging his numerous affairs about five years ago, Tiger Woods commented, "I felt I had worked hard my entire life and deserved to enjoy all the temptations around me."[9] His take on things would resonate with very few Canadian Millennials and other adults.

Table 4.1 Premarital and Extramarital Sexual Attitudes of Millennials and Other Adults

% Indicating "Not Wrong at All"

	ALL	Millennials 1986–plus (18–29)	Xers 1966–1985 (30–49)	Boomers 1946–1965 (50–69)	Pre-Boomers Pre-1946 (70-plus)
A man and a woman having sexual relations before marriage	69	59	72	75	55
A married person having sexual relations with someone other than their marriage partner	6	5	8	5	3

Sexual Behaviour

Generational and Trend Findings

Beyond attitudes, approximately 75 percent of Millennials say that they currently "engage in sex" — noteworthy in view of the fact that only about 25 percent are either married or living common-law. Their level of sexual activity is second only to 30- to 49-year-old Gen Xers. On the surface, the fact that 23 percent say premarital sex is "always wrong" or "almost always wrong," and 1 in 4 say that they *never* engage in sex seems consistent. However, further to our argument that "to approve is not necessarily to engage," approval readily exceeds sexual involvement

One "cause for pause" finding as we try to wade through all this data on attitudes and behaviour: no less than 48 percent of Canadian adults — 1 in 2 — acknowledge that they have lived with "a non-marital sexual partner." That's a lot of people engaging in sex outside of marriage. They include 39 percent of Millennials, 60 percent of Gen Xers, 48 percent of Baby Boomers, and 24 percent of Pre-Boomers.

Figure 4.4 **Sexual Activity by Age Cohort (%)**

"How often do you engage in sex?"

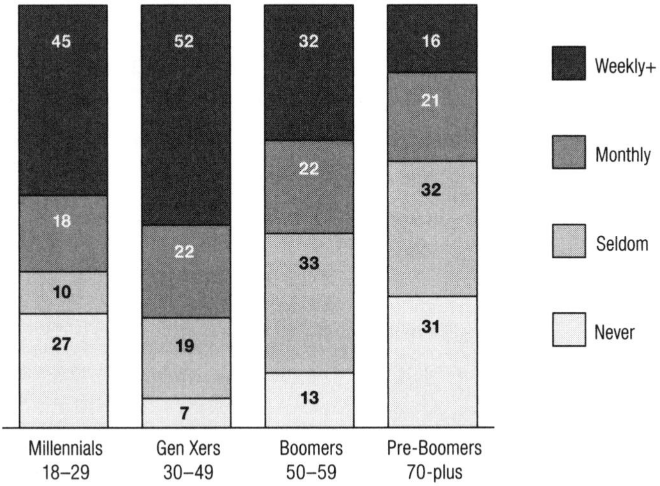

| | | | | | |
| Millennials 18–29 | Gen Xers 30–49 | Boomers 50–59 | Pre-Boomers 70-plus | | Weekly+ / Monthly / Seldom / Never |

Accounting for the Millennial Behavioural Anomaly

As seen in the big increases since the Boomers, Canadians have been basking in newfound sexual freedom. But, attitudinally and behaviorally, it also is freedom with limits. The Millennials probably feel more sexual freedom that any previous Canadian generation. But part of that liberation may be showing up in the inclination to be more reflective than any previous generation about the pluses and minus of sex outside of marriage.

These findings for Canada appear to be consistent with research in the United States. Contrary to the idea that Millennials are into a "hookup" culture and multiple partners fostered by online connections, a research team headed by Jean Twenge from San Diego State University has found that fewer Millennials under 25 are having sex (85 percent) than Gen Xers were having when they were the same age (94 percent). Twenge and colleagues Ryne Sherman from Florida Atlantic University and Brooke Wells from Widener University suggest the decrease may be tied to concerns over personal safety, health concerns, and even less interaction because of the Internet.[10] In Canada, public health experts claim that sexually transmitted infections are

Sexual Behaviour Among Youth: 1987 to 2016

The argument that freedom to engage in sex has not necessarily meant that everyone has seized the opportunity is borne out in trend data concerning sexual activity among young people.

In the 1980s, some 55 percent of 15- to 19-year-olds reported that they were sexually involved (see Figure 4.5). But through 2008, the level remained the same. Our latest survey — offering data on the slightly older, 18- to 23-year-old cohort — reveals a very similar level of sexual involvement.

Figure 4.5 **Sexual Activity of Youth, 1987–2016 (%)**

% Indicating They Have Been or Are Sexually Involved

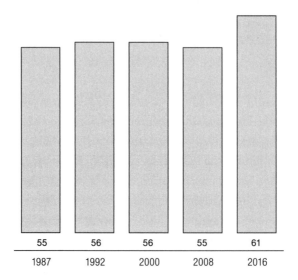

55	56	56	55	61
1987	1992	2000	2008	2016

The impact of the Sexual Revolution in Canada, it seems, was to make premarital sexual involvement a choice. What is still being debated, perhaps more so today than in the past, is not so much whether those choices are morally right or wrong, but whether or not they are good or not so good for people.

Sexting and Millennials

Considerable publicity has been given to the prevalence of sexting among young people. Sexting commonly refers to sending sexually explicit messages, pictures, and videos through text, email, or social media such as Facebook or Instagram. Sexting can include "intimate images" which, according to Canadian criminal law is a picture or video created in private circumstances that shows a person who is naked or semi-naked or is engaged in sexual activity.

In a 2014 study, "Young Canadians in a Wired World, Phase III: Sexuality and Romantic Relationships in the Digital Age," Valerie Steeves found that 15 percent of grade 11 students reported that they had sent a sext message. An even higher 36 percent said they had received a sext message, often from an original recipient who forwarded a sext message intended only for them. Messages were more common among males than females.

Sexting between adults 18 and over is legal in Canada when the people involved agree to participate. However, it is a criminal offence to post a picture without the voluntary permission of the person involved. For youth under 18, taking and sharing sexual images is against the law, except where the intimate image is for private use.

The Ontario Women's Justice Network is among the organizations that reminds individuals that sexting is risky: "Once you share an intimate image of yourself, it's almost impossible to control what happens to that picture/video. Pictures can be saved in phones, on computers, or stored online forever … sent to other people with one click, even by accident."

(Source: OWJN 2017)

continuing to rise. "In general, all the sexually transmitted infections have been increasing in the last 20 years," says Dr. Jason Wong of the B.C. Centre for Disease Control. Dating apps are a "suspected culprit," he says, although he acknowledges that no studies to date have documented the link.[11] Puzzling — since sexual activity in Canada is not seemingly on the rise. Alongside these kinds of explanations, we think a major factor is being overlooked that we have been emphasizing: the greater freedom to have or not have sex.

Abortion

In the 1960s, the theme of freedom included the assertion that women had the right to freedom over their bodies, including the right to terminate an unwanted pregnancy. That claim, of course, gave rise to an intense debate between so-called pro-choice and pro-life proponents in Canada, the United States, and many other places. In the U.S., the Supreme Court legalized abortion nationwide in the Roe v. Wade case in 1973.[12] In Canada, abortion was legalized in 1969 in cases where it was necessary for the physical or mental well-being of the mother. In 1988, the Supreme Court ruled that the existing law was unconstitutional. Since then, Canada has had no criminal laws restricting abortion.[13]

Nonetheless, remnants of the debate continue through today. From time to time, pro-life groups — led by Roman Catholics and evangelicals — attempt to resurrect the issue.[14] On some occasions, new lighting rods appear. In the spring of 2018, considerable controversy resulted from the federal government requiring that all employers applying to hire students as part of the Canada Summer Jobs project sign off on an "attestation." It stated that the job and the organization's core mandate would respect individual human rights in Canada, including "reproductive rights."[15] In defending the attestation, Prime Minister Justin Trudeau was unequivocal in stating the position of the federal government: "Women have fought for generations for the right to control their own bodies," he said, adding that any organization whose explicit purpose calls for removing the right to abortion "is not in line with where we are as a government and, quite frankly, where we are at as a society."[16]

We raised the abortion topic with our survey participants.

Generational and Trend Findings

Millennials have very similar responses regarding the availability of legal abortion as Gen Xers, Boomers, and Pre-Boomers. Variations are generally fairly small.

Some 8 in 10 Millennials support the availability of legal abortion when *rape*, a *mother's health*, or a *serious defect in the baby* are involved (see Table 4.2). The endorsement level drops to about 6 in 10 in situations where *low income, not wanting to marry the man*, or *not wanting more children* are

Table 4.2 **Attitudes Toward the Availability of Legal Abortion: Millennials and Other Adults**

% "Yes"

	ALL	Millennials 1986–plus (18–29)	Xers 1966–1985 (30–49)	Boomers 1946–1965 (50–69)	Pre-Boomers Pre-1946 (70-plus)
Her health is seriously endangered	85	82	85	86	86
There is a strong chance of a serious defect in the baby	81	74	80	85	82
The family has a very low income and cannot afford any more children	61	63	64	60	56
She is not married and does not want to marry the man	58	60	59	57	55
She is married and does not want to have any more children	57	57	61	55	50
For any reason	51	55	57	47	42

the key issues. About 5 in 10 Millennials support the availability of legal abortion *for any reason*, a level similar to Gen Xers that is higher than that of Boomers and Pre-Boomers.

Very often observers and commentators have portrayed the abortion debate as essentially involving two camps that are divided down the middle. These findings indicate that is not an accurate reading of the situation. In the cases of rape, health, and a defect in the fetus, a solid majority of 80 to 90 percent of Canadians, regardless of age, favour the availability of a legal abortion. The division on the issue surfaces when other situations are posed, such as low income and individuals not wanting more children. Where the country is divided down the middle is when it is proposed that legal abortion be a choice "for any reason."

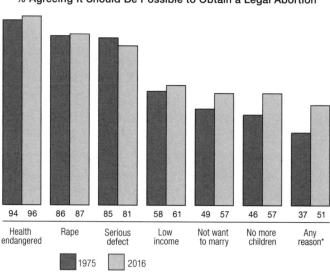

Figure 4.6 **Abortion Attitudes of Adults: 1975–2016 (%)**

% Agreeing It Should Be Possible to Obtain a Legal Abortion

94 96	86 87	85 81	58 61	49 57	46 57	37 51
Health endangered	Rape	Serious defect	Low income	Not want to marry	No more children	Any reason*

■ 1975   ☐ 2016

*1985 & 2016

The trend data for adults indicate that the high levels of agreement in the 1970s over the availability of a legal abortion when health, rape, and serious defect issues continue to exist today (see Figure 4.6). However, there have been slight increases in the agreement levels in other situations, including low incomes, a woman not wanting to marry the man, and a woman not wanting to have more children — significantly, all involving personal choices versus situations beyond personal control. Reflecting the greater openness to the abortion possibility, the percentage of Canadians indicating the option of a legal abortion should exist "for any reason" has increased from 37 percent in 1985 to a current level of 51 percent (see Figure 4.6).

Variations in Sexual and Abortion Attitudes

There are a number of fairly predictable differences in attitudes by a number of variables.

- *Millennial women* are slightly more likely than their male counterparts to endorse premarital sex. But that said, fewer Millennial women (69

Youth Abortion Attitudes over Time and as Young People Have Aged

These adult trend patterns are similar to the trend data for young people (see Figure 4.7). The proportion of younger people who felt that legal abortion should be possible in the case of rape hasn't changed much from the mid-'80s. But the percentage who favour the availability of a legal abortion when a woman does not want to have more children has increased significantly over the past three decades — reflecting the pervasiveness of prized cultural themes such as individual choice and freedom.

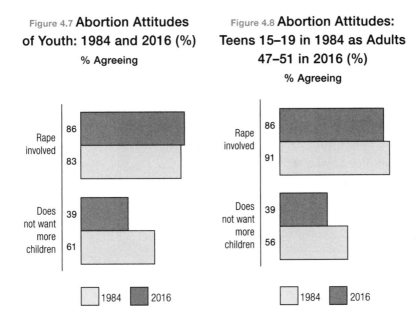

Figure 4.7 **Abortion Attitudes of Youth: 1984 and 2016 (%)**
% Agreeing

Figure 4.8 **Abortion Attitudes: Teens 15–19 in 1984 as Adults 47–51 in 2016 (%)**
% Agreeing

Those same patterns are reflected in what 15- to 19-year-olds in 1984 are telling us as 47- to 51-year-olds now (see Figure 4.8). Their level of agreement with the availability of a legal abortion when rape is involved has remained high. In addition, there has been a notable increase in this cohort's inclination to broaden its availability to include, for example, situations where a mother does not want to have any more children.

percent) than men (77 percent) are currently sexually involved. Here again we see an important distinction between sexual attitudes and behaviour: to approve in principle does not necessarily mean one personally engages in practice. Millennial women are also marginally more inclined than men to favour the legal availability of abortion.

- *Quebec Millennials* tend to be slightly more accepting of premarital sex than others, reflected as well in their higher level of sexual involvement (86 percent vs. 68 percent elsewhere).
- *Rural Millennials* are somewhat less inclined to endorse availability of legal abortion "for any reason."
- *Millennials who are religiously active* are considerably less likely than other youth adults to approve of premarital sex and abortion.
- Millennial *born outside of Canada* and — relatedly — those who are members of racialized groups are less inclined than other young adults to approve of premarital sex and, particularly in the case of immigrants, the availability of legal abortion.
- *Indigenous* young adults exhibit similar sexual and abortion attitudes as others, with the exception of being slightly more likely to approve of premarital sex.
- Members of the *LGBTQ* community express higher levels of approval than others of both premarital sex and the legal availability of abortion for any reason.

EQUALITY ISSUES

Sexual Orientation

Around 1995, Kevin Allen, gay and in his early 20s, was walking down a Calgary street in the Inglewood neighbourhood one afternoon when he was stopped by a police officer. Allen recalls the officer telling him "that he didn't like the wiggle in my walk." Such was the kind of harassment that LGBTQ people of his generation experienced. Now a leading voice for gays in the city, Allen observes, "I've met some great offices over the past few years," in working with the Calgary Police Service's diversity unity. "On the other hand, I have a visceral response to the institution."[17]

THE MAGNIFIED MOSAIC

Some Millennial Sexual Attitudes by Select Variables

	Premarital Sex	Extramarital Sex	Abortion: Rape	Abortion: Any Reason
	Not wrong at all	Not wrong at all	Yes	Yes
NATIONAL	59%	5	81	55
Women	62	3	82	56
Men	56	6	80	54
Quebec	61	6	86	52
Rest of Canada	58	4	79	56
Urban	57	4	80	57
Rural	66	7	83	42
Services: Monthly-plus	17	3	52	12
<Monthly	76	5	93	65
Born elsewhere	36	5	59	42
Born in Canada	64	5	86	64
Visible minority	42	10	71	51
Caucasian	64	3	84	57
Indigenous*	76	8	90	58
Non-Indigenous	67	7	84	56
LGBTQ*	74	12	87	73
Hetero-sexual*	66	6	84	57

*Millennials and Gen Xers combined because of small sample sizes.

Millennials have been emerging within a Canada where the presence of people who are gay and lesbian has become widespread — indeed, normative. Our current surveys have pegged the percentage of Canadians who identify variously as LGBTQ at about 7 percent.[18] They include some 17 percent of Millennials, around 7 percent of Gen Xers, and 5 percent of Boomers and Pre-Boomers. Those figures can be expected to increase as individuals feel both safe and inclined to go public about their sexuality.

Further, as more and more Canadians make their sexual orientations known, acceptance will undoubtedly become even more widespread. After all, who doesn't have a friend, a family member, or a colleague who is gay, for example? (See Figure 4.9.) Those relational bonds will only enhance the inclination to be accepting of sexual diversity, something evident in the United States as well where research has found that those who have a gay friend or family member are more likely than others to support gay marriage.[19]

Figure 4.9 **Personal Relationship to Gay, Lesbian, and Bisexual People (%)**

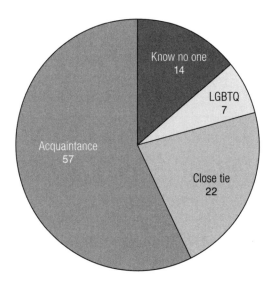

Generational and Trend Data

Since the 1960s, the emergence of same-sex orientations and lifestyles has been accompanied by a phenomenal transformation in attitudes. Today, more than 60 percent of Millennials, Gen Xers, and Boomers say that *two persons of the same sex having sexual relations* is "not wrong at all." The figure is lowest among Pre-Boomers, 70 and over. Our current figure of 62 percent compares to a mere 14 percent in 1975. Keep in mind, by way of comparison, that premarital sex currently receives the approval of about 70 percent of Canadians.

When it comes to equal rights, some 90 percent of people across the country — irrespective of age — maintain that gays and lesbians *are entitled to the same rights as other Canadians.*

Critics might be quick to say, "If that's the case, why was the country divided over the legalization of same-sex marriage" just over a decade ago in 2005? Actually, it is not at all clear that the country was and is as divided on the topic as many have thought.

In our current surveys, we worked from the assumption that "the all-Canadian way" of dealing with diversity is not just to approve or disapprove of what other people advocate but to also be willing to tolerate some things without necessarily approving. When we asked Canadians to respond to same-sex couples marrying and asked whether they (1) approve and accept, (2) disapprove but accept, and (3) disapprove and do not accept, what we found is that the first two acceptance responses came in at 84 percent — led slightly by Millennials (88 percent), Gen Xers (87 percent) and Boomers (83 percent), followed by a solid majority of Pre-Boomers (77 percent). Levels of acceptance of same-sex adoption of children were virtually the same (see Table 4.3).[20]

Significantly, about 1 in 4 Canadians across all general age cohorts say that their *acceptance of homosexuality has increased over the years.* It is noteworthy that Pre-Boomers are among those acknowledging such a shift.

Interestingly, when we compare these findings with the United States, particularly regarding gay marriage, we find that Canadians are more accepting — but the differences between the two countries have been shrinking in recent years. The Pew Research Center reports that the 2017 level of

Table 4.3 **Attitudes toward Same-Sex Individuals and Relationships:
Millennials and Other Adults**

	ALL	Millennials 1986–plus (18–29)	Xers 1966–1985 (30–49)	Boomers 1946–1965 (50–69)	Pre-Boomers Pre-1946 (70-plus)
Two persons of the same sex having sexual relations ("Not wrong at all")	62%	62	67	63	48
Homosexuals are entitled to the same rights as other Canadians ("Agree")	89	92	90	88	88
Same-sex couples marrying					
Approve & accept	63	72	68	60	47
Disapprove but accept	21	16	19	23	30
Disapprove & do not accept	16	12	13	17	23
Acceptance of homosexuality over the years ("Has increased")	24	30	20	25	27

support for gay marriage in the U.S. had reached 62 percent, up substantially from only 37 percent just 10 years earlier in 2007. In both countries, Millennials are more supportive of gay marriage than older cohorts. That said, Pew found — as we have in Canada — that changes have been taking place among all generational cohorts.[21]

Millennials are not only experiencing changing attitudes toward sexuality, but they also are demonstrating changing practices. The third annual Accelerating Acceptance report published by GLAAD revealed that 20 percent of Millennials now identify as LGBTQ (compared to 12 percent of Gen Xers, 7 percent of Baby Boomers, and 5 percent of Pre-Boomers). The report goes on to state that an increasing number of Millennials (12 percent) identify as transgender or non-conforming.[22] This may, in part,

Being Gay in the Canadian 1950s and 1960s

On display at the Canadian War Museum is a device that was known as "the fruit machine." In the Cold War era, the Canadian government feared that closeted gays in the civil service, military, or RCMP represented a security risk, so researchers at Carleton University began to develop "the fruit machine" as a means to detect homosexuality. In the 1950s and '60s, homosexuality was not only seen as shameful but thought it could also be a threat to national security. It was feared that if the Russians discovered someone's homosexuality, they could be blackmailed into giving up government secrets.

The RCMP therefore embarked on a mission to find and remove all gays from the civil service, targeting hundreds of suspected gay people. In Ottawa, an RCMP unit had the task of hunting them down, spying on gay hangouts, and finding informers. In Ottawa alone, some 400 people lost their jobs. One was John Wendell Holmes, a respected Canadian diplomat who, after admitting his homosexuality, was quietly removed from public service in 1960.

For "the fruit machine" to work, a suspected gay person was shown photos with images that supposedly would excite a homosexual, as reflected in their pupils dilating, skin reflexes, and breathing rate. It never became operational due to technical problems.

(Sources: Gardner 2005; Hauen 2017)

This just in ...

A federal judge has approved a major deal to compensate members of the Canadian military and other agencies who were investigated and sometimes fired because of their sexual orientation. Gay military veterans say they were interrogated, harassed, and spied on because of their sexuality. The discriminatory policies ruined careers and lives of people who were considered security risks. The final settlement includes up to $110 million in total compensation, with eligible individuals expected to receive between $5,000 and $175,000, depending on the gravity of their causes.

(Source: CTV News/Canadian Press, June 18, 2018)

be fuelled by the large number of celebrities who, in recent years, have declared that they are both gender and sexually fluid. Examples include Cara Delevingne, Kristen Stewart, Miley Cyrus, and Tom Hardy. This has led the *New York Post*, for example, to refer to Millennials as "the most bisexual generation of all time"[23]

Behaviourally, the 2016 census revealed that there are now 24,370 married same-sex couples in Canada — about one-third of the country's 72,880 same-sex couples. The married figure is up from 7,465 in 2006 — one year after it became available — and 21,015 in 2011. Half of all same-sex couples are living in four of the country's largest census metropolitan areas — Toronto, Montreal, Vancouver, and Ottawa-Gatineau.[24] Marriages among Millennial same-sex couples can be expected to increase; time will tell.

The Trend and Cohort Findings

The claim that their attitudes have been changing is readily borne out by the trend data we have for both adults and younger people. Each of the youth cohorts in 1984, 2000, and 2016 reported acceptance levels well above one another with respect to both their belief that people who identify as gay or lesbian are entitled to the same rights as everyone else and their acceptance of same-sex sexual relations (see Figure 4.10). As we have been emphasizing, these changes by cohort point to contextual changes in the culture rather than factors related to life cycle — a point emphasized by Western University's Robert Andersen and McMaster University's Tina Fetner in their analysis of cohort differences in both Canada and the U.S. between 1981 and 2000.[25]

Further indicative that more than life cycle is involved, our examination of the views of 15- to 19-year-olds back in 1984, compared to what they are now as 47- to 51-year-olds, shows that there has been a massive shift toward endorsing both gay and lesbian rights and relations over the past three decades (see Figure 4.11).[26]

Figure 4.10 **Attitudes of Youth Toward Gay and Lesbian Rights and Sexual Relations: 1984–2016**

(% "Yes")

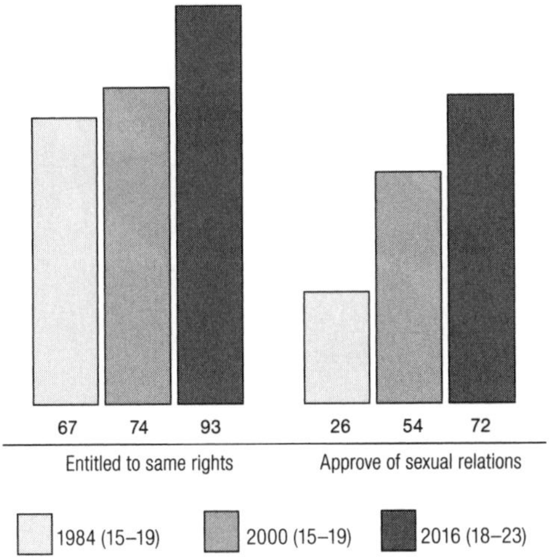

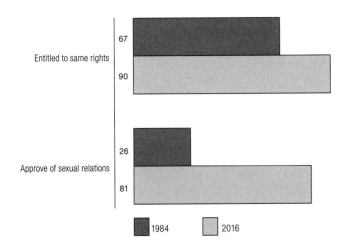

67	74	93
Entitled to same rights		

26	54	72
Approve of sexual relations		

☐ 1984 (15–19)   ▢ 2000 (15–19)   ■ 2016 (18–23)

Figure 4.11 **Attitudes of Youth Toward Gay and Lesbian Rights and Sexual Relations: Teens 15–19 in 1984 as Adults 47–51 in 2016**

(% "Yes")

Entitled to same rights
67
90

Approve of sexual relations
26
81

■ 1984   ▢ 2016

It's hard to imagine not only the social stigma that gays and lesbians experienced in the past but also the magnitude of the difficulties they faced in the course of trying to live out life. Apart from problems of employment and equal rights, a poignant reminder of what they faced is the fact that, up until 1969, homosexuality was punishable by up to 14 years in prison. Even after decriminalization, people in the public service would simply be demoted or have no possibility of getting promoted.[27] Much of the last three decades of the twentieth century was given to gays working to procure employment and family rights taken for granted by other Canadians. While resistance still exists, it is clear that the vast majority of Canadians — led by Millennials — believe that sexual orientation should not be a barrier to full participation in Canadian life.

Gay-Straight Alliances

An increasing number of Canadian Millennials have been exposed to gay-straight alliances during their high school and university years. Part of the LGBTQ student movement with 1980s origins in the United States, gay-straight alliances have been created to provide safe environments for LGBTQ young people and their heterosexual, "straight" allies. They are often now called "gender and sexuality alliance" to be more inclusive.

Needless to say, such organizations have sometimes been met with resistance in both the U.S. and Canada. Nonetheless, similar clubs have sprung up across the country, notably in New Brunswick, Ontario, Saskatchewan, Alberta, and British Columbia.

In Alberta, for example, the Department of Education describes them as existing to "promote welcoming, caring, respectful and safe learning environments for lesbian, gay, bisexual, transgender, and queer (LGBTQ) students and their allies." They are run by students and supported by school staff. The department encourages students to locate student or staff allies to help in getting the club launched and provides resources for establishing and running the venture.[28]

The alliances are believed to have the potential to contribute to the personal and social well-being of LGBTQ youth. They also appear to

Two-Spirit People

A concept that is receiving increasing attention by mainstream culture is that of "two-spirit people." According to Zachary Pullin, a Chippewa Cree writer, a large number of Indigenous cultures historically recognized and respect individuals with a balance of both feminine and masculine qualities. "Many of the great visionaries, dreamers, shamans or medicine givers," he says, "were two-spirit people."

The term itself began to gain traction in 1990, "when 13 men, women, and transgender people from various tribes met in Winnipeg to find a term that could unite the LGBTQ Native community." Recognizing that many tribes identify third genders in their cultures, they settled on "two-spirit" to describe the balance of masculine and feminine characteristics. The two-spirit tradition, Pullin emphasizes, centres primarily on gender and not sexual orientation, reflecting roles rather one's relationship to another person.

Pullin uses the example of one prominent Crow tribe individual, Ohchickapdaapesh, who was dubbed a "boté" — a term for a two-spirit person in Crow — and also known as Woman Jim. He gained prominence in the 1870s as both a warrior and an accomplished craftsperson who made intricately decorated leather goods.

Another Indigenous writer, Tony Enos, says that two-spirit people "have both a male and female spirit within them and are blessed by their Creator to see life through the eyes of both genders." While the term was coined in 1990, the concept has a long history and is not specific to gender or sexual orientation. "Two-spirit," he says, "acknowledges the continuum of gender identity and expression." The term is specific to Indigenous Peoples: "Two-spirit is a role that existed in a Native American/First Nations/Indigenous tribe for gender queer, gender fluid, and gender non-conforming tribal members. If you don't have a tribe, you can't claim that role." Clarifying its relationship to sexual orientation, Enos writes that gay "is about attraction to a person of the same sex," while two-spirit refers to "the embodiment of two genders residing within one person."

(Sources: Pullin 2014; Enos 2017)

contribute to healthier interpersonal school life. Extensive research carried out by McMaster's Tina Fetner and her colleagues, for example, have found that students who have participated in gay-straight alliances have benefitted from the support of staff and friendships and an enhanced quality of life.[29]

Gender

In early 2015, the mother of a seven-year-old student in an Edmonton Catholic school filed a complaint with the Alberta Human Rights Commission. The school district had refused to let her daughter, assigned male at birth, use the girls' washroom. In an interview with the CBC, the parents noted that they knew from the beginning that something was different about their child. At age six, the child made it clear: "I just told my mom I felt like a girl." The parents realized their child wasn't "a boy who liked girl toys — she was a girl who had a penis," said the child's mother. "Allowing a transgender individual into the bathroom that they identify with, there is no harm that will come to anybody," she said, except "my daughter's mental health."[30] In the short-term, the board relented and allowed the student to use the bathroom of her choice.

The Edmonton incident triggered a provincial-wide debate about gender identity. In response to the controversy, Alberta's Education Minister David Eggen instructed all of the province's 61 school boards to submit drafts of new or updated policies by March 31, 2016, to explicitly protect the rights of LGBTQ students and staff. The directive came after the province passed laws that allowed the minister to overrule school boards that deny a student's request to form a gay-straight alliance at school or that discriminate against gender identity and expression.[31] The province's expectations were made explicit with the minister's release of a document, *Best Guidelines*, in January of 2016.[32]

The Complexities of Gender

The debate in Alberta is just one illustration of a major awakening to the complexities of gender and gender identity — and a reminder of the key roles that choice and individualism in a pluralistic society play in modern-day identity politics. Such a rethinking and reconceptualization of gender is having important effects in a wide variety of other places, with the impact potentially of a magnitude that may justify *Time*'s prophecy that transgender rights will be "the next civil rights frontier."

Far from an issue restricted to academic settings, we are starting to become aware of the fact that far larger numbers of people may be transgender than we ever realized — in part because many of us have thought of such individuals as a relatively small number of transsexuals who have undergone sex surgery. It is troubling to learn that, in reality, a significant number of individuals are finding life very difficult.

Research to date on their experiences in Canada is limited and sample sizes small. Yet preliminary probes tell a troubling story. Data collected by Egale Canada for Ontario and released in 2015, for example, indicate the following:

- 9 in 10 transgendered individuals have felt unsafe in places at school;
- 7 in 10 have been targets of mockery;
- 7 in 10 have seriously considered suicide and 4 in 10 have attempted suicide;
- 4 in 10 believe they have been turned down for a job due to being transgender; and
- 5 in 10 are living on less than $15,000 per year.[33]

In a country like Canada, where we take pride in our emphases on pluralism and inclusion, there is a great need to better understand the complexities of gender. Those complexities — led by the clearer recognition of transgender persons — are starting to have a significant impact on Canadian life. The impact is already being felt throughout our major institutions — schools, universities, governments, the police, the medical profession, the legal system, the media, major businesses, leisure industries, religious groups, and by any number of other organizations and individuals. Even survey researchers are grappling with the basic methodological task of how to ask "the gender question" which for decades was simply a binary item.

Given the importance and confusion surrounding gender, there may be value in providing a succinct bit of background before we look at how Millennials and other Canadians are viewing the topic.

Historically in Canada, the United States, and much of the world, gender has been seen as a product of biology where sex is determined at birth and takes one of two forms — male or female. Up until fairly recently, the terms sex and gender have been used in common speech as interchangeable. A standard dictionary like *Webster's* offers what it calls a "medical definition of gender" as "the behavioral, cultural, or psychological traits typically associated with one sex." Its definition for "sex" is "the state of being male or female."[34] *Webster's* defines sex as "either of the two major forms of individuals that occur in many species and that are distinguished respectively as female or male especially on the basis of their reproductive organs and structures."[35]

In recent years, academics have led the way in challenging the accuracy and adequacy of these two age-old concepts. The reason is fairly simple: sex as a dichotomized variable doesn't take into account some individuals who have both male and female biological features. Early in the twentieth century, the term "intersex" was introduced to describe babies born with chromosomes or sex characteristics that are neither exclusively male nor female. While estimates vary, some experts think intersexuality occurs in perhaps one in 1,500 births.[36]

In contrast to sex, gender — as with other arenas of modern-day identity politics where individuals claim authority and choice over self-identity — has been increasingly viewed either as a pure social construction or, more recently, a self-definition which is not necessarily directly related to sex. One can biologically "be" a male or a female. But one's self-definition or identity may not necessarily correspond to one's biological makeup. Scholars increasingly have been emphasizing the need to see gender as a spectrum or continuum between masculine and feminine. Here *gender identity* includes identifying as a man, a woman, both (non-binary), or neither (agender nor genderfree). *Gender expression* is used to refer to the manner in which individuals "perform" their gender identity (e.g., identify as a particular gender, but express that gender in ways that include transgender and cisgender — one's biological sex).

The Unique Gender Research of a
University of Lethbridge Professor

Paul Vasey, who holds a research chair in psychology at the University of Lethbridge, has been at the forefront of research on transgender individuals for close to two decades. "Right now, debate about transgender individuals and their place in society is omnipresent," says Vasey. There consequently is considerable interest in his cross-cultural work.

There are some places in the world, including South Asia, Nigeria, Mexico, Samoa, Thailand, and Hawaii where third genders are recognized. Vasey has studied Samoan third gender individuals – known as "fa'afafine" – for some time. In fact, his partner of close to 15 years, Alatina is a fa'afafine individual. Someday they plan to marry and retire in Canada. "There we'd be perceived as an ordinary same-sex couple," Vasey points out.

National Geographic writer Robin Henig, who has visited Vasey and Ioelu in Samoa, comments, "It dawned on me how deeply bound in culture gender itself is. The gender classification of Ioelu would change, as if by magic, from fa'afafine to gay man, just by crossing the border."

(Sources: UNews 2017; Henig 2017)

Some individuals who have felt that they were "trapped" in the wrong body have undergone sex reassignment surgery. In a more general sense today, with or without undergoing surgery, individuals who feel dissonance between their sex and their gender have come to be known as "transgender" or "trans" people. As of mid-2017, experts had identified some 60 gender identities. In addition, complicating quantification attempts, many researchers have been positing gender to be "fluid," changing any number of times in a lifetime.[37]

The addition of variables like race — being a person of colour or an Indigenous two-spirit person — further expands the gender portrait. Age is also of central importance. As we noted earlier, some two decades ago sociologist Susan McDaniel spoke of "gendered generations" in drawing attention to the internal diversity of age cohorts.[38] The important concept of intersectionality, popularized by American law professor Kimberlé Crenshaw, has underlined the need to see how co-existent traits such as race, gender, sexual orientation, and lack of power can interact with one another.[39] In Calgary, for example, the request that the police who marched in the 2017 Pride Parade not be in uniform reflected not only concern on the part of the LGBTQ community generally but Indigenous and racialized members of that community in particular.[40]

In Canada, the U.S., and many parts of the world, movements to recognize and respond to trans individuals have received considerable media attention — and have known considerable success. Those initiatives have sought to ensure that transgender people are able to live their lives free from discrimination. That means ensuring that they do not face barriers in life, ranging from employment to access to bathrooms to freedom from harassment and violence.

This is no peripheral development that is restricted to academic corridors. As of late 2018, legislation protecting gender identity was in place in all Canadian jurisdictions, and gender expression legislation has been passed everywhere except Manitoba, Saskatchewan, and the Northwest Territories. Federally, Bill C-16 has added "gender identity or expression" to the Canadian Human Rights Act as a prohibited ground of discrimination. Effective August 31 of 2017, the federal government allowed individuals to identify themselves with an "X" if they do not identify as female or male in acquiring passports and other government-issued documents. In making the announcement, the Minister of Immigration, Refugees and Citizenship Ahmed Hussen had this to say:

> All Canadians should feel safe to be themselves, living according to their gender identity and express their gender as they choose. By introducing an "X" gender designation in our government-issued documents, we are taking an important step towards advancing equality for all Canadians regardless of gender identity or expression.[41]

Table 4.4 **Personal Relationship to Transgender People: Millennials and Other Adults**

	ALL	Millennials 1986–plus (18–29)	Xers 1966–1985 (30–49)	Boomers 1946–1965 (50–69)	Pre-Boomers Pre-1946 (70-plus)
Are transgender yourself	<1%	2	<1	<1	0
Have close relationship with one or more trans people	4	9	5	2	2
Acquainted with someone who is transgender	23	24	26	22	21
Do not know any transgender people	72	65	69	76	77

(Source: Computed from Angus Reid Institute, Transgender Survey, August 2016)

Some Canadian and Global Data

A 2016 survey carried out by the Angus Reid Institute found that Millennials are slightly more likely than older age cohorts to be transgender or have a close relationship with transgender individuals. Perhaps surprisingly, variations by gender, region, and community size are fairly small. Age-wise, about 1 in 4 Millennials and Gen Xers and 1 in 5 Boomers and Pre-Boomers say they know someone who is transgender (see Table 4.4). That's an important finding, attesting to the fact that the number of trans individuals is well above the 1 percent or so Canadians who currently are making their gender identities known.

Global Data. In 2016, three UCLA law researchers teamed up with Ipsos Reid to explore public support for transgender rights in 23 countries. The sample was comprised of more than 17,000 people.[42] Andrew Flores, Taylor Brown, and Andrew Park found support for transgender rights to be around 70 percent in Sweden, Spain, Germany, Britain, Argentina, and Canada. A number of other countries followed at about 60 percent, among them the United States, Australia, India, France, Brazil, and Mexico. A third tier, with a support level of about 50 percent, included Japan, China, South Korea, Turkey, and Poland. Russia came in at around 40 percent.

More specifically, the right for transgender people to marry was supported by majorities in 16 of the 23 countries, the right to adopt children by 14, and allowing access to public restrooms consistent with a transgender person by a majority in 15 countries. Younger individuals, women, and people with higher levels of education and income were more approving of transgender rights than others.

In the case of Canada, 81 percent indicated support for discrimination protection, 77 percent for the right to marry, and 74 percent for the right for transgender people to adopt children. The number supporting access to public restrooms based on one's gender was 64 percent.

A Closer Look at Canada. Because the transgender issue has only recently received widespread recognition, we do not have trend data to report. That said, thanks to our close association with Angus Reid, we do have access to the data from the institute's 2016 national exploration of transgender attitudes from 1,416 Canadians.[43] That survey allows us to look at how Millennials view the topic, along with other Canadian adults.

Overall, the data show a remarkably high level of acceptance of transgender individuals — perhaps enhanced by the faces of children such as the seven-year-old in Edmonton, let alone high-profile celebrities such as Caitlyn Jenner or Chaz Bono.

Some 9 in 10 Millennials and other adults maintain that *the increasing acceptance of transgender people* is a positive development, reflecting less emphasis on differences between men and women (see Table 4.5). A solid majority of Canadians of all ages seem acutely aware of the fact that trans individuals *face considerable discrimination* and therefore *require protection and accommodation*. There is widespread acknowledgment of the need to *reconsider the way life is structured*, including things like *gender-specific washrooms*. Millennials and Gen Xers are somewhat more inclined than Boomers and Pre-Boomers to endorse the specific idea that transgender people should be able to *choose the washrooms they feel most comfortable using*. Still, those two cohorts are just as likely to maintain that solutions need to be found.

Tension in the Mosaic over Gender

All persons, including those who identify as "transgender," must always be treated with compassion, respect, and love. While the Canadian Conference of Catholic Bishops supports Bill C-16's intention to protect Canadians from harm, some of the principles behind the legislation – even if widely accepted in our society – cannot be endorsed by Catholics.

The most serious of these is the claim that gender is separable from biological sexuality and is to be determined by the individual. This central tenet of contemporary gender theory is not in accord with natural law or Christian revelation and has therefore been explicitly rejected by Pope Francis and by Pope Benedict XVI.

In the words of the Catechism of the Catholic Church, each man and woman "should acknowledge and accept" his or her biological sexuality identity, including "physical, moral, and spiritual difference and complementarity."

Questions about freedom of speech, freedom of association, and freedom of religion are also likely to arise in connection with this legislation. We urge those of Catholic faith, and all people of good will, to be diligent in defending these freedoms.

(Source: Excerpted from Canadian Conference of Catholic Bishops 2017)

This is not to say that things are anywhere near perfect. About 1 in 3 Millennials, Xers, and Boomers say that *a worker who identifies as transgender in my workplace will be discriminated against.* Similar proportions of Millennials and others maintain that *being transgender is just unnatural.* That said, even 61 percent of Canadians who hold the "unnatural" view support the federal government's legislation prohibiting discrimination against trans people, reflecting once more the Canadian proclivity to tolerate difference even if a person does not personally agree with someone different than themselves.

All these seemingly "positive" developments, however, are not necessarily greeted with enthusiasm by everyone. A July 2017 national poll by the Angus Reid Institute found Canadians divided down the middle when asked if they think that *allowing gender-neutral identification is a good thing* (49 percent)

Table 4.5 **Attitudes Toward Transgender People:**
Millennials and Other Adults

% Agreeing

	ALL	Millennials 1986–plus (18–29)	Xers 1966–1985 (30–49)	Boomers 1946–1965 (50–69)	Pre-Boomers Pre-1946 (70-plus)
Increasing acceptance of transgender people is a positive sign, where less emphasis is placed on the differences between men and women	87	91	87	86	83
Transgender people face a lot of discrimination in their daily lives	85	83	88	83	85
I support federal legislation prohibiting discrimination against transgender people	84	88	86	80	87
Canada should work to accommodate and protect transgender people in society	78	82	79	75	75
It's appropriate that society is reconsidering the way it organizes things like gender-specific washrooms	73	75	73	73	75
Transgender people should choose the washrooms they feel most comfortable using	58	63	61	56	49
A worker who identifies as transgender in my work-place will be discriminated against	30	33	29	31	-
Being transgender is just unnatural	29	26	26	32	31

(Source: Computed from Angus Reid Institute, Transgender Survey, August 2016)

versus *a bad thing* (51 percent). A slight majority were opposed to the idea of provinces issuing gender neutral birth certificates (58 percent) versus favouring it (42 percent). Significantly, in both the general and birth certificate instances, Millennials were more supportive than older Canadians.[44]

Organizationally, some religious groups — notably Roman Catholics and evangelical Protestants — have expressed concern about moving beyond binary gender categories.[45] Moreover, some have felt that, ironically, they have been excluded from the discourse on inclusion. There also have been some academics who have questioned the idea of gender diversity. None have been more outspoken in Canada than University of Toronto psychologist Jordan Peterson. A high-profile outspoken critic of gender neutral language and government protection of transgender people, Peterson has described Bill C-16 as "an assault on biology and an implicit assault on the idea of the objective world."[46]

Variations in Gay and Transgender Attitudes

A growing majority of people are supportive of gay and transgender individuals. There are, however, some significant attitudinal differences among Millennials. Here are some highlights.

- *Women* are generally more accepting than *men* of gay and transgender behaviour.
- Millennials in *rural Canada* are slightly less accepting of same-sex marriage and far less likely than their counterparts in urban areas to feel transgender individuals should be able to choose washrooms or be accommodated.
- Fairly predictably, *education* is associated with somewhat higher levels of acceptance, *religious involvement* with lower levels.
- With greater numbers of immigrants in recent years arriving as active Catholics, Muslims, and evangelicals,[47] support of gay and lesbians and same-sex marriage specifically is lower among both *immigrants* and *visible minorities.*
- Indigenous Canadians exhibit high levels of support for gays and lesbians and same-sex marriage and similar majority levels of support for trans individuals. It therefore is not surprising that in June of 2018, Allan (Chicky) Polchies Jr. was elected as the first openly LGBTQ Indigenous chief in Atlantic Canada. He identifies as two-spirit. He and his partner of eight years are the foster parents of a toddler.[48]

- As would be expected, Canadians who identify as *LGBTQ* are more likely than people who identify as straight to express positive attitudes toward gays and transgender individuals.
- The inclination to agree with accommodation and protection, along with trans people being allowed to choose the washroom they are comfortable using, does not differ by the *extensiveness of contact* with transgender individuals. Here individuals seem to be reflecting a Canadian principle, rather than a guideline based on personal experiences with transgender individuals.

ASSESSMENT

Canada's Millennials have appeared at a time when the Sexual Revolution is well behind them. For this cohort, sex has been "normalized." While their grandparents and many of their parents wrestled with the question of sex outside marriage, the Millennials have known the legacy of the revolution and the debates, where Canada's "moral mosaic" sees premarital sex as something that is a matter of personal choice. Obviously, there are some people — led by many of the religiously devout — who continue to insist that sex be restricted to marriage and to straight people. To the extent they believe that, their choice is generally respected. But, simultaneously, many other Canadians believe sex can be practised outside of marriage as well.

Personal sexual freedom is not without its limits, however. Extramarital sex continues to be widely condemned — and that is not too strong a word. Few people, young and old, view sex with someone other than one's marital partner as appropriate. It was bypassed by the Sexual Revolution.

In keeping with the entrenchment of personal freedom, Millennials have been even more inclined than earlier generations to approve of the availability of legal abortion. That is not to say they endorse abortion, just that they favour its legal availability in a wider range of situations than their predecessors.

Indicative of their pervasive belief in the rights of diverse Canadians, Millennials have been following in the footsteps of Boomers and Xers in particular in asserting the importance of equal rights and opportunities for LGBTQ Canadians. They believe they should be able to marry, adopt children, and participate fully in Canadian life. Here, perhaps surprisingly, the views of Millennials are also shared by many people in the three older age cohorts.

In short, consistent with the framework we have been using throughout the book, these findings show that, as Millennials live out life in the sexual sphere, their diversity and pluralistic mindsets are readily evident. They endorse individualism and freedom and expect that — with the sole exception of extramarital sexual activity — Canadians will be accepting of the wide range of choices that people make when it comes to sexual activity, reproduction, sexual orientation, and gender.

Such a mosaic mindset is further evident when it comes to family life.

THE MAGNIFIED MOSAIC

Some Millennial Homosexual and Transgender Attitudes by Select Variables

	Gay sexual relations	Same-sex marriage	Accommodate & protect	Choose washroom comfortable using
	Not wrong at all	Approve & accept	Yes	Yes
NATIONAL	62%	72	82	63
Women	68	78	83	71
Men	56	65	81	56
Quebec	64	75	77	68
Rest of Canada	62	72	83	62
Urban	62	75	84	66
Rural	66	67	72	46
Degree-plus	70	84	84	81
Some post-secondary	49	75	82	56
High school or less	65	68	81	64
Services: <Monthly	78	85	84	67
Services: Monthly-plus	24	38	75	47
Born elsewhere	35	40	78*	68*
Born in Canada	69	77	82*	64*
Visible minority	53	61	---	---
Caucasian	65	78	---	---
Indigenous*	78	83	79	62
Non-Indigenous	64	69	80	62
LGBTQ*	80	86	96	90
Heterosexual*	64	69	78	59
Trans or know someone	---	---	82	65
Do not know someone	---	---	82	62

*Millennials and Gen Xers combined because of small sample sizes.

CHAPTER 5

Families: Salience/Attitudes/ Aspirations

There is an old line in sociological lore to the effect that "a sociologist goes to a football game and watches the crowd."[1] If you expand your concept of football to include the immensely popular global game played with the round ball, a sociologist sitting in the stadium notices a peculiar phenomenon as the teams walk on to "the pitch." Each player is walking hand in hand with a child. The obvious question is "Why?"

People in the know tell us that the children are viewed as "mascots" and the practice dates back about two decades. Football's international association (FIFA) announced in 2001 that it was partnering with UNICEF in a "Say Yes for Children" campaign aimed at improving and protecting children's lives everywhere. The hand-in-hand practice began with World Cup 2002 matches in South Africa and has subsequently expanded widely.[2]

Motives are viewed as ranging from protecting the players ("fans are less likely to throw things at them when they walk in with children") to teams making money ("sometimes charging families to have their kids be mascots"). But the overarching utility lies in public relations. In the words of one observer, "It looks good to have your team walk out with children, and it allows teams to showcase values."[3] We would add, as sociologists watching the crowd, the practice poignantly symbolizes the link between soccer and families. To be able to do that is to touch large numbers of people — a fairly ingenious marketing manoeuvre.

THE SALIENCE OF FAMILY LIFE

Extensive research on families in Canada has demonstrated conclusively that there is nothing much more important to Canadians than family life.[4] Our current surveys have found that almost 90 percent of people across the country say that they are receiving "a great deal" or "quite a bit" of enjoyment from families. Further, 75 percent of Canadians tell us that family life is "very important" to them, matched only by freedom. Beyond that dead-heat for first, a comfortable life comes in second (51 percent) and success third (46 percent).

Generational Comparisons

In an Environics report released in February 2017, 56 percent of Millennials said *having good relations with parents and family* was essential to being an adult — second only to having a full-time, steady job. An additional 37 percent said good relations with parents and family was "important, but not essential."[5] In our latest survey data, 63 percent of Millennials say that they place a very high level of importance on family life — a level somewhat below that of Xers, Boomers, and Pre-Boomers (see Table 5.1). If we broaden the response to include "somewhat important," the Millennial total is 94 percent — and close to 99 percent for everyone else.

Enjoyment of family life, as compared to stated importance, is actually a bit higher across the board — 80 percent for Millennials, slightly higher for Xers and Boomers (about 88 percent), and highest for Pre-Boomers (94 percent).

Families and Life in the Good Old Days

Veteran Canadian observer and pollster Michael Adams points out that, in the 1960s, the revolution in Canadian families had yet to dawn. Divorce was difficult to obtain and homosexuality could earn a person a prison sentence. Even traditional families looked and felt different, he says, "with Dad being much more often the unquestioned head of the household" and sharing little in the domestic chores. "Common-law arrangements were rare and mixed unions were scandalous."

The roles of children and how they were disciplined were also different. Given such differences in how family life was lived out in "the good old days," little wonder that many want a home that is somewhat different from the kind of home they grew up in.

(Source: Adams 2012)

We would expect that the inclination to value and enjoy family life would be related to one's own experiences as a child. We asked Canadians to respond to a simple, pointed statement: "I always wanted a home like the one I grew up in."

- What we found is 61 percent of people of all ages agreed — the cause for pause perhaps being that 39 percent, or about 4 in 10, disagreed.
- Here the agreement level is slightly higher for Millennials (66 percent) than others (around 60 percent). Those who think that parents and grandparents are more inclined than Millennials to wistfully think back to positive family upbringings in days gone by — when more couples stayed together, more moms stayed home, and more grandmas were "baking cookies likes grandmas used to make" — need to think again.

Table 5.1 **Salience of Family: Millennials and Other Adults**

	ALL	Millennials 1986–plus (18–29)	Xers 1966–1985 (30–49)	Boomers 1946–1965 (50–69)	Pre-Boomers Pre-1946 (70-plus)
"Very important"	75%	63	74	78	85
Receive "a great deal" or "quite a bit" of enjoyment	87	80	87	88	94
I always wanted a home like the one I grew up in	61	66	63	57	56

Marriage and Cohabitation

In the same Environics report that we referenced in the previous section, just 14 percent of Millennials identified getting married as "essential to being an adult," followed by 42 percent who said it was "important, but not essential." Only slightly higher proportions singled out having children (17 percent and 48 percent respectively). At the same time, nearly half of Millennials identified marriage or children as major life goals and aspirations.[6]

With these data in mind, we know that Canadians are getting married later in life. In the 1960s, the average age of a woman's first marriage was 23, and a man's was 25. In 2011, these figures were 29.6 and 31 respectively.[7] Currently, about 15 percent of Millennials are married or cohabiting (see Figure 5.1). Another 35 percent indicate that they are currently in relationships. This 50 percent total compares to about 75 percent for Gen Xers, Boomers, and Pre-Boomers (see Table 5.2). In 1981, approximately 25 percent of 25- to 29-year-olds had *never* been married.[8] As of 2016 — 35 years later — our survey figure for never married 25- to 29-year-olds is close to 65 percent.

Reflecting significant changes in sexual attitudes and practices, 1 in 2 Canadians say that they have lived together with a non-marital sexual partner (see Table 5.2). They include around 40 percent of Millennials, 60 percent of Gen Xers, and some 50 percent of Baby Boomers — the latter two generations having emerged during and just after the Sexual Revolution of

Figure 5.1 **Marital Status of Millennials (%)**

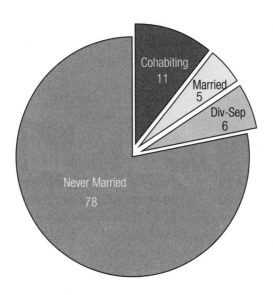

the 1960s. Even a noteworthy segment of some 25 percent of Pre-Boomers acknowledge that they have lived with a non-marital sexual partner. The overall total for Quebec (66 percent) is much higher than for the rest of the country (31 percent), on par with some of the leading nations in the world such as Sweden. Moving forward, we think it is important to pay close attention to growing cohabitation levels in Canada. In 2016, 21 percent of all couples were in such unions (versus 6 percent in 1981).[9] And Millennials are at the front edge of this trend. In 2011, 23 percent of 25- to 29-year-olds were in common-law relationships, compared with 8 percent in 1981.[10]

Somewhat remarkably, 9 in 10 Millennials in relationships describe them as "very happy" or "pretty happy." Further, those same levels hold across *all four* age groups (see Table 5.2). And about 2 in 3 Millennials say it is important for them to marry at some point in their lives — a level similar to Xers and Boomers, if slightly below Pre-Boomers. Incidentally, in the U.S., Millennials also have been slower than other generations to marry; nonetheless, more than 2 in 3 who are unmarried say they would eventually like to marry.[11] So much for the popular media emphasis on Millennials not wanting to marry.[12]

Table 5.2 **Marriage and Other Relationships**

	ALL	Millennials 1986–plus (18–29)	Xers 1966–1985 (30–49)	Boomers 1946–1965 (50–69)	Pre-Boomers Pre-1946 (70-plus)
In a marriage or relationship	71%	51	77	75	72
Importance of you marrying in your lifetime	61	64	59	59	72
Have lived together with a non-marital sexual partner	48	39	60	48	24
Relationship generally: "very happy" or "pretty happy"	92	91	91	92	93
Concerned about it "a great deal" or "quite a bit"	27	35	29	23	23
Have you ever been divorced: "Yes"	21	5	17	30	25

"Alright," you say. "How can I take all that data seriously when divorce is taking place all over the place?" A good point. For several decades, Reg has asked Canadians, "Have you ever been divorced?" In 1975, the figure was 7 percent; in 1995, it doubled to 14 percent; and by 2015, tripled to 21 percent. Those figures, of course, refer to the entire Canadian population. Statistics Canada, using data through 2008, has suggested that as many as 43 percent of marriages entered into in 2008 will end before couples reach their fiftieth anniversary.[13]

Maybe. But that projection could be on the high side. The reason is that, what many people don't know, the divorce rate actually has been *declining* since the late 1980s. In 1926, the divorce rate was 0.06 per 10,000 population and 5.5 in 1968. With the liberalizing of divorce laws in 1968, the rate jumped to 12.4 per 10,000 population in 1969 and, following a further liberalizing of divorce laws in 1986, peaked at 36.4 in 1987. By 2000, the rate had declined to 22.9, and as of 2008, it stood at 21.1.[14] The common-law option for many people seemingly has not only resulted in fewer people choosing to marry but also in fewer people subsequently opting for divorce.

Incidentally, if all this sounds a bit confusing, it's also more than slightly confusing for StatsCan as well. The agency announced in 2011 that 2008 would be the last year for which it would provide information on marriage and divorce rates, in part due to costs but also because relationships have become increasingly fuzzy and more difficult to track.[15]

In the midst of all these complexities, the bottom line is this: at any given point in time when a survey snapshot is taken, people who are married and in other comparable relationships say they are experiencing a measure of happiness from their ties. Tomorrow or next week? No guarantees that things will remain the same. And for many, things obviously don't stay the same.

That's why Millennials, despite their 91 percent level of apparent relationship happiness, acknowledge in no less than 35 percent of cases that they have "a great deal" or "quite a bit" of concern about their relationships — a level that exceeds that of Xers, Boomers, and Pre-Boomers. Those are some clear signals that some relationships could be in trouble.

Speaking of relational difficulties, some interesting research just in. It has been widely recognized that one predictor of relational hopes and expectations is the marital experiences of one's parents. But a newly released study has underlined the specific importance of what mothers have encountered. Two Ohio State University family researchers, Rachel Arocho and Claire Kamp Dush, maintain that a good predictor of Millennials' marital and cohabitation choices and timing are strongly associated with the marital experiences of their mothers. They maintain that even though Millennials have grown up at a time when divorce is widespread, those "whose parents divorced likely think about and experience relationship formation somewhat differently than those whose parents did not."[16] Monetta quips that when it comes to such decisions, some Millennials think that "Mother knows best."

Children

A major source of enjoyment for Canadians of all ages, of course, is children.... Otherwise, the naive observer might say, why do people keep having them?

More than 80 percent of Millennials say the ideal number of children is between 1 and 3 — a view held by similar numbers of older adults as well (see Table 5.3). Only 6 percent of Millennials — both female and male — say that the ideal is not to have any children at all. To this point, 11 percent of this 18- to 29-year-old Millennial cohort have kids — and, true to their word, so far the average number is 1.8!

A quick note on "not having children." The media have given considerable attention to the idea that Millennials increasingly are opting not to have kids. Our findings show that the inclination to see "childless by choice" as an ideal is still very low (6 percent) — about the same as it is for Gen Xers (5 percent), albeit slightly above Boomers (2 percent) and Pre-Boomers (<1 percent). The small increase hardly warrants sensationalist media declarations to the effect that the "Choice to be childless is bad for America" (*Newsweek*)[17] or that "Millennials are choosing pets over people" (*Washington Post, Hamilton Spectator*).[18] *Newsweek* poetically if crudely put things this way: "The lack of productive screwing could further be screwing the screwed generation."[19]

Eye-catching headlines, precarious data.[20]

Zoomer guru David Cravit adds some generational perspective in writing that Boomers "loved sex but didn't love big families." The arrival of the pill in 1963 gave them "an irresistible win-win. Sex became more convenient, birth control became more reliable. What could be better?"[21]

Another headline that has been run extensively is that large numbers of Millennials are still hanging out at home. Statistics Canada has reported that, as of 2016, 35 percent of young adults between the ages of 20 and 34 were living with at least one parent — up from 31 percent in 2001. They were led by young people in Ontario (42 percent) and Toronto specifically (47 percent). Some other figures: Vancouver, 39 percent; Winnipeg, 35 percent; Montreal, 33 percent; and Calgary, 29 percent.[22]

Consistent with the Statistics Canada data, our surveys corroborate those findings: all the budding birds have not left the nest on time. In some cases, they have made a return stop. About 1 in 2 Gen Xers — who as of 2016 were 30 to 49 years old — have offspring living at home. In addition, 1 in 4 Boomers likewise have "aging kids" at home, as do almost 1 in 10 70-plus Pre-Boomers.... They can be forgiven for wondering if the kids "will ever leave home"!

Table 5.3 **Children: Millennials and Other Adults**

	ALL	Millennials 1986–plus (18–29)	Xers 1966–1985 (30–49)	Boomers 1946–1965 (50–69)	Pre-Boomers Pre-1946 (70-plus)
Ideal no. of children:					
1–3	86%	83	85	87	87
4–6+	10	12	10	11	13
None	4	6	5	2	<1
Have children?	57	11	55	73	85
Number of children: 1–3	52	11	52	68	69
Have children currently living with you	28	11	50	23	8

The prevalent explanation? Economic necessity.[23] We'll return to this question when we look at Millennials' aspirations for the future in Chapter 7. But we would be remiss if we did not briefly speak to the growing social reality, and even concern in some areas of society, with "emerging adulthood" — a phrase popularized by psychologist Jeffrey Arnett[24] — or more recently referred to, often in a pejorative sense, as "delayed adulthood." This is the elongated period of time it takes young adults to stand on their own in the world.

Lest we become nostalgic about the good old days, all three of us moved out of our parents' homes in our late teens or early 20s. This was the cultural norm. This is when Joel, for example, learned to grocery shop. When apples were a mere $1.46 a pound, he didn't realize he had to make sure they weighed exactly one pound before heading to the cashier — who would proceed to weigh the apples and charge him for precisely 1.2 pounds, if necessary.

Yet things have changed as children live at home longer, and in some circumstances, children are coddled through life by "helicopter" or "snowplow" parents and teachers alike. As noted earlier with respect to getting married or having children, the typical markers of independence among young adults are appearing, for some, later in life.

Why Some Young Gen Xers, Boomers, and Pre-Boomers Did Not Have Children

... partner did not want any ... no future for them ... did not find suitable mate ... I could not have any ... not married ... too old ... didn't want them ... poor health ... I'm too selfish ... low priority ... we wanted our freedom from that responsibility ... not important to me ... I would be too strict on them ... it just didn't work out ... world is too shitty ... no time for children ... didn't marry until I was 59 ... it was illegal at the time ... haven't had the right partner to have children with ... I wouldn't be a good parent ... money ... too many other things I want to do in life ... parents mess up kids, mine did, why continue that? ... the more I'm around them, the more I dislike them ... the world is not a very nice place ... can't afford to pay my own bills, not ready for that kind of commitment ... I'm afraid I'll hurt them emotionally ... I have too many other priorities ... I'm scared of the pain, the commitment, everything ... too much work ... I would be a bad mother ... not a priority ... work situation would make it difficult ... not ready ... planet of crazies ... sexual orientation ... lack of time to invest ... overpopulation ... I didn't think we'd be good parents ...

(Source: Bibby 2004:40)

We see these changes with our students and their parents. For instance, some well-intentioned parents are selecting their university-aged children's courses, coming in to pay their fees, speaking with professors about how to best help their children succeed, and, in rare cases, to contest their 20-year-old's research paper grade. We show documentaries in our classes of people in their late twenties whose mothers still make their lunch and do their laundry and, dare we say, come to their child's place of employment to negotiate their first salary.

Amidst the growing discourse surrounding mental health in Canadian society, including rising anxiety among university students, we notice that many students are ill-prepared to deal with life's expected hurdles and disappointments at this stage of life. Far be it for us to reduce all of these

Family Diversity in the Media

In the American show *Modern Family*, we see nuclear families, a second marriage between an older man and younger woman that includes adults and teenage children from previous relationships plus a newborn between the two of them, and a same-sex couple with an adopted Vietnamese child.

Kim's Convenience is a Canadian sitcom featuring a Korean-Canadian family. The parents fit many stereotypes of a conservative immigrant family, while the university-aged children epitomize more progressive and liberal leanings of mainstream Canadian society.

Black-ish portrays an upper-middle-class African-American family, including grandparents, parents, and grandchildren, all under the same roof. With fears that their family is assimilating too much to "white America," this family seeks to re-assert strong ethnic roots and identity in how it sees itself and hopes others see them.

Programs like these illustrate the diversity of family life in contemporary society. They tap into what Millennials take for granted: there is no one-size-fits-all approach to family life as society and individuals alike negotiate the various choices before them. In doing so, individuals and family units hold on to notable autonomy in constructing identities for themselves.

realities to children living at home longer. However, such an interpretation should not be easily dismissed either. As much as young Canadians benefit economically and otherwise by living at home longer, there are other social impacts arising from these broad social changes that we ought to pay close attention to in the coming years and decades.[25]

The flip side, as JoAnn Lee reminds us, is that some young adults are impacted by "accelerated adulthood" too.[26] Many who find themselves in marginalized positions in society, whether due to gender, socioeconomic background, family background, or sexual orientation, are forced to grow up much quicker than their peers in response to their respective hardships. In many ways we have already seen this, and will continue to see this, in our "Variations" sections at the end of each chapter. We would add that

Figure 5.2 **Enjoyment and Concerns, One's Children: Millennials and Other Adults (%)**

% Indicating "A Great Deal" or "Quite a Bit"

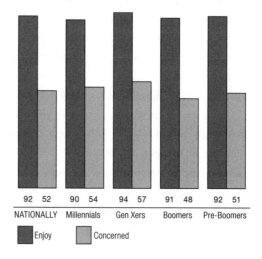

92	52	90	54	94	57	91	48	92	51
NATIONALLY		Millennials		Gen Xers		Boomers		Pre-Boomers	

■ Enjoy   ■ Concerned

despite the all-encompassing label of "delayed adulthood" being assigned to Millennials, many young people today are rising up well against the hand they are being dealt by society. We will have more to say about this in Chapter 7.

Regardless of how one thinks about the pros and cons of delayed adulthood, the good news is that some 9 in 10 Millennials who have their own children say that they are receiving "a great deal" or "quite a bit" of enjoyment from them — about the same proportion as reported by Gen Xers, Boomers, and Pre-Boomers (see Figure 5.2).

That's not to minimize the obvious — that 5 in 10 Millennials and older adults also acknowledge that their children sometimes are a source of strain. Most of the sources of anxiety are fairly predictable: concern about health and safety, concern about not getting in trouble, concern about them "turning out okay," concern about remaining okay.[27] The old adage that parents "never stop worrying about their kids" is borne out in the finding that concern about children doesn't decline much with age; even about 1 in 2 Pre-Boomers who are 70 and over say they are troubled "a great deal" or "quite a bit" by their kids. Reg remembers well how his beloved mother,

Enjoyment of Family Members Over Time

In 1984, 65 percent of 15- to 19-year-olds said that family life was very important to them. The figure slipped to 59 percent in 2000 but has rebounded to 64 percent among today's slightly older, 18- to 23-year-old Millennials.

Today's younger Millennials are expressing renewed levels of enjoyment of their mothers and fathers, after a slight dip among young people between 1984 and 2000 (see Figure 5.3). Perhaps that reflects parents doing a better job of combining employment outside the home with parenting. The widespread idea in the 1970s and '80s was that women and men "could do it all." But Canadian research suggests that some offspring — unlike their parents — were not at all convinced that their parents were doing a particularly good work–home balancing act. Their offspring — the parents of today's Millennials — may have figured out how, in fact, to achieve a better balance, contributing to more positive relations with their own children.

Current Millennials who are 18 to 23 differ little from their slightly younger 1984 and 2000 cohorts in the enjoyment they say they are receiving from both their siblings and their grandparents. Both seemingly have remained fairly stable resources over the years, functioning as important family resource complements to time-pressured moms and dads.

Figure 5.3 **Enjoyment of Family Members: 1984, 2000, 2016 (%)**

% Indicating Receive "A Great Deal" or "Quite a Bit" of Enjoyment

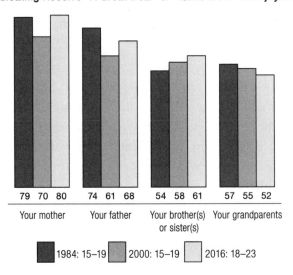

| 79 70 80 | 74 61 68 | 54 58 61 | 57 55 52 |
| Your mother | Your father | Your brother(s) or sister(s) | Your grandparents |

■ 1984: 15–19 ▨ 2000: 15–19 ☐ 2016: 18–23

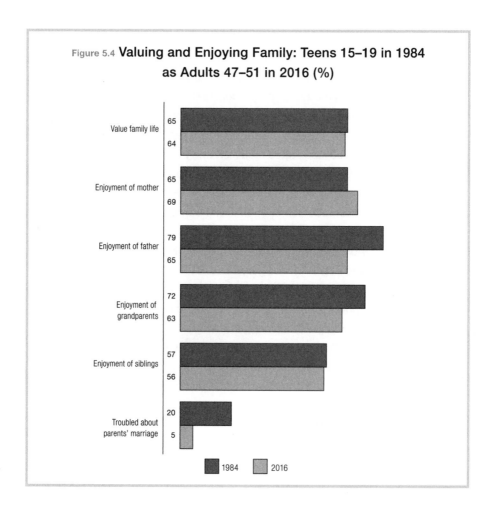

Figure 5.4 **Valuing and Enjoying Family: Teens 15–19 in 1984 as Adults 47–51 in 2016 (%)**

well into her eighties, was — paradoxically — proud of him but still wondered if, in the long run, he was going to turn out okay!

That's our way of saying that Millennial parents are on course to match the anxiety levels of their own parents and grandparents.

Undoubtedly there is something about leaving home and establishing one's own family that results in some slippage in the amount of time one spends enjoying parents. Yet, it's interesting to see that the levels of enjoyment do not decrease when it comes to enjoying siblings, again not unexpected given that life is often experienced in expanded ways after one's teen years. The steady and even increased level of enjoyment of grandparents is also not surprising, given that interaction is frequently tied to special occasions, and the growing realization of grandchildren that Grandma's and Grandpa's years are winding down. They therefore are all the more cherished.

Taken together, the bottom line of these findings is clear: family — in its wide variety of shapes and forms — remains of central importance to Millennials and other Canadians.

ATTITUDES AND ASPIRATIONS

The Generational and Trend Findings

Discipline, Sex, Parenthood, and Views of You

Our surveys offer considerable additional data on how Millennials and other Canadians view family life, including their hopes and dreams.

An age-old lament is that *discipline in most homes is not strict enough.* In 1955, Gallup found that 81 percent of Canadians agreed with the statement. In 1965, the figure was exactly the same.[28] Today, the figure is virtually unchanged at 83 percent (see Table 5.4). Some 7 in 10 Millennials concur with the need for stricter discipline in homes, only slightly below the 8 in 10 level for Gen Xers and 9 in 10 level for Pre-Boomers.

And the idea that *it would be a good idea to have a curfew for young people under 16* is still being endorsed by almost 50 percent of Canadians. They include about 1 in 3 Millennials and 1 in 2 older adults. The 50 percent figure — while obviously high — is nonetheless below the 62 percent Reg found in 1995 and well below the 81 percent figure that Gallup recorded in 1955.[29]

Seemingly strictness is increasingly preferred within homes, rather than outside of them.

Two brief findings on sex and parenthood. In keeping with Millennials' widespread acceptance, they — along with Gen Xers — are considerably more likely than Boomers and Pre-Boomers to approve of *young people having sex when they are under the age of 18.* Some 7 in 10 Millennials, along with Xers and Boomers, also say that they approve of *unmarried adults having children* — levels far above that of Pre-Boomers (45 percent).

Table 5.4 **Varied Family Attitudes of Millennials and Other Adults**

	ALL	Millennials 1986–plus (18–29)	Xers 1966–1985 (30–49)	Boomers 1946–1965 (50–69)	Pre-Boomers Pre-1946 (70-plus)
Discipline and Youth					
Discipline in most homes today is not strict enough	83%	69	83	87	91
It would be a good idea to have a curfew in this community for young people under the age of 16	46	36	44	51	49
Sex and Parenthood					
People having sex when they are under 18 (Approve)	36	51	44	28	11
Unmarried adults having children (Approve)	70	72	76	70	45
Views of Parents and Children					
Very important what your children think of you	67	64	65	66	75
Very important what your parents think of you	47	47	40	50	64

The importance of family — including parents and children — is further underscored by the fact that more than some 65 percent of Millennials, Xers, and Boomers say that *what their children think of them* is very important. Among Pre-Boomers the figure is an even higher 75 percent.

And we never seem to cease being affected significantly by *what our parents think of us*, regardless of how old we are. At this point in time, looking at Canadians who have parents who are still alive, we find that about 5 in 10 Millennials and Boomers, along with more than 6 in 10 Pre-Boomers, say that what their parents think of them is very important. The same sentiments are expressed by a slightly fewer 4 in 10 Gen Xers, where psychological autonomy from parents is — we predict — going to be short-lived.

Among young people, the importance of parental approval has remained steady since 2000, even if relationships with parents have "bobbed and

Figure 5.5 **Importance to Young People of What Their Parents Think of Them by Gender: 2000, 2008, 2016 (%)**

% Indicating "Very Important"

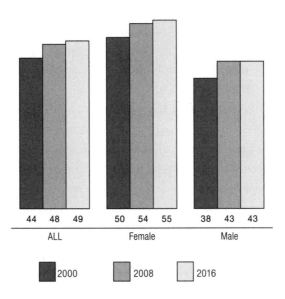

	ALL			Female			Male		
	44	48	49	50	54	55	38	43	43

■ 2000   ■ 2008   □ 2016

weaved" (see Figure 5.5). Approval has consistently been more important to females than males.

American psychologist Carl Pickhardt has noted the paradox of young people simultaneously courting parental approval and disapproval. He distinguishes between parental approval and love: "Approval is awarded. Approval is earned. Love, on the other hand, is constantly anchored in parental commitment. It never varies. Approval is conditional upon performance; love is unconditionally given."[30] Following his thinking, young Canadian women — generally speaking — seem to feel a greater need than their male counterparts to please their parents. Conversely, males — in keeping with widely documented evidence[31] — continue to place a higher value than females on aggressiveness, independence, and the overt expression of their feelings.[32] Whatever the precise reasons, the gender differences in the importance of parental approval continue to exist.

Interracial Marriage

We already saw in Chapter 4 that Millennials are leading the way in approving of same-sex marriages and same-sex parenting. This acceptance, we noted, is another example of the enshrinement and pervasiveness of a pluralistic Canadian mindset that places supreme value on diversity and choice.

In addition to growing acceptance of our LGBTQ population, Canadians have experienced profound changes in outlook when it comes to interracial marriage.

It's hard to believe that in the mid-1970s, more than 40 percent of Canadians did not approve of marriages involving white people and either black people or East Indians/Pakistanis (see Figure 5.6). Similarly, some 35 percent disapproved of white–Asian marriages, and 25 percent of white and Indigenous people marrying.

Today Millennials lead the way in almost unanimously stating their approval of all forms of racially or culturally mixed unions (see Table 5.5). Further, their approval levels are pretty much matched by Gen Xers and Boomers. Even Pre-Boomers, born before 1946 and now 70 and over, have also experienced dramatic attitudinal shifts over the past several decades. In 1975, people in this older grouping were 30 and over. At that time, just 55 percent of Canadians 30 and over approved of white–Asian unions,

Figure 5.6 **Canadian Racial Intermarriage Attitudes, 1975–2015 (%)**

% Indicating Approval

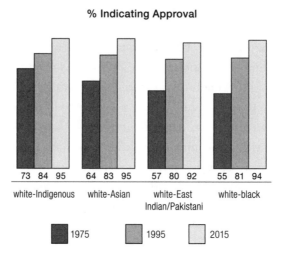

73 84 95	64 83 95	57 80 92	55 81 94
white-Indigenous	white-Asian	white-East Indian/Pakistani	white-black

■ 1975   ■ 1995   □ 2015

Back to the Future with Home Gender Expectations

Joel and Reg's disclaimer: Monetta is solely responsible for this ...

In her 2012 article in *The Atlantic*, "Why Women Still Can't Have It All," Anne-Marie Slaughter noted that her "commitment to the feminist cause" led her to question the ability of women to "have it all" including a career, family, and a broader life. Since this article appeared, there has been a wave of Millennial women abandoning the idea that women can and should be successful mothers and wives, while still being able to "climb the work ladder." The appearance of recent articles with titles such as "Fewer Millennials Want Gender Equality at Home" and "Do Millennial Men Want Stay-at-Home Wives?" suggest a good number of Millennial women are opting for "traditional gender roles."

Further, recent research involving young Millennials has found growing acceptance of egalitarian relationships between men and women among older Millennials (those born in the 1980s and 1990s), compared to younger Millennials (those born in the 2000s) who indicate a preference for traditional family roles at home, with men the breadwinners and decision-makers. Could we be seeing the beginnings of a change in attitudes with the younger generations?

The sociologist in me would suggest that backlash against feminism is in part fuelling this movement, with notable celebrities like Kelly Clarkson, Shailene Woodley, and Sarah Jessica Parker denouncing feminism and claiming to be "humanist." While these claims are made with one version of feminism in mind, they suggest that some Millennial women are wanting something different and are open to embracing at least some elements of traditional gender roles.

(Sources: Slaughter 2012; Donnelly et al. 2016)

66 percent approved of white–Indigenous marriages, 49 percent approved of white–East Indians/Pakistanis marriages, and 45 percent approved of white–black marriages.

Without question, the shifting of attitudes has been influenced by the growth in the proportion of the population identifying themselves as racialized people.[33] Statistics Canada census data show that the *visible minority* figure jumped from 5 percent in 1981 to 13 percent in 2001 to 19 percent in 2011. The number is projected to reach 30 percent by 2031.[34]

As we saw in Chapter 4 with gay marriage, it appears, in keeping with longstanding sociological observations about diverse people groups, that Canadians tend to increase their acceptance and practice of interracial unions as Canada becomes more multiracial. Though the majority of people still form romantic relationships with those who are like themselves (e.g., racially, religiously, socioeconomically), Statistics Canada data in 2011 reveal that 4.6 percent of all Canadian couples are in mixed unions, up from 2.6 percent in 1991. As expected, those in younger generations (e.g., 25 to 34 years old, 7.7 percent) are more likely to be in a mixed union versus older generations.[35] This is hardly a massive social shift, but it is a small sign that the attitudinal shifts regarding interracial marriage among Canadians, and Millennials especially, are reflected in practice for some.

Significantly, in the U.S. as well, the softening of interracial marriage attitudes[36] has undoubtedly been influenced by the fact that close to 45 percent of Millennials are not white.[37] As of 2016, Millennials were already forming the largest number of multiracial households.[38]

Hopes, Dreams, and Realities

Our trend and cohort data also provide us with an intriguing reading of the hopes and dreams of earlier youth cohorts and how things have turned out — at least to date. Beginning in 1992, we asked young people about their expectations in a number of areas. What we have done in our latest surveys is see how well those 15- to 19-year-old teenagers in 1992 have fared as 39- to 43-year-old Gen Xers in 2016.[39]

With the cautionary reminder that this is simply how "the teens of 1992 have turned out so far," let's open the curtain on the family-related outcomes.

- In 1992, 85 percent said they expected to *get married* and close to the same percentage anticipated *having children*. As of 2016, 75 percent had married, and 65 percent said they had children (see Table 5.6).

Table 5.5 **Racial Intermarriage Attitudes of Millennials and Other Adults**

% Approving of Marriages Between...

	ALL	Millennials 1986–plus (18–29)	Xers 1966–1985 (30–49)	Boomers 1946–1965 (50–69)	Pre-Boomers Pre-1946 (70-plus)
white and Asian people	95	98	95	96	89
white and Aboriginal people	95	98	95	95	91
white and black people	94	98	95	95	85
white and East Indian or Pakistani people	92	96	93	92	79
any other kinds of racial or culturally mixed unions	93	97	95	93	81

Mixie Me

"Mixie" is a sibling word, a term my sister and I adopted to describe people like ourselves. We used the term because as kids we didn't know another one.

At my elementary school in Toronto, I was the only mixed-race kid in my grade. Today the school is thick with mixies bearing features from all over the map. You don't look for your tribe in the faces of people over a certain age — after all, how much mixing really went on in Toronto bedrooms in the 1940s?

Historically, mixing the races was a sin and then a crime and then, after years of slow progress, merely a terrible thing to do to an innocent child who would be forever torn between two worlds. Well into the 1980s, psychologists claimed that biracial individuals were inevitably confused, anxious, and poorly adjusted. Multiracialism was seen as a pathology.

It's easy to imagine a future in which upwardly mobile Asians and whites mix more frequently, while other minorities are left out of a trendy mixed-raced future. Marriage across racial lines is increasingly possible, but mixing across class has always been tricky. And class, it goes without saying, remains stubbornly tied to skin colour.

(Source: Hune-Brown 2013)

Table 5.6 Family Expectations and Outcomes
15- to 19-Year-olds in 1992 as 39- to 43-Year-Olds in 2016

	Expectations	Outcomes
"Do you expect to..."	1992	2016
Get married	85%	75
Have children	84	65
Stay with the same partner for life	86	82

- Some 86 percent said in 1992 that they expected to stay with the *same partner for life*. So far that's been the case for 82 percent who have married. But they are only 39 to 43 years old. Obviously that figure is only going to continue to fall — perhaps considerably.

We'll look at the expectations and outcomes regarding education, careers, and finances as well very shortly in our discussion of the future in Chapter 7.

Variations in Family Attitudes

Millennials are relatively uniform in their attitudes about family life, with some notable differences between those in Quebec and elsewhere. As with our previous Magnified Mosaic tables, we are highlighting some findings; pertinent details are available for interested readers.

- *Quebec Millennials* are just as likely as others to place a high level of importance on family life. But their highly publicized emphasis on personal autonomy comes through in their being less inclined than others to place a high level of importance on what their parents think of them (females 39 percent, males 23 percent). Relationally, they are more likely than other Millennials to expect their current relationships to last a lifetime but less likely to place importance on getting married at some point in their lives.

- Nationally, more *women* than men place a high level of importance on family life and maintain they are going to stay with their current partners for life.
- There are minimal differences between Millennials *born in Canada and those born elsewhere* as well as those who are *visible minorities and others*. One exception: those *born elsewhere* and *visible minorities* are less likely to believe they will stay with their present partners for life, primarily because they more often say they "don't know."
- Millennials who are actively involved in *religious groups* differ somewhat from others in being somewhat more inclined to highly value family life, wanting homes like they grew up in, and anticipating marrying during their lifetimes.
- *Indigenous Millennials* are somewhat more likely than others to report high levels of happiness with their relationships and to anticipate they will be lasting.
- Millennials who identify as *LGBTQ* place somewhat lower levels of importance on family life but no less likely to report happy relationships. Differences on other items tend to be small. Overall, much larger samples of LGBTQ youth are needed to build on these preliminary findings.

ASSESSMENT

Family life is extremely important to Canada's Millennials, just as it has been so very important to generations before them. They deeply value parents, partners, and children, along with siblings, grandparents, and other individuals who are part of their family networks.

Once again reflecting the Millennial mosaic, what characterizes these family arrangements is the wide variety of options that are available to young people, as well as other adults. Having such family choices is deeply valued and championed by Millennials — undoubtedly to a greater extent than at any time in Canadian history. Millennials assume that individuals are free to relate to whoever they want and however they want. That includes being able to choose whether to be in a relationship or not be in a relationship, to choose whether to have or not have sexual involvement, to variously choose whether or not to cohabit, marry, or have children — in whatever sequence people want. It also means individuals can choose to follow in the family footsteps of their parents — or create new family pathways of their own. What people choose to do is also to be respected, regardless of how far removed those choices might be from one's own personal preferences.

Pluralism and choice are among the hallmarks of life for Canadian Millennials when it comes to family life — and pretty much everything else. Those themes also carry over into how Millennials approach religion and spirituality. That's the topic we turn to next.

THE MAGNIFIED MOSAIC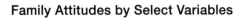

Family Attitudes by Select Variables

	Family life is highly valued	Wanted home like one grew up in	What parents think of you very NB	Relationship very/ pretty happy	Expect stay same partner for life**	NB to marry
NATIONAL	63%	67	47	91	65	64
Outside Quebec	63	71	49	92	61	68
Quebec	63	65	39	88	71	49
Urban	62	68	47	86	62	---
Rural	70	51	45	91	69	---
Women	74	67	50	89	75	64
Men	50	65	44	95	49	63
Born elsewhere	70	70	52	89	46	58*
Born in Canada	62	65	46	92	67	58*
Services: Monthly-plus	74	74	47	96	66	88*
Services: <Monthly	61	62	58	91	62	60*
Visible minority	66	61	45	91	48	---
Caucasian	62	67	47	92	68	---
Indigenous*	74	56	43	96	90	---
Non-Indigenous*	70	65	42	85	70	---
LGBTQ*	39	61	39	95	65	50
Heterosexual*	63	65	43	88	72	59

*Millennials and Gen Xers combined because of small sample sizes.
**Of those currently in a relationship.

CHAPTER 6

The Gods: Religion/Spirituality

Did you know that religion, spirituality, and superstition are part of the sports world?

It's not uncommon during a Super Bowl celebration to have one of the American stars of the game uninhibitedly declare, "I have to give praise and glory to My Lord and Saviour, Jesus Christ."[1] Baseball players — notably those from Latin America frequently give the sign of the cross following a game.[2] Others point to the sky when they hit a home run, allegedly thanking, in one writer's playful phrase, "the Fan Upstairs."[3]

Some observers emphasize that spirituality is a central part of sports. Shirl Hoffman, who taught at the University of North Carolina, has written, "Along with movies, media, literature, drama, advertising, television, and other agents of popular culture, sport, for better or worse, adds form and texture to our hearts." Moreover, says Hoffman, sport "shapes our spirits and creates alternative realities and states of consciousness."[4] Arnold

Palmer, the legendary golfer, once put it this way, "What other people may find in poetry or art museums, I find in the flight of a good drive."[5]

Hockey players — primarily from Canada and Europe — are not particularly well-known for their religious or spiritual phrases or practices. But, significantly, they are known for their rituals. Sidney Crosby eats a peanut butter and jam sandwich before he hits the ice. He also doesn't speak to his mom or sister on game days because, when he does, it seems he gets injured.[6] It was well known that Wayne Gretzky invariably tucked his sweater into the right side of his hockey pants. What was less known was that he had the equipment manager carry baby powder that was sprinkled on his taped sticks to "soften" his passes. "The Great One" also had to deliberately miss the net to the right at the beginning of each pre-game warm-up.[7] And then there are all those players in a variety of sports who don't shave or change their socks while the team is on a winning streak.... We hope for the sake of the environment and everybody present that the Cleveland Indians didn't follow that socks ritual when they went on their unprecedented 22 game winning streak in 2017!

As with sports, so with culture more generally. Much has been made of the possibility that Millennials in the United States are less religious than older Americans. According to the reputable Pew Research Center, the U.S. public as a whole has been becoming less religious in recent years. But many measures suggest that the nation's youngest adults are much less religious than everyone else. For example, Pew maintains that Millennials born since approximately 1980 are much less likely than older Americans to identify with a religion, pray, attend services regularly, or consider religion to be an important part of their lives.[8]

Such patterns have led to the inevitable comparative question: what is the religious situation with Millennials in Canada? Are they likewise inclined to be less religious than other adults? If so, is this a new development that is reflecting significant changes in Canadian life, or is it something that is largely a reflection of life stage that will turn out to be short-lived? And if they are not "into" religion, where are they with respect to spirituality and supernatural beliefs?

Our surveys provide us with considerable data to address these questions.

RELIGION

In recent decades, organized religion in Canada has not exactly been a growth industry. Led by Mainline Protestants — the United, Anglican, Lutheran, and Presbyterian churches — organized religion in Canada has been losing numbers and influence since approximately the 1960s. In sharp contrast to the past, large numbers of Canadians are not actively involved in religious groups. The percentage of Canadians who explicitly said that they had "no religion" increased from under 1 percent in 1960 to 20 percent by 2000. During approximately the same period, regular service attendance dropped from over 50 percent in 1950 to under 20 percent.[9]

Nonetheless, religion continues to be important to sizable numbers of Canadians. In addition, many religious groups — led by Catholics, evangelicals, and Muslims — are benefitting from accelerated levels of immigration. In turn, this is resulting in greater religious diversity and greater religious choices.[10]

Then there is the seemingly anomalous reality that, apart from their posture toward organized religion, many Canadians continue to hold a wide range of supernatural beliefs and engage in a variety of religious practices. To add to the confusion, surveys have found that significant numbers of people across the country continue to say that they value spirituality, frequently offering the qualifying phrase that they "are spiritual but not religious."[11]

In light of such varied developments and data, there is considerable value in gaining a clearer understanding of where Millennials are with respect to religion and spirituality, and what the possible impact will be on Canadian life.

Generational Comparisons
Beliefs

Our surveys show that, like adults and young people before them, a majority of Millennials hold a wide range of supernatural beliefs. Close to 7 in 10 say that *God or a higher power exists* (see Table 6.1). But many go much further: 5 in 10 maintain that God *cares about them* personally, and close to the same number claim that they actually have *experienced God's presence*. Similar to what Pew has found in the United States, their levels of belief about God, while high, are slightly lower than the levels for Xers, Boomers, and especially Pre-Boomers (see Table 6.1).

Canadian Millennials, however, are actually more likely than older cohorts to believe in *life after death* and just as inclined to believe in *heaven* and *angels*, including the belief that they themselves have been protected by *a guardian angel*. Belief in *hell* continues to be held by about 40 percent of Canadians. Perhaps surprisingly, belief in hell is slightly higher among Millennials (46 percent) than older age groups. Then again, maybe we shouldn't be surprised: many of these themes have been an increasing part of popular culture in recent years.

Table 6.1 **Select Conventional Religious Beliefs of Millennials and Other Adults**

"Do you believe ... "

% Indicating "Yes, I definitely do" or "Yes, I think so"

	ALL	Millennials 1986–plus (18–29)	Xers 1966–1985 (30–49)	Boomers 1946–1965 (50–69)	Pre-Boomers Pre-1946 (70-plus)
God or a higher power exists	73	66	72	76	80
God or a higher power cares about you personally	61	53	59	63	70
That Jesus was the Divine Son of God	59	50	57	63	68
You have experienced God's presence	47	44	46	48	54
In life after death	66	70	66	65	59
In heaven	63	62	62	65	64
In hell	42	46	44	39	35
In angels	62	59	62	64	58
That you have been protected from harm by a guardian angel	56	52	55	60	57

These findings suggest that supernatural beliefs continue to be highly pervasive in Canada among adults of all ages, including Millennials. In some instances, the levels are slightly lower for younger adults, in other cases slightly higher.

Those varied "lower and higher" patterns are also evident when we look at "less conventional" supernatural beliefs (see Table 6.2).

- For example, some 6 in 10 Millennials say they believe that *miraculous healing* sometimes occurs — slightly below the levels of older adults.
- But they exhibit similar levels of belief to Gen Xers, Boomers, and Pre-Boomers when it comes to *communication with the dead* and the assertion they will be *reincarnated.*
- Further, Millennials are more inclined than others to maintain that we can have *contact with the spirit world* and also more likely to assert belief in *astrology.*

Hell and Pop Music

The high level of belief in hell among both Millennials and Gen Xers may, in part, reflect an emphasis on hell in heavy metal music in recent decades. Don Jamieson, the co-host of the popular and long-running *That Metal Show*, on the American cable television network VH1 Classic, recently offered a top 10 list of "Songs About Hell." He writes that "Hell can be a fiery underworld inferno. But it can also be used to express one's own personal torment, express anger and disbelief or to describe attractiveness." He cites the words of the late lead singer of AC/DC, Bon Scott: "Hell ain't a bad place to be."

Jamieson's Top 10 Songs About Hell: (10) "See You in Hell," Grim Reaper; (9) "Hell Awaits," Slayer; (8) "To Hell With the Devil," Stryper; (7) "Welcome to Hell," Venom; (6) "Hotter Than Hell," Kiss; (5) "Saints in Hell," Judas Priest; (4) "Earth on Hell," Anthrax; (3) "I Am Hell," Machine Head; (2) "Heaven and Hell," Black Sabbath; and number 1 — "Highway to Hell," AC/DC.

Note: Don, Reg wants to know where's Meatloaf's "Bat Out of Hell" – a Gen X rock classic?
(Source: Jamieson 2015)

Table 6.2 **Select Less Conventional Supernatural Beliefs
of Millennials and Other Adults**

"Do you believe ... "

% Indicating "Yes, I definitely do" or "Yes, I think so"

	ALL	Millennials 1986–plus (18–29)	Xers 1966–1985 (30–49)	Boomers 1946–1965 (50–69)	Pre-Boomers Pre-1946 (70-plus)
Miraculous healing sometimes occurs	69	61	67	71	79
We can have contact with the spirit world	50	53	57	48	31
We can communicate with the dead	42	44	48	42	25
Some people have psychic powers enabling them to predict events	51	39	54	57	44
You personally have experienced an event before it happened (precognition)	49	45	52	52	37
In astrology	35	39	38	32	30
That you yourself will be reincarnated	33	36	33	33	27

We are reminded when we look at these findings that supernatural beliefs have many sources beyond religious groups, with those sources — if anything — expanding in recent years. In case anyone has missed it, the supernatural realm has been getting a fair amount of play in movies, television programs, and in the packaging of pop artists and their songs. The supernatural has been given extensive attention in computer games and via a wide array of websites. Themes relating to life after death, hell and evil, angels and demons, and contact with the spirit world and the dead are rampant. In days gone by, they may have been "the stuff" of sermons and broader religious group teachings. These days, they have an unprecedented number of cultural sources.

The result? The survey findings show that, for better or worse, no one needs to fear for the demise of supernatural beliefs among Millennials — and presumably their offspring. The topics might be changing a bit. But interest in supernatural phenomena remains extensive.

Practices

Beyond beliefs, Millennials and other Canadians continue to engage in a wide range of religious activities, both public and private.

Our surveys corroborate the census findings of Statistics Canada in revealing that close to 8 in 10 people across the country continue to *identify* with a religion of some kind (see Table 6.3). The largest group by far is Roman Catholicism (about 40 percent), followed by other Christian groups (some 30 percent). Just under 10 percent of Canadians identify with other major world faiths, led by Islam (2 percent). Some 7 in 10 Millennials identify with a religious group. However, as in the U.S., that level is somewhat below the identification levels of Boomers and Pre-Boomers in particular (about 9 in 10 each). That said, it's important to note that only about 3 in 10 Millennials say they have *no religion*.

Active participation in religious groups, however, lags well behind religious identification. Currently, close to 3 in 10 Millennials indicate that they attend services at least once a month. A tip-off that a segment of Millennials is religiously involved is that both monthly and weekly levels are actually slightly higher than the levels reported by both Gen Xers and Boomers (see Table 6.3) — a level, as we will see shortly, that is due in part to immigration. About 4 in 10 Millennials say they never attend services. The remaining 3 in 10 or so attend occasionally (see Figure 6.1).

Levels of *private prayer* are down somewhat for Millennials and Gen Xers compared to older cohorts. But levels of other *practices* — table grace and Scripture reading — are similar.

- The numbers of Canadians who say they are engaging in *worship services* or *other spiritual practices online* are small — but are led by Millennials, suggesting this could be a potential "growth area" for digital platforms. What remains less clear is whether these activities are in addition to or in place of face-to-face worship gatherings. Moreover, we know little about the content or context for these online spiritual practices among Canadian Millennials.

- Private devotional practices seemingly are associated with personal enrichment and experiencing the divine. Noteworthy numbers of Millennials and other adults are claiming such effects (see Table 6.3). About 1 in 4 Millennials, similar to the levels of Gen Xers and Boomers, say that they are being personally "strengthened" *by their faith* and are *experiencing God* — on a weekly-plus level, no less. These findings serve as a reminder that faith, for some, is far from only cognitive: it is also highly experiential.

Our findings on religion and spirituality resonate with other studies that reveal a range of religious beliefs and practices among young people in North America. A good number, at this stage in life, seem to be setting religion aside in order to focus on more pressing and tangible "this world" concerns such as education, career, and family life.[12] Expressed differently, some Millennials seem to continue to engage in private practices like prayer from time to time, but their formal ties to religious organizations are fading into the background for what at this point is an unknown period of time.

Figure 6.1 **Frequency of Service Attendance: Millennials (%)**

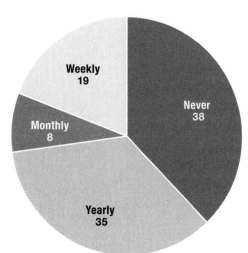

Table 6.3 **Religious Identification and Select Practices of Millennials and Other Adults**

	ALL	Millennials 1986–plus (18–29)	Xers 1966–1985 (30–49)	Boomers 1946–1965 (50–69)	Pre-Boomers Pre-1946 (70-plus)
Identification					
Identify with a religion	79%	72	76	83	88
Weekly-plus					
Service attendance	14	18	12	11	25
Private prayer	38	33	33	41	47
Table grace	19	24	17	16	22
Scripture reading	13	18	12	11	16
Watch worship services online	4	7	5	3	1
Practise other spiritual activities online	6	9	7	4	3
Feel strengthened by your faith	29	27	27	28	39
Feel you experience God's presence	25	23	22	26	33

One variable that is having a noteworthy impact on the religious vitality of Millennials is immigration. Between 2001 and 2011, for example, almost 500,000 Roman Catholics arrived from other countries, along with close to 400,000 Muslims. The median age of the Catholics was 43, and of Muslims, 29.[13] Keep in mind that these large numbers of additions are not tied to growth factors that leaders and the media frequently emphasize, namely outreach in the form of proselytism and evangelism. Those kinds of efforts at recruitment take a lot of work and are not particularly effective; just ask evangelicals, Mormons, or Jehovah's Witnesses. These huge

Figure 6.2 **Millennial Practices by Birthplace (%)**

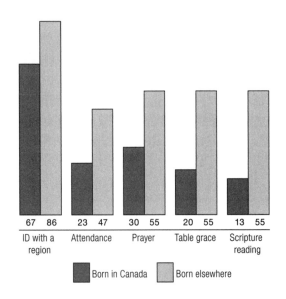

	67	86	23	47	30	55	20	55	13	55
	ID with a region		Attendance		Prayer		Table grace		Scripture reading	

■ Born in Canada   ■ Born elsewhere

numbers of new people are arriving in Canada as "ready-made" Catholics and Muslims. What a tremendous stimulus for both religious bodies.

But, these days at least, it's not just that huge numbers of newcomers, led by Catholics and Muslims, are bolstering the ranks of the host groups. Millennials born outside of Canada are considerably more conservative and devout in their faith and more likely than those born here to identify with a religion and attend services, as well as engage in private practices such as prayer, table grace, and Scripture reading (see Figure 6.2).[14] This is primarily because increasingly large numbers of immigrants in recent years have been coming from Asian and African countries where Christianity and Islam are thriving.[15] What remains to be seen is how religious these immigrants will remain with each successive generation in the Canadian milieu. Research to date suggests that we might expect these higher levels of religiosity among first generation immigrants to taper over time.[16]

In understanding increasing religious diversity in Canada, it also is very important to note that immigration is having an important impact on the number of people with "no religion" inclinations. During the 2001–11 period just noted, no less than some 450,000 new arrivals indicated they had "no religion," particularly those of Chinese and Japanese origin. They also are very young: their median age was 33. There is no guarantee, of course, that their offspring will mirror such low identification and commitment levels. The outcomes, especially beyond the offspring's early adult years, are worth watching. The literature to date suggests some intergenerational stability among young "nones" and their parents[17] but also a measure of "defection" to the ranks of the affiliated.[18]

Still, however these socialization patterns play out in the future, what is important is that immigrants are adding significantly to the size of some religious group pools and creating the possibility of ongoing retention. The onus will be on the groups to sustain such salience and neutralize secularization inclinations.

The Trend and Cohort Findings

Seemingly reflecting period effects — where the Canadian social context has become increasingly secular since the 1980s — the trend data shows that young people have been less inclined to embrace traditional beliefs about God, life after death, and the divinity of Jesus (see Figure 6.3). They also have been less likely to believe that some people have psychic powers.

Signs of the Times: Immigration Growth in Toronto

The Catholic Archdiocese of Toronto is building one brand-new church per year to keep from bursting at the seams. "We have opened what we call a mega-church, a large 1,000-person church, once a year for the last 14 years," said Cardinal Thomas Collins of Toronto. "The Archdiocese of Toronto is certainly very much influenced by tremendous immigration from all around the world." Mass is celebrated in 37 languages every Sunday in its 225 parishes.

Communications director Neil MacCarthy says that most newcomers have recently been arriving from China, Korea, Vietnam, the Philippines, Sri Lanka, and India. "We often refer to the Archdiocese of Toronto as the United Nations of our faith." Many new arrivals, he notes, bring a strong awareness of faith with them. Cardinal Collins says the diversity means "we have a richness in this diocese."

(Source: Krawczynski in Bibby and Reid 2016:51)

Figure 6.3 **Select Beliefs and Practices of Youth: 1984, 2000, 2016 (%)**

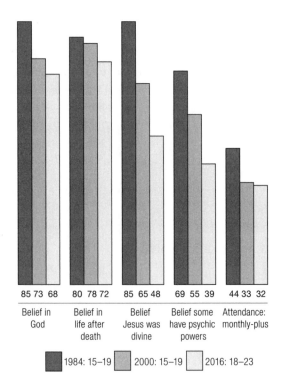

85 73 68	80 78 72	85 65 48	69 55 39	44 33 32
Belief in God	Belief in life after death	Belief Jesus was divine	Belief some have psychic powers	Attendance: monthly-plus

■ 1984: 15–19　■ 2000: 15–19　□ 2016: 18–23

That's not to say traditional beliefs have been abandoned. Some 7 in 10 express belief in God and life after death. But the numbers have been dropping in recent decades. As Reg has put things, "God has been slipping in the polls."[19]

Monthly-plus service attendance for young people was 44 percent in 1984 and dropped to 33 percent by 2000. However, the decline has not continued. The figure today for young Millennials, 18 to 23, is a very similar 32 percent.

When we look at what 15- to 19-year-olds were reporting in 1984 and compare that to what they were telling us as 47- to 51-year-olds in 2016, we find some similarities and some differences (see Figure 6.4).

- Their current levels of *prayer* and *service attendance* are similar now to what they were in the '80s.
- The belief that they *have experienced God* is, if anything, up slightly. That idea — based on the perception of an experience — seems to persist over time.
- However, the cognitive-based beliefs in *God, life after death*, the *divinity of Jesus*, and *psychic powers* seem far more vulnerable to change — and levels are down in each instance.
- One belief exception is the idea that we can *communicate with the dead* — which, as we just noted, has a fair amount of cultural support. Here the endorsement level has in fact increased since the 1980s.

To sum up what we have been seeing so far, Millennials are exhibiting considerable variations in their tendencies to hold beliefs, engage in private practices, and be involved in religious groups. Those different inclinations are further evident when it comes to spirituality and attitudes toward religion.

Figure 6.4 Select Beliefs and Practices: Teens 15–19 in 1984 as Adults 47–51 in 2016 (%)*

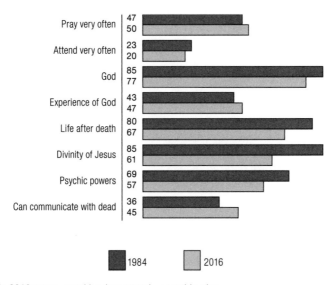

*In 2016: pray = weekly-plus; attend = monthly-plus.

Are you a "Belieber"?

Justin Bieber is a household name across Canada. Bieber, who is seen in the media one day for supposed immoral and sometimes illegal behaviour and the next day attending a Hillsong campus in the United States, describes what he thinks Jesus wants: "I do not want to shove this down anyone's throat. I just wanna honestly live like Jesus. Not be Jesus — I could never — I don't want that to come across weird. He created a pretty awesome template of how to love people and how to be gracious and kind. If you believe it, he died for our sins. Sometimes when I don't feel like doing something, but I know it's right, I remember, I'm pretty sure Jesus didn't feel like going to the cross and dying so that we don't have to feel what we should have to feel. What Jesus did when he came to the cross was basically say, 'You don't have to feel any of that stuff.'" He goes on to say, "It doesn't make you a Christian just by going to church. I think that going to church is fellowship, it's relationship, it's what we're here on the earth to do, to have this connection that you feel there's no insecurities. I think that's where we need to be. Like I said, you don't need to go to church to be a Christian. If you go to Taco Bell, that doesn't make you a taco."

Whether it is Justin Bieber, or U2 whose songs pay homage to religious themes, or social media hashtags in response to tragic global events (e.g., #PrayforParis), young Canadians are constantly exposed to and engaged with the supernatural in the media and pop culture figures that they follow.

(Source: La Puma 2015)

SPIRITUALITY

Highly regarded *Vancouver Sun* columnist Douglas Todd has been examining religion and spirituality for some four decades. Recently, Todd drew attention to an anomaly in the first decade or so of the twenty-first century. In the midst of the numerical problems of organized religion, the top ten selling books in Canada included three bestsellers dealing with spirituality — two by Vancouver's Eckhart Tolle and the third by Alberta-born author William Paul Young. Todd raised the question of whether the Canadian media, in rarely covering religious and spiritual issues, is overlooking an important component of its potential audience.[20] The same "coverage" criticism could be levelled at academics.

In recent years, various observers in Canada, the United States, and elsewhere have drawn attention to the idea that many individuals are distancing themselves from religion in favour of spirituality. The dichotomy is summed up in the inclination for people to say that they are "spiritual but not religious." The phrase has received considerable media play and, not surprisingly, has spawned a large number of spiritual-but-not-religious (SBNR) organizations, websites, blogs, and other social media expressions.

Generational Comparisons
Spiritual Needs

What our surveys show is that 67 percent of Canadians openly acknowledge that they have spiritual needs. They include a majority of 60 percent of Millennials — a level slightly below that of Gen Xers (69 percent), Boomers (68 percent), and Pre-Boomers (74 percent). Previous research suggests that what people have in mind when they use the word "spiritual" is extremely subjective and varied. Nonetheless, the general consensus is that the term does point to traits that transcend everyday life, including such diverse characteristics as "needing God's spirit" and "nourishing our souls" through "oneness with the earth" and "inner awareness."[21]

As for the relationship between spiritual needs and religion, our surveys also show that a minority of about 25 percent of Millennials and others say that they are *neither religious nor spiritual* (see Figure 6.5). That's important to note in that the figure represents close to 1 in 4 Millennials and other Canadians. The question of the remaining 3 in 4 is the extent to which they embrace one, the other, or both. We asked them pointedly.

- What we found is that some 40 percent of Millennials, Xers, and Boomers describe themselves as *spiritual but not religious* while another 25 percent or so say they are both *religious and spiritual.* Just 10 percent indicated they were *religious but not spiritual.*

- Pre-Boomers differ somewhat from the others in being more inclined to say they are both *religious and spiritual* (33 percent), and less likely to report either that they are *spiritual but not religious* (29 percent) or *neither* (23 percent).

Incidentally, the Pew Research Center found in polling Americans in early 2017 that a lower proportion — 27 percent — viewed themselves as "spiritual but not religious." A higher level of 48 percent viewed

Figure 6.5 **Religion & Spirituality Self-Descriptions of Millennials and Other Adults (%)**

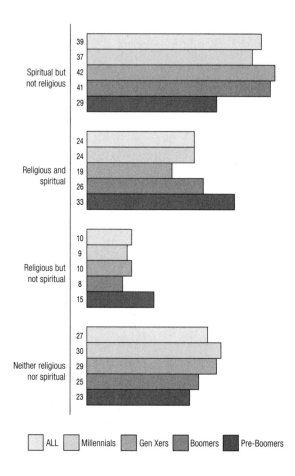

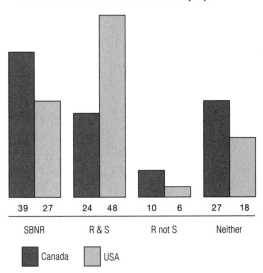

Figure 6.6 **Self-Descriptions of Spirituality: Americans and Canadians (%)**

	SBNR	R & S	R not S	Neither
	39 27	24 48	10 6	27 18

◼ Canada   ◻ USA

themselves as "religious and spiritual," 6 percent as "religious but not spiritual," and a lower figure of 18 percent as "neither religious nor spiritual." At this point in time, Canadians appear to be somewhat more inclined to experiment with spirituality than Americans. Here again, what seems to be an important differentiating factor is the much higher proportion of people in the U.S. who identify with evangelical expressions of Christianity (about 30 percent) than in Canada (around 10 percent).

We would maintain that the major takeaway from all this is the fact that the majority of Millennials and other Canadian adults have hardly abandoned religion *and* spirituality. That said, some 30 percent indicate they are *neither* religious nor spiritual. Clearly both the pro-religious and no-religious camps have considerable room to expand their numbers.

The Trend and Cohort Findings

Reg first asked young people about spirituality in his Project Teen Canada survey of 15- to 19-year-olds in 1992. At that time, 58 percent indicated that they had *spiritual needs*. In 2000, the figure was 52 percent, followed by 54 percent in 2008, and 58 percent for 18- to 23-year-olds in 2016 (see Figure 6.7). Clearly the expression of spiritual needs has remained fairly constant over at the least the last three decades or so.

In looking more closely at the 1992, 2000, and 2008 teen cohorts as of 2016, it is interesting to see that in all three instances, there has been about a 10 percentage-point increase as these teenagers moved, respectively, into their 20s, 30s, and 40s. These increases would seem to be the product of both life-cycle and contextual effects — people becoming more spiritually inclined as they get older, combined with a fairly pro-spirituality emphasis in the culture. Apart from the two explanations, the bottom line is that

What People Mean by Spirituality and Spiritual Needs

In early 2017, Joel was invited by the Royal Canadian Chaplain Service to address Canadian military chaplains on a myriad of topics. One of those subjects concerned the differences between "religion" and "spirituality." More to the point, what do people mean when they say "spirituality"?

Sociologist Nancy Ammerman of Boston University provides insightful clarity in her book *Sacred Stories, Spiritual Tribes*. She notes that "spirituality" is typically a boundary marking concept against institutionalized forms of religious life, which people associate with external religious authority and dogma that is problematic for the individual. Conversely, "spirituality" represents a posture *for* personal spiritual experience and authority. It is not surprising then that as Canadians have increasingly embraced values of individualism, personal autonomy and authority, and choice in a diverse society, Boomers, Gen Xers, and Millennials describe themselves, above all, as "spiritual but not religious."

Here are just some of the common descriptors that people have in mind when they say they are "spiritual": belief in the divine; connected to nature; mystery and awe to surroundings and experiences (e.g., beauty or community); something more than our earthly/physical beings; meaning and purpose and connectedness in life events; inner wisdom; ethical spirituality by treating others with compassion; prayer and meditation; connection to others and the spiritual realm. For those familiar with Reg's writings over the years, there are many points of overlap between Ammerman's findings and his work.

Figure 6.7 **Spiritual Needs of Teens: 1992, 2000, 2008, versus 2016 (%)**

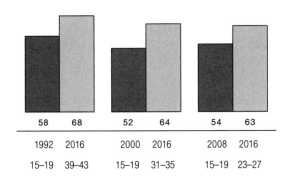

58	68		52	64		54	63
1992	2016		2000	2016		2008	2016
15–19	39–43		15–19	31–35		15–19	23–27

spiritual needs are persisting in Canada. But once again we need to empha-size that spirituality is not for everyone. About 1 in 3 Millennials and older adults do not indicate they have such needs.

General Attitudes: Religion and Spirituality

We also had the opportunity to ask Millennials and other adults about their thoughts on an array of religion-related topics. Their responses help to fill out our understanding of their thoughts and feelings about religion and spirituality.

Religion's Impact. There is little doubt that organized religion is viewed with caution by large numbers of Millennials. That's not to say that it does not have its young fans. As we have just seen, the pro-religion numbers are noteworthy, led by young adults who have been arriving from other countries. But, for many Millennials, "the caution flag" is up — especially compared to the three older cohorts (see Table 6.4).

- Just over 6 in 10 Millennials agree that *the Ten Commandments still ap-ply today* — but that number is well below the figures for Pre-Boomers (91 percent), Boomers (77 percent), and slightly below that of Xers (68 percent).
- Millennials are considerably less likely than older Canadians to say that *religion's overall impact on the world is positive* (44 percent versus 68 percent for Pre-Boomers, for example).

- They also are far less inclined than older age cohorts to think *the decline in religious involvement has been a bad thing for Canada* (38 percent versus 52 percent for Gen Xers and 69 percent for Pre-Boomers) — and far more likely to agree that *the growth in atheism is a good thing for Canada* (47 percent versus 25 percent for Boomers and 16 percent for Pre-Boomers).

Table 6.4 **Outlook on Religion of Millennials and Other Adults**

	ALL	Millennials 1986–plus (18–29)	Xers 1966–1985 (30–49)	Boomers 1946–1965 (50–69)	Pre-Boomers Pre-1946 (70-plus)
Religion's impact					
The Ten Commandments still apply today	73%	63	68	77	91
I think that religion's overall impact on the world is positive	51	44	47	52	68
I think the decline in religious involvement has been a bad thing for Canada	48	38	42	52	69
I think the growth in atheism is a good thing in Canada	33	47	40	25	16
Religion's importance					
It's important for parents to teach their children religious beliefs	61	53	56	65	78
I'd be open to more involvement with religious groups if I found it worthwhile	39	42	41	35	43
I prefer to live life without God or congregation	33	47	40	25	16
When you die, you want to have a religious funeral	41	45	40	38	45
You feel you experience God's presence	25	23	22	26	33

Religion's Importance. The fact that Millennials are divided in their sentiments toward religion is further evident when we focus on religion's place in their lives. One in two agrees that *it's important for parents to teach their children religious beliefs*; obviously the other 1 in 2 disagrees. Almost 1 in 2 also says that they "prefer to live life without God or congregation."

But just about when we conclude that large numbers of Millennials don't want much to do with God or religious groups, no less than 42 percent tell us that they would *be open to more involvement with religious groups if I found it worthwhile*. That 42 percent includes no less than 1 in 3 of those who just indicated that they prefer to take a pass on *God or congregation*.

Joel is quick to add that his extensive research into people who say they "are open to greater involvement" — summed up in his recent book, *The Meaning of Sunday*[22] — shows that the depth of their receptivity is questionable.

The Gods in the Movies

In the last two decades, movies with religious or spiritual themes have been knowing considerable success, led by Millennial movie-goers. They have included Mel Gibson's *The Passion of the Christ* (2004, U.S. box office $612 million), *The Nativity Story* (2006, $46.4 million), *God's Not Dead* (2014, $62.6 million), *Heaven Is for Real* (2014, $101.3 million), *War Room* (2015, $73.7 million), and *The Shack* (2017, $96.4 million). These movies are also attracting actors with star power such as Greg Kinnear, Dennis Quaid, and Jennifer Garner. They are gaining further popularity in Canada. Toronto reviewer John Semley has put things this way: "Faith-based films have always had a small but strong niche in the North American market. In Canada, select filmmakers are redefining the genre and producing an edgy form of faith-based films that appeals to a broader audience while maintaining traditional messages."

(Sources: Faughnder 2016; Semley 2017)

When we are under the age of 30, it's a bit difficult to project what we will want or not want by way of a rite of passage when we die. Nonetheless, we asked our survey participants the blunt question: "When you die, do you want to have a religious funeral, a non-religious service of celebration, or no service?" For all their reservations about religion, 45 percent of Millennials said they would want to have a religious funeral. Another 43 percent said they would want a non-religious celebration. The remaining 12 percent think that they would prefer not to have any service.

Here again, what's readily apparent are the diverse takes on religion that Millennials have. A solid core seems to be pro-religious and another solid core wants little to do with religion. A third segment appears to be somewhere in the middle. This pattern is consistent with what Reg has been finding in his recent analyses of religion in Canada, summed up in his 2017 book, *Resilient Gods: Being Pro-Religious, Low Religious, or No Religious in Canada.*[23]

Aware of what seems to be accelerated "religious polarization" in Canada, Reg — in partnership with Angus Reid — put the question to Millennials and other Canadians, to see to what extent they identify with the diverse positions toward religion:

> Some people say Canadians variously (1) embrace religion, (2) reject religion, or (3) are somewhere in between the two extremes. Where would you tend to locate yourself?

Consistent with our findings on beliefs, practices, spirituality, and outlook, about 30 percent of Millennials are inclined to embrace religion, 30 percent reject it, and some 40 percent are in-between (see Figure 6.8). Those proportions are very similar to those of both Gen Xers and Boomers. Pre-Boomers differ from the three younger cohorts in having a higher proportion of people who say they embrace religion and lower proportions who both reject religion or take a middle position.

The extent to which Millennials and others identify with what we might call "the religious middle" is intriguing. Many observers simply dichotomize between people being religious and not being religious. While those two groupings clearly exist, it also is clear that sizable numbers of Canadians

Figure 6.8 **Religious Inclinations of Millennials and Other Adults (%)**

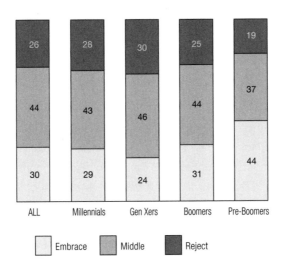

— both younger and older — are somewhere in between those two polar opposites. The inclination for them to gravitate in either direction is something worth watching.

The resilience of religion should not be underestimated. Durkheim poetically commented a century ago that "The old gods are growing old or are already dead. There are no gospels which are immortal." He then added a poignant qualifier: "But neither is there any reason for believing that humanity is incapable of inventing new ones."[24]

If religion is "down," it can be expected to rebound in any number of ways. One example is the appearance since around 1990 of what is referred to as the Emerging Church Movement. This highly diverse initiative originated in New Zealand, Australia, and the United Kingdom and has subsequently spread to the United States, Canada, and elsewhere. Its defining traits include informal relationships and limited structure, experimentation and flexibility, community and service.[25] British researcher Katharine Sarah Moody and American Randall Reed recently have argued that emerging churches are particularly popular among Millennials who have shied away from traditional Christianity and frequently identify

The Irrelevance of Religion for a Solid Segment of Millennials

There is a growing amount of research on young people who say they have "no religion." In 2017, Joel and colleague Sarah Wilkins-Laflamme teamed up to examine the situation in Canada in an article entitled, "Becoming a Religious None." Several findings stand out which they are exploring further in a new book on religious nones in Canada and the United States.

Many Millennials who currently say they have no religion were raised in religious traditions, led by Christianity. Why did they leave? Reasons include: greater social acceptance of having no religion; more parents giving their teenage offspring the choice of being involved or not involved; social ties that discouraged group ties; disagreements with religious teachings (e.g., on issues such as gender and sexuality); concern in the U.S. about the fusion of the Christian Right and politics; and life transitions, such as residential moves that resulted in lower levels of involvement. Such factors have contributed to Millennials believing that religion is of little importance in day-to-day life.

More generally, it is becoming more common for children to be raised without religion in the home – and this is only likely to increase in the future as "no religion" becomes more widespread. Large numbers of Millennials in turn are not exposing their children to religion. In some cases, individuals are hostile toward religion and in other instances have no strong feelings for or against religion. Either way, religion is seen as irrelevant at best and divisive at worst for a growing segment of Millennials.

(Sources: Thiessen and Wilkins-Laflamme 2017 and forthcoming)

themselves as religious nones. Emerging Christianity, they say, is a form of religious life enacted by individuals and groups with a variety of religious identities. In contrast to their disenchantment with traditional groups, the appeal of Emerging Churches lies with their placing importance on themes such as tolerance, pluralism, authenticity, relationships, community, and participation.[26]

Signs of religion's resurgence in the face of apparent decline are worth watching for.

Variations in Beliefs, Practices, Spirituality, and Outlook

The diversity in responses to religion and spirituality are underlined when we look at a sampling of variables, such as religious group, region, community size, gender, education, birthplace, race, and sexual orientation. Here are some highlights; again, the details are there as wanted.

- Predictable differences exist between Millennials who *identify with a religious group* and those who do not. Variations between Catholics, Protestants, and those who identify with other major world faiths are fairly random, depending on the item posed. Put succinctly, the religious are a varied lot. So much for stereotypical generalizations.
- *Quebec Millennials* match or exceed *other Millennials* when it comes to a variety of beliefs. Involvement is another matter, but only a minority actually rejects religion. Most remain Catholics, even if they are not actively involved in parishes.[27]
- Beliefs and involvement levels are similar for Millennials in *urban and rural* areas. Openness to greater involvement is higher among those living in urban areas.
- Differences between Millennial *women and men* are generally small. Men are reporting higher levels of involvement than women, perhaps in part reflecting recent immigration patterns. Women are somewhat more inclined than men to acknowledge spiritual needs.
- *Educational differences* are limited primarily to service attendance and the embracing of faith, where levels are inversely related to education. However, even Millennials with university degrees are not more likely than others to actually reject faith.
- Consistent with what we noted earlier, Millennials *born outside Canada* are consistently more likely than others to believe, practise, acknowledge spiritual needs, and embrace religion. Given that 8 in 10 Millennials in our surveys who were born elsewhere are also members of *visible minorities*, it is not surprising that many of the birthplace findings for beliefs, attendance, spiritual needs, and the embracing of faith are similar for *visible minority–Caucasian* comparisons as well.
- Canadians who are *LGBTQ* consistently exhibit lower levels of

conventional beliefs and practices, as well as a lower inclination to have spiritual needs and be open to greater religious group involvement. Asked pointedly, 1 in 2 say they have rejected religion — almost twice the proportion of *heterosexuals*. Such findings are consistent with findings for the United States. The Pew Research Center has reported that LGBTQ adults are almost twice as likely to be religiously unaffiliated (41 percent versus 23 percent). Pew found that some 30 percent felt personally unwelcome in a religious organizations.[28]

ASSESSMENT

Throughout this chapter, what we have been finding and underlining is the fact that for large numbers of Millennials, religion and spirituality continue to be present. Beliefs, practices, involvement, and the expression of spiritual needs characterize the lives of many young adults.

But that's only part of the picture. Things are different. A noteworthy core of about 1 in 3 Millennials frankly has little use for organized religion. Religious polarization is more blatant than perhaps at any time in Canadian history. Further, just as Millennials and other Canadians have an unprecedented number of choices as they live out life in Canada, today's emerging generation has all kinds of choices when it comes to religion and spirituality. So there is less consensus on conventional beliefs, a greater sense that organizational involvement is optional, and a recognition that spiritual needs can be met in extremely diverse ways — if they have to be met at all. Millennials have the choice of opting for faith, bypassing it, or drawing on some of its features when they find it is expedient to do so.

What stands out to us from our findings and other studies is how pervasive individualism, choice, and subjectivity are in how Millennials — regardless of religious tradition — approach religion and spirituality. Our findings are consistent with those of Peter Beyer and Rubina Ramji's findings for young Canadian Muslims, Hindus, and Buddhists.[29] Similar inclinations have been documented in research in Europe and the United States.[30] Although parents and family are invariably the most influential source in the faith development of children,[31] Millennials do not want to simply accept what their parents hand down to them. They want control and choice, with technology, the Internet, and social media assisting in exposing them to the limitless religious and spiritual options available. Significantly, our survey findings suggest that there is limited interest in organized religion on the part of two very visible and vocal groupings — Indigenous Peoples and the LGBTQ community.

Diversity and pluralism have not eradicated religion in Canada. But such centrally important cultural features have radically increased one's choices, and those choices are being exercised by Millennials. With pluralism's blessing, what they choose is expected to be respected by everyone else. As is readily evident, their choices are not always the same choices as their parents and grandparents.

The fact that Canadian Millennials have innumerable choices as they live out life is also contributing to them holding a fascinating outlook. Regardless of what might be happening in the world and the country and to everyone else, and regardless of what so many prophets of doom are saying about their dismal futures, the country's youngest adults believe that they personally have bright futures.

To that surprising finding we now turn.

THE MAGNIFIED MOSAIC

Millennial Beliefs by Select Variables

	God or higher power exists	Commu- nicate with dead	Attend monthly+	Have spiritual needs	Open to involve- ment	Embracing	Rejecting
NATIONAL	66%	44	26	60	42	29	28
Catholic	81	54	22	60	48	33	10
Protestant	83	35	54	77	49	51	10
Other world faith	67	67	32	74	37	33	9
No religion	32	31	2	34	33	3	66
Outside Quebec	67	40	30	59	49	31	27
Quebec	65	57	14	64	20	21	30
Urban	65	43	26	59	43	27	29
Rural	73	46	27	67	32	39	19
Women	67	47	23	66	39	26	28
Men	66	40	33	54	45	33	27
Degree- plus	66	40	19	58	47	15	29
Some post- secondary	65	41	25	66	36	28	30
High school or less	67	47	30	57	46	33	26
Born elsewhere	78	34	49	76	48	41	20
Born in Canada	65	45	22	58	41	27	29
Visible minority	75	47	36	63	48	34	22
Caucasian	62	43	22	59	39	27	30
Indige- nous*	71	55	12	60	37	17	37
Non-Indig- enous*	70	46	23	66	41	26	29
LGBTQ*	51	44	4	49	24	9	52
Heterosex- ual*	73	46	21	65	40	26	27

*Millennials and Gen Xers combined because of small sample sizes.

CHAPTER 7

The Future: The Paradox/
So Far/Great Expectations

Much has been written and said about what the future holds for Millennials. There also has been considerable conjecture about the impact that Millennials are going to be having on Canada and, for that matter, the world. Our surveys have a fair amount to say about what possibly lies ahead.

THE PARADOX

Young people in Canada supposedly have never had it so bad. Yet their resilience is evident in the fact that most of them think they eventually are going to have it extremely good.

Living with the Bad

First, why they have it so bad.

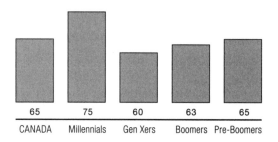

Figure 7.1 **It's Tougher for Youth Today**

"Young people starting out today have it harder than past generations" (%)

65	75	60	63	65
CANADA	Millennials	Gen Xers	Boomers	Pre-Boomers

For starters, the world doesn't seem to be as safe as it once was. Terrorism and conflict seem to be rampant across the planet. Those are not just developments that are taking place in far-off regions of the world. In recent years, terrorism has touched down in places like Toronto, Ottawa, Montreal, and Edmonton.

Precarious global conditions have significant implications for the quality of life everywhere, including Canada. Older Canadians are especially troubled about what is happening worldwide — with 90 percent feeling the world as not as safe as it used to be. But some 2 in 3 Millennials share those feelings (see Table 7.1).

Life is also not particularly easy on the Canadian *economic and employment* front. Incomes are embryonic and money is frequently scarce. It's also hard for young adults to make headway on the job market. Recent Pew Research in the U.S. reminds us that U.S. Millennials have been particularly hard hit by economic downturns in recent years, often being "among the last hired and the first to lose their jobs."[1]

Large numbers of Canadian Millennials have not fared much better. A 2017 *Globe and Mail* survey of some 2,600 Millennials led to the conclusion that "a significant number are not prospering in today's economy."[2] Paul Kershaw of the University of British Columbia has summed up Millennials' predicament as being like "an escalator going down faster than young people can run up. They go to school longer, they work longer hours, they delay starting families. But," says Kershaw, "those adaptations aren't enough to spring up faster than the escalator is going down."[3]

Some observers say that things have become tighter because of factors including the elimination of mandatory retirement, the influx of immigrants, machines replacing human workers, and student loan debt. It is no wonder then, as we saw in Chapter 5, that more young people than ever before continue to live with Mom and Dad or boomerang back home after leaving home the first time — for the second or third time in some cases!

Monetta reminds us that, despite their optimism and willingness to work hard, Millennial women, like women before them, continue to face

Table 7.1 **Many View Life as Difficult: Millennials and Other Adults**

% Agreeing

	ALL	Millennials 1986–plus (18–29)	Xers 1966–1985 (30–49)	Boomers 1946–1965 (50–69)	Pre-Boomers Pre-1946 (70-plus)
General					
The world is not as safe a place as it was when I was growing up	81	65	77	87	90
Concerned about the future	55	71	54	50	51
Canada's uncertain future makes it hard to plan for the future	56	60	58	54	50
It's hardly fair to bring children into the world with the way things are	34	46	39	27	23
Concerned about so many things changing	32	42	34	27	29
Finances					
The lot of the average person is getting worse, not better	70	65	69	73	66
Concerned about lack of money	47	64	54	40	28
During the last few years, my financial situation has been getting better	22	34	26	17	10

Figure 7.2 **Home Ownership Status of Millennials and Others (%)**

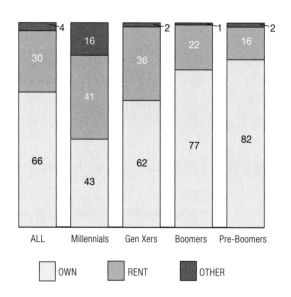

difficulties in the workplace. Drawing on the current research of Nancy Worth of the University of Waterloo,[4] she notes the following:

- Despite their increasing presence in the workforce, women continue to be faced with navigating a disproportionate number of precarious and insecure jobs.
- They report widespread gender and age stereotyping that requires considerable social agility. But most remain positive and believe they can transcend such barriers once they "prove themselves."
- Nonetheless, power and privilege operate in the workplace specifically and the labour market more generally, posing ongoing challenges for women. And the wage gap, while decreasing somewhat for Millennial women, still exists.[5]

In addition to having to live in an increasingly unsafe world and tough economic and employment conditions, Millennials are living at a time when change seems to be everywhere, stimulated by the arrival of the

---

Generation Squeeze

Dr. Phil Kershaw, a professor in the Faculty of Medicine's School of Population & Public Health at the University of British Columbia has founded Generation Squeeze to speak for younger Canadians in the market place and the world of politics. Kershaw's work has focused on generational inequality.

The movement's website states that Canadians in their 20s, 30s, and 40s need more influence in politics and the market. Taking its cue from the Canadian Association for Retired Persons that lobbies governments on behalf of Canadians 50-plus, Generation Squeeze lobbies for Canadians in their 40s and younger. It emphasizes that it is not working against the interests of parents or grandparents but believes "in a Canada that works for all generations." It wants governments to provide "a better generational deal" that will elevate life for young people who are currently facing difficulties.

Presently, governments are spending about $35,000 per person age 65 and over and less than $12,000 on adults under 45. Over the past four decades, older generations have been prioritized, as younger Canadians have fallen behind. Generation Squeeze wants to pressure all political parties to narrow the gap, while protecting spending on aging parents and grandparents.

(Sources: Kershaw 2018a, 2018b, and 2018c)

Internet and the geometric jump in digital devices. It's all a bit daunting. Some 3 in 10 Canadians say they are troubled "a great deal" or "quite a bit" by *so many things changing.*

The tight *housing* market, particularly in major centres, has made it almost impossible for young adults to buy their own homes. Renting is also increasingly unaffordable. As would be expected, owning versus renting versus other arrangements is directly related to age: Millennials (43 percent) are on the bottom of the home ownership ladder, below Gen Xers (62 percent), Boomers (77 percent), and Pre-Boomers (82 percent).

Some 7 in 10 people of all ages say that *things are getting worse* for average people, and concern about the lack of money is highest among Millennials, followed by Gen Xers. Yet here is a preview of the Millennial paradox: they lead the way in saying they are troubled about not having enough money.

However, they also are more likely than any other age cohort to say that during the last few years, their financial situations have been *getting better*.

In short, many Millennials see things as tough as they "start out."

Pursuing the Good

In the midst of all this, the general Millennial mood is hardly one of despair. The times might be difficult, but they are making progress. And even if many of their peers may struggle, the majority of Millennials — individually — feel they can live successful lives. Research on American Millennials by Vision Critical has found the same thing: "Perhaps the most surprising aspect revealed by our study of Millennials," it says, "is their optimism, which is hard to square with their reputation as perpetually-dissatisfied moaners. It's a mistake to think they are moping their way through life as though the decks have been stacked against them." Vision Critical found the most common words Millennials used to describe their current situation were "happy," "excited," and "confident." Vision Critical, like us, noted that the sunny outlook "persists despite the fact that younger Millennials live paycheck to paycheck and many still receive financial assistance from their parents. They're convinced that better days lie ahead."[6] Similarly, the Pew Research Center has noted that, despite being more burdened by financial hardships than previous generations, Millennials are optimistic about the future in general and "extremely confident about their financial future."[7]

One of the apparent reasons why most Millennials are so upbeat about their personal futures is their belief that the key to what happens in their lives is what they themselves are capable of accomplishing. Asked about the extent to which certain factors determine what happens in their lives, some 9 in 10 Millennials — as with Xers, Boomers, and Pre-Boomers — emphasize the importance of *their own efforts* (Table 7.2). *Health* is clearly acknowledged as an important factor. In addition, Millennials in particular see *other people* as playing important roles in their lives. To a greater extent than older cohorts, Millennials also see *chance* and *luck* as influencing their lives; to a lesser extent, they acknowledge *God* as having an impact.

Table 7.2 **Views of Key Sources of Influence:**
Millennials and Other Adults (%)

% Indicating Influenced "A Great Deal" or "Quite a Bit"

	ALL	Millennials 1986–plus (18–29)	Xers 1966–1985 (30–49)	Boomers 1946–1965 (50–69)	Pre-Boomers Pre-1946 (70-plus)
Your own efforts	89	87	90	90	92
Your health	84	79	82	86	90
Other people	45	55	45	41	43
Chance	40	50	43	34	34
God	39	36	34	42	51
Luck	33	41	35	28	30

However, relative to other factors, number one is what they themselves bring to their lives. Millennials place great stock in their agency as individuals to make things happen. As long as health holds, other determinants play far less important roles in who they become and what they accomplish.

Incidentally, the teenage predecessors of Millennials have been inclined to buy into the well-worn idea that "anyone who works hard can rise to the top." From 1984 through 2008, Reg's Project Teen Canada surveys found that some 75 percent of 15- to 19-year-olds agreed with the statement. Interestingly, among adults, from 1975 through 2015, the figure was only about 45 percent to 50 percent (see Figure 7.3). Today, for example, the agreement level for 18- to 23-year-olds is 53 percent.

Still, even if Millennials join other adults in realizing that hard work alone will not guarantee success, they *do* believe that their own efforts are critical to knowing success.

SO FAR ...

As we saw in the family chapter, teens in 1984 and 1992 had high hopes when it came to things like getting married, staying married, and having children. We also can readily take a peek, by way of teen cohort illustrations, at how "the class of 2000" is looking as of 2016.

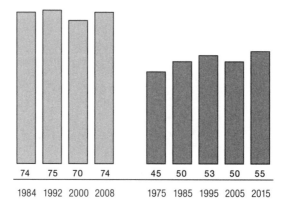

Figure 7.3 **Belief That Hard Work Results in Success: Teenagers, 1984–2008 and Adults 1975–2015 (%)**

"Anyone who works hard will rise to the top"

| 74 | 75 | 70 | 74 | | 45 | 50 | 53 | 50 | 55 |
| 1984 | 1992 | 2000 | 2008 | | 1975 | 1985 | 1995 | 2005 | 2015 |

The Cohort Findings

Both the 1992 and 2000 cohorts were top-heavy with young people who felt they would graduate from university, as well as get the jobs they wanted when they graduated from school — whatever the level of graduation to which they aspired.

Well, to this point, *graduation from university* has been elusive for all but about 30 percent (see Table 7.3). That's not surprising, given that in 1985, only about 15 percent of Canadians had graduated from university and that the present level stands at 28 percent.[8] The education dreams of young people in both 1984 and 2000 far exceeded realistic projections and were well out of reach for most young people. Statistics Canada, in a 2018 report on youth, points out that a large gap in post-secondary education remains between youth from lower and higher income families.[9] What's more, young women and men, StatsCan reminds us, continue to enter different types of programs and fields of study. Women are well represented in the social sciences, public administration, health, the humanities, and education. But they are underrepresented in the physical sciences, math and computer science, and engineering and architecture. Making things worse, Statistics Canada notes that the costs of education have been increasing and many graduates continue to be burdened with heavy debt. For example, recent data show some

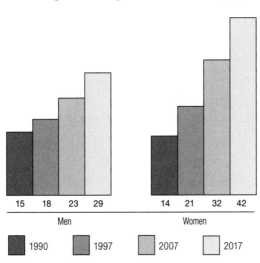

Figure 7.4 **Women and Men, 25–34 with Bachelor's Degree or Higher: 1990–2017 (%)**

15	18	23	29		14	21	32	42
Men					Women			

■ 1990   ■ 1997   ■ 2007   □ 2017

(Source: Statistics Canada 2018)

50 percent of those who graduate with a bachelor's degree leave convocation ceremonies with an education debt that averages more than $26,000.[10]

Young people in the 1980s and 2000 were not unaware of the employment and economic realities of their respective eras. The early '80s were characterized by severe recession and crippling interest rates, with the Bank of Canada rate, for example, hitting 21 percent in August of 1981.[11] In Alberta, mortgage rates soared to 20–25 percent and had to be subsidized for a period of time by the provincial government. Nationally, the federal debt more than tripled between 1975 and 1992. Around 2000, the economic times again were rough, with Canada in the aftermath of having to deal with a global financial crisis.[12]

Nonetheless, 8 in 10 were convinced in both the '80s and 2000 that they could defy the odds and not only find work but "get the job they want" when they graduated. As they look back, only about 3 in 10 admit that they actually were able to find those jobs (see Table 7.3).

It will be interesting to see how today's Millennials will one day assess their jobs as they likewise age, given a recent Environics report. Some 50 percent said their education, training, and skills were a good match for their current jobs. About 30 percent reported that their jobs were not closely related to their education or skills. The balance either felt they were overqualified (13 percent) or underqualified (7 percent).[13] In light of growing concerns about student debt, and awareness of the precariousness of the education–job fit, young Canadians may become more cautious about "automatically" pursuing post-secondary education. Incidentally, Environics found that only 1 in 3 Millennials felt their post-secondary education was "essential" to having a fulfilling life, and half said that if they could do things again, they would have pursued a different type of post-secondary education.

Perhaps these findings reinforce what social psychologists have reported in several areas of life regarding having too many choices — in this case, between dozens of education programs and career options — where we begin to regret the decisions that we make.[14] Maybe this is one of the downsides of choice, individualism, and autonomy that seem so important in Canadian society today, especially for Millennials.

One thing 15- to 19-year-olds were convinced of in both the 1980s and 2000 was that they eventually would *own their own homes*. No less than 96 percent of the young people in both cohorts didn't just "hope" to own their homes; they said they *expected* to own homes.

To date, about 55 percent of those from 1992 and 50 percent of those from 2000 have achieved the goal of home ownership. Not bad — especially when we keep in mind that those from 1992 are still only 39 to 43 and those from 2000 are merely 31 to 35. But clearly there is quite a distance to go to close in on 96 percent. Many, it seems, will never realize their home ownership expectation.

Financial comfort relative to one's parents is an interesting topic that yields predictable findings in the 2017 Environics Millennial study. Nearly 4 in 10 believe that they are worse off financially compared to when their parents were at the same stage of life. Yet Environics found that Millennial optimism shines through in that half expect to be better off than their parents when they reach later stages of life.

The goal of being *more financially comfortable than their parents*, as indicated earlier, was put to our youth cohorts beginning in 1992 because

Table 7.3 **Educational, Employment, and Economic Expectations of 15- to 19-Year-Olds in 1992 and 2000 and Outcomes as of 2016 (%)**

	EXPECTATIONS		OUTCOMES	
	1992 (15–19)	2016 (39–43)	2000 (15–19)	2016 (31–35)
Graduate from university	61	32	62	23
Get the job I want when I graduate	83	26	86	30
Own my own home	96	57	96	51
Be more financially comfortable than my parents	78	36	79	32
Had to work overtime to get ahead	41	50	44	48
Travel extensively outside of Canada	73	37	72	38
Get married	85	57	88	45
Have children	84	65	94	48
Stay with the same partner for life	86	61	88	60

experts have been claiming since at least the 1980s that "this will be the first generation in history that will have to settle for less than their parents." Reg and his original collaborator, Don Posterski, wanted to see to what extent young people themselves were holding such a view.

In 1992 and again in 2000, about 8 in 10 teens said that, yes, they expected to be more comfortable than their moms and dads. In our latest surveys, we were able to ask those 1992 and 2000 "teenagers-now-adults" — and everyone else, "Are you more financially comfortable than your parents?" Alas, only 36 percent from 1992 and 32 percent from 2000 said such is the case. Again, they still have time to pass their parents. But the decades to do so are now down to just two or three. That said, we know that parents, as in the past, are often helping their Millennial children financially — for university or college, getting married, or purchasing a home — sometimes at their own financial peril.[15] Such generosity in some cases is contributing to a diminishing intergenerational gap. Incidentally, both the

Millennials in the Workplace

If you Google "Simon Sinek on Millennials in the Workplace," you will come across a humorous and provocative 15-minute interview viewed by some 10 million people. At the outset, he jokingly says, "Apparently Millennials are tough to manage … and they are accused of being entitled, narcissistic, self-interested, unfocused, and lazy." He goes on to describe the "bad hand" that Millennials have been dealt via poor parenting strategies during their upbringing, technological dependency, the social pressure for instant gratification, and a society unwilling to invest in the long-term maturation of young people. Simply put, Millennials are a product of the environment they have been raised in, and maybe Millennials should be given more credit for trying to navigate these turbulent waters as bright, capable, and promising members of society.

Several studies on Millennials in the workplace contribute to this overview.

- Extremely likely to switch careers, possibly several times, in their lifetime – very much reflective of their proclivity for choice and autonomy in contemporary society.
- Desire employment that pays well and provides opportunities for skills development and career advancement; they want to learn, grow, and contribute.
- Value work/life balance and flexible work options, so much so that they would leave a job if these criteria were not met. They "work to live" rather than "live to work."
- Contrary to public perception, are not overwhelmingly drawn to companies that positively contribute to society. They are not opposed to such things, but this variable does not drive their employment decisions.

The question that is yet to be fully answered is how Millennials will navigate the workplace over their lifetimes, and how workplaces will navigate Millennials. The script is unfolding before our eyes.

(Sources: Environics 2017; Harrington, Van Deusen, Fraone, and Morelock 2015; Human Resources Professionals Association 2016; Pew Research Center 2010; Twenge 2014)

1992 and 2000 cohorts have been realistic about having to work overtime in order to get ahead — so far. Then again, those overtime admissions are only going to increase.

The dream of *travelling extensively outside of Canada* was held by about 73 percent of teens in both 1992 and 2000. To date, just over one-third say they have been able to do that so far — although, to be fair, the oldest are now only in their early 40s. Interestingly, Vision Critical says that today's Millennials "love to travel, and they're not about to wait for it. They are resourceful travellers who Google a lot in the course of shopping online for good deals and unconventional accommodation arrangements." Online services like Airbnb[16] "have triggered an explosion of available rooms,

---

The Single Life Is Not for All Singles

Statistics Canada data for the 2016 Census show that the single household has increased dramatically over the last 150 years, led by younger females.

An interesting "take" on this trend in North America was offered a few years back by *Forbes* magazine writer Larissa Faw, a single Millennial. Faw wrote that she and her Millennial-aged girlfriends confidently accomplished their educational and career goals, have friendship networks, nice apartments, and the accessories they like. But, after not giving a high priority to romance, a growing number are now becoming troubled over "prioritizing our careers before love."

They are not willing to settle for less than they think they deserve, but they also have a lax attitude toward searching for potential mates. "We're busy dominating the world. We don't have time to hang out at bars. While some of us explore online dating, or take a more proactive approach, the majority of Millennial women have long assumed we would meet Prince Charming via friends, or through our own social circles."

What's making things worse is that there now aren't enough quality men to go around. Eligible Millennial women now outnumber their male counterparts. Millennial women aren't sure if they need to lower their standards or try to remain patient. But the years are going by.

(Sources: Statistics Canada 2017e; Faw 2012)

---

posing a threat to the industry's traditional players."[17] Millennials have unprecedented resources for exploring travel possibilities; time will tell how well they exceed the travel dreams of their predecessors.

Finally, as we saw in the family chapter, age is still a factor in teens from the '80s and 2000 either *marrying* or *having children*. Both may still happen, though the gaps are pretty significant. The expectation of *staying with the same partner for life* has already come up short. There's currently a 25 percentage-point deficit for the class of 1992 and a 28-point gap for the class of 2000. Things are only going to get worse since the deficits cannot be reversed.

Generational Comparisons

Fulfillment. We asked Millennials and other adults for something of an assessment of where things are against where they would like things to be. The item read, "At this point in your life, *how fulfilled* do you feel with respect to your aspirations concerning a number of areas." We posed eight: your life as a whole, family, education, what you want out of life, finances, marriage or relationship, children, and career.

- It's important to note that, *regardless of age*, large numbers of Millennials, Xers, Boomers, and Pre-Boomers express relatively high levels of fulfillment in all of these centrally significant areas of their lives (see Table 7.4).
- A majority of Millennials, for example, say they are "very fulfilled" or "fairly fulfilled" with their lives as a whole, and with family life, education, and what they want out of life. Young adults understandably are less fulfilled when it comes to finances and three specifically age-related areas: their marriages or relationships, careers, and children.
- It's also important to underline what may seem obvious to many readers — or maybe not so obvious: *one's sense of fulfillment* with life as a whole and each of these specific areas *is directly related to age*. As we get older, we are more likely to express higher levels of fulfillment with life as a whole — and everything else.

Table 7.4 **Fulfillment Levels of Millennials and Other Adults as of 2016**
% "Very Fulfilled" or "Fairly Fulfilled"

	ALL	Millennials 1986–plus (18–29)	Xers 1966–1985 (30–49)	Boomers 1946–1965 (50–69)	Pre-Boomers Pre-1946 (70-plus)
Your life as a whole	75	64	70	81	92
Your family life generally	82	75	79	84	91
Your education	73	71	65	77	85
What you want/ wanted out of life	66	54	60	72	86
Your finances	54	42	47	58	78
Your marriage/ relationship	59	37	59	66	68
Your career	48	34	48	52	54
Your children	54	16	51	68	78

In short, large numbers of Millennials are expressing fulfillment. But, overall, their fulfillment numbers rank fourth behind Gen Xers, Boomers, and Pre-Boomers. Some things, it seems, take years to attain — or at least years to develop a state of mind that results in one feeling fulfilled.

By the way, further to our reflections on the difficulty Boomers have had in balancing careers with family life, it is worth noting that their reported level of fulfillment with respect to their children falls behind that of Pre-Boomers — while career fulfillment is no higher. More generally, Pre-Boomer levels of fulfillment of life as a whole and family life specifically exceed the levels of Boomers.

Perceptions of How One Has Changed. In trying to get a clearer sense of how Millennials and other Canadians have or have not been changing over time, we raised a number of personal and social themes and asked, "Over the years, would you say there has been *an increase, a decrease*, or *no particular change*" in their attitudes and behaviour (see Table 7.5).

The personal items pertained to time, happiness, and money. What we found is that Millennials are more inclined than others to feel that the pace of life has been increasing over the years and are less inclined — along with Gen Xers — to feel they have been finding time to do the things they want.

This is not particularly surprising with the rise of young adults simultaneously attending university and working part-time or full-time jobs in order to pay for their studies.[18] Of course many will debate the merits of how effective a person can truly be trying to juggle these taxing and stressful social roles. We see this first-hand with our students in the classroom.

Nevertheless, contrary to widespread perception, many Millennials are working extremely hard to keep up with the demands of everyday life, leaving them with very little extra time.

Table 7.5 **Perception of Change over Time: Millennials and Other Adults as of 2016 (%)**

% Indicating There Has Been "an Increase over the Years"

	ALL	Millennials 1986–plus (18–29)	Xers 1966–1985 (30–49)	Boomers 1946–1965 (50–69)	Pre-Boomers Pre-1946 (70-plus)
You					
The general pace of life	46	58	47	42	32
Your general happiness	35	44	34	34	26
The extra money you have on hand	29	34	25	31	30
The time you have to do the things you want	28	20	15	37	49
Others					
Your awareness of what is happening around the world	56	67	48	57	60
Your concern for other people	34	45	31	32	34
The acceptance of people who are different from you	28	44	26	24	22
Your acceptance of homosexuality	24	30	20	25	27

We have already seen that money is a particular concern for Millennials. But on the positive side, about 1 in 3 say that they have been experiencing an increase in the extra money they have on hand — about the same proportion as Xers, Boomers, and Pre-Boomers.

And with respect to happiness, a cohort-leading 44 percent of Millennials maintain that their happiness level has increased.

As for interpersonal relations, the news is all good for Millennials. They readily outdo Gen Xers, Boomers, and Pre-Boomers in claiming that there has been an increase in recent years in their awareness of what is happening in the world (67 percent), their concern for other people (45 percent), and their acceptance of people who are different from them (44 percent). In addition, the increase in their acceptance of gays and lesbians is slightly higher than that of the other three cohorts.

Two caveats are worth noting here. First, stage of life matters. We would expect Millennials to have an increase in these areas because, in all likelihood, global awareness, concern for others, and acceptance of others tend to increase with life experience. Second, as we observed and highlighted in Chapter 1, believing that one has changed in these areas does not necessarily mean one *actually* has experienced such changes.

Still, at minimum, there is evidence of positive growth and positive intent. All in all, good signs, it would seem, with respect to interpersonal life in Canada. Now if only Millennials had more time and money....

Perceptions of Changing Priorities. We also identified a number of areas of life that Canadians of all ages value and asked our respondents, "With the passage of time, would you say that the following have become *more important* to you, *less important* to you, or have remained at about *the same* level of importance?" (see Figure 7.5).

The findings here are both illuminating and intriguing, providing considerable "cause for pause."

- To begin with, the top three areas that Millennials say have become more important to them with the passage of time are *intellectual growth* (56 percent), *being successful* (50 percent), and *family life* (49 percent). Only family life is cited as becoming more important to people in the three older age cohorts.

- About 40–45 percent of Millennials also cite four other areas as becoming more important with the passage of time: *friendships, getting along with others*, their *marriage or relationship*, and their *physical appearance*. All four seem to be related to life stage.
- Three areas accorded lower levels of importance with time: *sex* (27 percent), *material comfort* (22 percent), and *God* (also 22 percent).
- Both *Gen Xers* and *Boomers* emphasize the growing importance of family life, relationships and friendships, while *Pre-Boomers* emphasize the increasing importance of family life and friendships.

Figure 7.5 **Changing Priorities of Millennials and Other Adults (%)**

% Indicating Have Become "More Important" with the Passage of Time

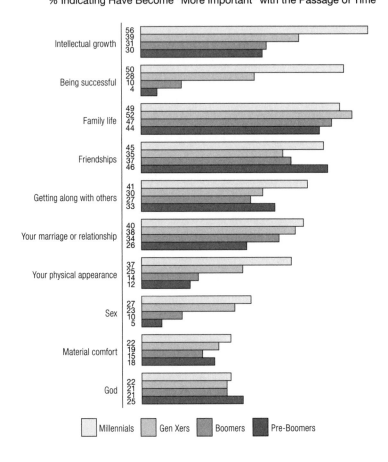

Gen Xers, Let's Step Aside for the Millennials —
One Radical Take

This summer I caught up with an old friend from college by phone. He mentioned that "our turn" — that is Generation X's — is coming up, as the Baby Boomers are reaching the end of their run. I believe I can speak for much of Generation X when I say, "It's about time!"

About time that the Boomers get out of the way, that is. But not necessarily for Gen X to step up. I have come to believe that even though we have the right of way, we should yield and hand the torch directly to the Millennials instead. Previous generations have made quite a mess of the world, to put it mildly, and the multiple crises that we face today threaten all life on earth. Nuclear radiation, pesticides, deforestation, water, and air pollution: these are the legacies of the Boomers. Things are looking grim.

I see this situation and look at my generation, and it strikes me that we are not up for the task. We lack imagination, inspiration, and idealism. We are behind the times. We [white men] needed to be convinced that gays weren't perverts, that blacks weren't crooks and that women were fully human. Millennials grew up in a different world. Sexuality, race, and gender that isn't hetero, white, and male is no big deal to them. There's nothing scandalous about a mixed-race couple of whatever orientation. Millennials have helpful characteristics and admirable traits for the challenges that face us.

Of course, some people will insist that the Millennials aren't ready for leadership, that they are too young. My counter to that is simple: letting the geezers run things certainly hasn't been working out too well, has it? And we Gen Xers are already over-the-hill. Old dogs can't learn new tricks, and it's new tricks that we desperately need now. Basically it boils down to this for me: the Millennials will be bearing what Boomers manufactured and Xers insist on maintaining. This could be our legacy: that we made the best choice we could by just getting out of the way.

(Source: Sonnenblume 2016)

Figure 7.6 **Top 10 Less Important Areas: Everyone (%)**

10	Family life	4
9	Intellectual growth	5
8	Getting along with others	8
7	Friendships	8
6	Marriage or relationship	9
5	Material comfort	15
4	Physical appearance	18
3	God	19
2	Successful	20
1	Sex	26

GREAT EXPECTATIONS

Having taken a number of readings on how younger Canadians dating back to the 1980s have fared so far, over against what they had hoped for, we asked Millennials and other Canadians about their expectations as they look to the future. Here we emphasize that we didn't ask about those proverbial "hopes and dreams." Rather, we asked explicitly about expectations: "As you look to the future, do you expect that you will" … and completed the question with a list of 10 far-ranging areas.

Finances and Family. The 2017 Environics report on Canadian Millennials revealed that fewer than 4 in 10 thought they currently had enough money to lead the lives that they wanted. However, of those who felt things were not where they wanted them to be, over 70 percent believed that they would have enough money in the future. Even fewer American Millennials believe they earn enough money (68 percent). Yet more American than Canadian young adults expect to earn enough in the future (88 percent).[19]

In our research, some 7 in 10 Millennials tell us they expect to be better off financially than they are now (see Table 7.6). But reality does seem to set in as the years wind down. The "better off" expectation drops off for Xers (52 percent), Boomers (33 percent), and Pre-Boomers (20 percent). Close to the same 7 in 10 proportion of Millennials expect that they will have close ties with family. Here the expectation increases with Boomers (75 percent) and Pre-Boomers (85 percent).

Table 7.6 **Future Expectations: Millennials and Other Adults**

"As you look to the future, do you expect that you will ..." (% "Yes")

	ALL	Millennials 1986–plus (18–29)	Xers 1966–1985 (30–49)	Boomers 1946–1965 (50–69)	Pre-Boomers Pre-1946 (70-plus)
Be better off financially than you are now	45	72	52	33	20
Have close ties with your family	73	71	69	75	85
Be in good health	56	69	55	49	54
Be living in the province or territory you want	73	62	69	78	87
Have the time to do the things you want to do	63	65	57	66	68
Stay with your present partner for life	79	63	74	85	93
Be in the kind of relationship you want	62	61	62	63	61
Have the job you want to have	34	56	43	24	9
Have enough money in retirement	45	51	37	44	67
Be well looked after in old age	40	43	36	39	56

Health. The fact that no one can be presumptuous about health is reflected in the finding that more Millennials than others expect to be in good health (69 percent). But that level is only slightly higher than that of the three older cohorts (about 50–55 percent). Then again, the harsh reality is that those older Canadians who were in particularly poor health are no longer with us. The rest are hoping for better things, at least in the short run.

Region of Residence. Many Canadians are not living in the province or territory of their choice. Our surveys and that of Gallup have shown for decades that a disproportionate number of people would live in places like British Columbia, Ontario, and the Maritimes if they could. Millennials are realistic: just 6 in 10 expect to live where they want to live. Here, the levels rise to 7 in 10 for Gen Xers, 8 in 10 for Boomers, and 9 in 10 for Pre-Boomers. That's hardly surprising: people in these older cohorts are more likely to already be where they want to be. Millennials are not as optimistic that they will have that residential luxury.

Time. We have seen that being short on time is a major concern for Millennials and many other people. About 2 in 3 Millennials expect to eventually have time to do the things they want to do. The cause for pause is that 1 in 3 have no illusions they are ever going to solve the "lack of time" problem. They may be in touch with reality: just 68 percent of Pre-Boomers who are 70 and older ever expect to capture the "enough time" medal.

Relationships. We have seen throughout our examination of the data that Canadians immensely value relationships. Even when ties don't last a lifetime, people move on with the hope that the second or third or fourth try will be "a charm." Few seem to give up altogether.

Some 6 in 10 Millennials say that, as they look to the future, they expect to be in the kind of relationship they want. That level is almost exactly the same for everyone else. For all the relational ups and downs, only about 15 percent of people across the country tell us that they do not expect to eventually be in the kind of relationship they want; the remaining 25 percent are not sure. Those who express little hope for better relational ties stand at only 10 percent for Millennials and about 15 percent for Xers, Boomers, and Pre-Boomers. A cause for pause: only 63 percent of Millennials say they expect to stay with their present partners for life — understandably progressively below that of Xers (74 percent), Boomers (85 percent), and Pre-Boomers (93 percent).

Jobs. You will remember that when adults were teenagers, some 9 in 10 expected to find the jobs they wanted when they completed school. As we have seen, those aspirations have fallen far short of what young people had in mind. These days, more than 5 in 10 Millennials say that, in the future, they expect to have the jobs they want to have. Among Gen Xers, the levels have been adjusted downwards in all but about 4 in 10 cases, among Boomers still in the paid workforce to just over 2 in 10. For almost all Pre-Boomers,

Millennials and Money

As we've been emphasizing, Millennials are extremely optimistic about their financial futures. Vision Critical reminds us that their financial dreams aren't much different from previous generations. "They see themselves owning a home or two, paying off their loans, covering their own expenses, saving, investing, and being able to pass along an inheritance to their loved ones. On paper that would make them ideal bank clients."

Then comes the punchline: "There's just one problem. Millennials don't use traditional banks." Vision Critical maintains they are twice as likely as the general population to hold no bank accounts or credit cards. They're more comfortable with electronic transactions and more likely to use digital financial tools and twice as likely as other cohorts to trust tech firms with their money. Some 1 in 2 also turn to Google for their financial information.

(Source: Vision Critical 2016: 24, 26–27)

of course, the ship has sailed. Still, 1 in 10 who are employable continue to think they will find the jobs they want to have. That's tenacity.

In Old Age. As they attempt to do some long-term projecting, as in retirement, 5 in 10 Millennials expect to have enough money in that post-retirement phase of their lives. That expectation level is slightly above that of both Gen Xers and Boomers, and considerably below the 7 in 10 level for the group which is already top-heavy with retirees — the Pre-Boomers. In a more general sense, only about 40 percent of Millennials say that they expect to be well looked after in old age — about the same level as expressed by both Gen Xers and Boomers, but again well below the 55 percent level for today's Pre-Boomers. Incidentally, comparatively, only some 50 percent of U.S. Millennials and Gen Xers believe they will be able to receive Social Security benefits due to long-term problems with funding the program, compared to almost 75 percent of Boomers.[20]

Happiness and satisfaction obviously are highly subjective. Still, whether "real" or "imagined," Canadians 70 and over are expecting life to be good in their final decades. As we have seen, most — contrary to widespread fears — are feeling pretty content: these days 97 percent of Pre-Boomers are describing themselves as "very happy" (25 percent) or "pretty happy" (72 percent). The comparable total for Millennials is 83 percent ("very happy" 19 percent, "pretty happy" 64 percent). Gen Xers and Boomers are in between (86 percent and 89 percent respectively).

Specific retirement plans are all over the place, in large part because of an extremely important development consistent with the emphasis on freedom and choice in Canadian society: the elimination of mandatory retirement.

At this point, 20 percent of Millennials plan to retire before they reach 65, a level similar to Gen Xers (see Figure 7.7). About 10 percent of Millennials and Xers maintain they don't intend to retire. Understandably, large numbers of people in these two younger cohorts currently have no retirement plans. Interestingly, about 1 in 3 Boomers aren't looking at retiring until after 65, if they plan to retire at all. As David Cravit, the expert on Zoomers aka "Boomers with energy," has put it, "Boomers are not retiring on schedule, in part because they don't want to, in part because they can't afford to."[21]

Figure 7.7 **Retirement Plans of Millennials and Others (%)**

"At what age do you plan to retire?"

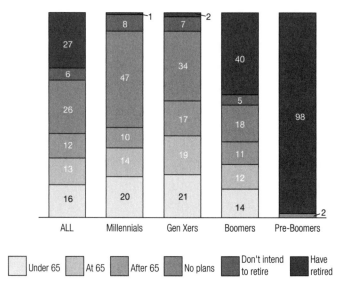

Variations in Outcomes and Expectations

Millennials are fairly uniform when it comes to outcomes and expectations. There are, however, some interesting exceptions. Here again we highlight some and provide the data for those who want to examine variations in more detail.

- The feeling that their lives are *highly fulfilled* at this point in time is slightly more prevalent in Quebec than elsewhere, among women, those with higher incomes, and the religiously devout. Conversely, it is somewhat lower among marginalized Millennials, including those with lower incomes, those born outside of Canada, racialized people, and those who identify as LGBTQ.

- The goal of *home ownership* is considerably more common in rural communities with populations under 1,000 than elsewhere. A considerably lower proportion of LGBTQ Millennials than straight Millennials own their homes — presumably reflecting not only income differences but also the fact that may prefer large urban areas such as Toronto, Vancouver, and Montreal where home ownership is an elusive dream for large numbers of younger adults.

- *Concern about the future* varies little — typically not reaching 10 percentage points. The same is true for placing increasing importance on *success*.

- The belief that one *will be better off financially* in the future is somewhat more pronounced among Quebec and Caucasian Millennials.

- At least 1 in 2 Millennials in almost every social and demographic category we are exploring say that they will eventually be able to *find the jobs that they want* in the future. The belief varies significantly by only one variable, and it's an important one — income. It also is slightly higher among young people born outside of Canada along with Indigenous Millennials. In their 2017 report on Millennials, Environics offered partial corroboration: Millennials "born outside the country and those with non-white ethnicity" stood out in "expressing greater motivation to succeed and optimism about their future prospects."[22]

ASSESSMENT

We started out this chapter by drawing attention to a paradox: Millennials are often portrayed as a generation that will find life to be more difficult than previous generations. Our research has shown that, indeed, Millennials readily acknowledge that life is not easy for them. The levels of concern that they express about personal and social life are high. They are troubled about a variety of personal matters, ranging from money and time through purpose and loneliness. They also are concerned about a good number of social issues and are not at all convinced that our institutional leaders are capable of responding effectively. And they definitely are troubled about the future — some 75 percent strong.

Yet, in the midst of all of this, today's Millennials — like their youth cohort predecessors — continue to believe two things. First, they themselves as individuals are capable of turning things around. Second, for all the hurdles facing their generation, they as individuals can be exceptions to the dominant negative rule.

So it is that Millennials — again like their cohort predecessors — are not lacking for hopes and dreams; what they tell us are in fact *expectations*. They eventually are going to have the jobs and relationships they want; own their own homes; live comfortable lives; have children, good health, success, time to enjoy life; and be looked after well after retirement. Our take is similar to that of Environics as they sum up their findings: "Despite the challenging economic climate facing young adults today, Millennials are notably optimistic about their lives generally and their long-term financial prospects."[23]

The fact that our extensive trend data show that their cohort predecessors are still coming up short on all those expectations doesn't seem to slow down most of them one bit. "Life might be tough," Millennials say, "but if I do everything I can, I am going to succeed."

That's why Canada's future is bright. Millennials and other adults — even those Pre-Boomers in the twilight of their lives — continue to have hope and determination.

"The kids are alright. And Canada will be alright!"

Well, to be honest, there's more to the story. Beyond the blue skies of diversity and choice, resilience and optimism, there are a handful of clouds on the Canadian horizon. There is much to celebrate. But there also are a few loose ends we need to take care of. That is the subject of our final chapter.

THE MAGNIFIED MOSAIC

Future Topics by Select Variables

	Fulfilled life whole	Currently own your own home	Concerned about the future	Success has become more important	Future: better off financially	Future: have job you want
NATIONAL	64%	17	71	51	72	56
Outside Quebec	61	16	70	53	69	61
Quebec	75	21	79	40	83	55
Urban	62	14	71	51	72	57
Rural	71	32	75	45	68	53
Women	68	18	74	53	71	55
Men	59	16	68	48	73	57
<$50,000	58	11	70	52	73	57
$50–99,000	69	33	75	47	76	57
$100,000+	76	18	76	64	80	72
Services: Monthly-plus	73	22	64	41	72	61
Services: <Monthly	60	15	74	54	71	54
Born else-where	55	23	76	50	66	64
Born in Canada	66	15	70	50	73	54
Visible minority	57	40	78	55	63	48
Caucasian	66	31	69	49	75	59
Indigenous*	74	41	60	41	62	57
Non-Indige-nous*	67	44	60	35	59	47
LGBTQ*	58	28	67	40	63	55
Heterosex-ual*	68	45	60	35	58	47

*Millennials and Gen Xers combined because of small sample sizes.

CHAPTER 8

Conclusion: The Good, the Bad, and the Wildcards

There's a lot of good news coming out of the mountain of data we have been looking at. For all the anxiety about Millennials, they are looking pretty much like generations before them. Our friends at Environics have concluded the same thing. Having likewise "spoken" to a large number of Millennials in 2016, they concluded that "Millennials in many respects are not all that different from older generations of Canadians." They too noted that there are predictable life cycle differences: "But in terms of life goals, career aspirations, and community engagement, Millennials do not appear to differ much from their parents and grandparents."[1] Relative to Gen Xers, Boomers, and Pre-Boomers, we don't have much to worry about.

THE GOOD

Interpersonally, they may well be a significant upgrade from previous generations.

A Pluralistic Society

Millennials know the reality of human diversity. They have grown up with all kinds of social, demographic, and lifestyle variations. As one prominent web developer, Victoria-based North Studio puts it, "Gay couples, mixed race families, and gender-nonconforming individuals," for example, "can be featured in advertising and marketing materials without much risk of offending this generation."[2]

But Canadian Millennials are not only emerging in a milieu of diversity: they *are* the diversity. They are also responding to diverse individuals with a pluralistic mindset. At minimum they are exhibiting tolerance, commonly interacting with people who are different, from time to time co-opting something that is different. Pluralism — traditionally summed up in our classic ideal of the integrated mosaic — has, of course, been one of the hallmarks of Canadian life for some time. At this point in our history, our latest generation of young people, the Millennials exude it, indeed breathe it. Pluralism is part of their DNA.

A JUST SOCIETY

But Millennials are not merely endorsing diversity. Accompanying their pluralistic outlook is the belief our diverse society also has to be a just and fair society. All people have to be treated well, regardless of who they may be. These ideals were underlined in embryonic form by Pierre Trudeau when he introduced the multiculturalism policy in the House of Commons in 1971.[3] Two of the three foundational emphases involved ensuring the full participation of diverse people in Canadian life and assuring them that valued parts of their national cultures could be and should be retained. We'll remind everyone of his third emphasis shortly.

So it is that Millennials recoil at the idea of intolerance. Any negative, let alone vicious, targeting of people, particularly those who are disadvantaged in any way — women, people of colour, Indigenous Peoples, the physically or mentally challenged, the poor, the homeless, the young, the elderly, the LGBTQ community — is deplored and met with aggressive and sometimes angry calls for corrective responses.

One only has to look at the dominant reactions to any number of issues over the past while:

- In an interview with the CBC in June of 2017, the governor general at the time, David Johnston, commented that "We're a country based on immigration, going right back to our Indigenous people, who were immigrants as well, 10, 12, 14,000 years ago." His words produced a firestorm of criticism on social media, with some saying they revealed a deep-seated colonial mentality. Within two days, Johnston tweeted, "I want to clarify the miscommunication. Our Indigenous peoples are not immigrants. They are the original peoples of this land."[4]
- Around the same time, a video went viral showing a white woman in a Toronto-area walk-in clinic demanding a "white doctor" for her son. During a four-minute argument with staff and patients, she complained that she waited five-and-a-half hours to see a "brown doctor" who she said did not help her child with his chest pains. "He was not speaking English. His teeth were brown." She added, "We want somebody Canadian to see him." People across the country — led in large part by Millennials using social media — were outraged.[5]
- In Lethbridge, Alberta — home of Reg's university — less than a week after "rainbow" crosswalks were painted in mid-2017, enthusiastic national and local applause quickly dissipated when it was discovered that both crosswalks had been vandalized via vehicle skid marks and paint — not once but twice in four days. But things hardly ended there. Emphatic public support for the original Millennial-driven initiative was reiterated, with city repairs of the crosswalks immediate.[6]
- And then there was the case of the Hamilton Tiger-Cats announcing on Monday morning, August 28th of 2017, that they had hired Art Briles, the former head coach of Baylor University's football team, as an assistant head coach. He had been fired at Baylor following an investigation finding the football program under Briles had mishandled allegations of sexual assault against a number of players. By 9:30 p.m., the team reversed the decision in the face of a major national

backlash, including a significant Millennial outcry on social media[7] — a demographic cherished by the CFL and all sports leagues.

We've come a long way from the days when women were not defined as people, when Chinese workers were assigned "a pigtail tax," when Indigenous people were variously seen as savages and backward individuals who needed to have their cultures eradicated, when immigrants were routinely referred to as "DPs" (displaced persons). Millennials automatically wince when people with disabilities are described as "crippled" or children with learning delays are referred to as "retarded." Ours is a Canada that aspires to respond with compassion to the poor and homeless, that has no patience with the exploitation or abuse of children or the elderly, a society that calls for acceptance of all people regardless of social characteristics.

Millennials' sensibilities about what is right and fair extend into the economic and consumption realms. Vision Critical says that their research into Millennials in the U.S. and Canada confirms that they "like nice stuff." But large numbers also care about where items are made, where they are shipped from, and whether manufacturers and retailers are committed to things like fair trade and organic and sustainability principles and make such information available. "They actively seek out brands that align with their values." What's more, the social consciousness of Millennials is targeting them in a method that matters to them. There is an ever-increasing number of fair trade and ethical shopping phone apps. Vision Critical says such emphases and activities are having an impact, "as more and more clothing manufacturers," for example, "go public with new sustainability commitments," including, for example, "promises to reduce or eliminate fabric fibers that come from endangered forests."[8]

A Multiple Mosaic Society

But it's not just a matter of the pluralistic Millennial mindset focusing on themes such as equality, justice, and social compassion. It extends much further. The entrenchment of pluralism accounts for why Millennials, *like so many — but not as many — people before them*, view virtually everything the way they do. All of life is seen and lived out through pluralistic eyes

— what's important, what's enjoyed, personal and social concerns, our takes on individuals and institutions, sexual activity, sexual orientation, gender, family life, religion, spirituality. What started out as an emphasis on respecting cultural differences has expanded well beyond "the multicultural cradle." As Reg and others have observed, over time the multicultural infant has grown up, left home, and touched virtually all of life. Today, we have not only a cultural mosaic but a value mosaic, a leisure mosaic, a concern mosaic, a sexual mosaic, a gender mosaic, a family mosaic, a religion mosaic, and so on.[9]

So it is that pluralism and its key correlates of diversity and choice have become the axiomatic themes that define Canadian life for Millennials. What Vision Critical says of American Millennials is applicable to Canada as well: "All social issues are important to them, be they LGBT rights, racial and gender equality or global warming." It warns that employers, for example, "must tread carefully, and pay more than lip-service to the causes that Millennials believe in."[10]

These emphases can routinely be observed on a daily basis. Take religion, for example. In June of 2017, Global News reported the results of an Ipsos poll that claimed some 50 percent of Canadians believe that "religion does more harm than good in the world." Yet the same poll found that only 13 percent indicated that they lose respect for someone when they find out they are religious.[11] Even if people do not like something very much, they still are tolerant. One's personal values and choices are not allowed to override the values and choices of others. It has become "the Canadian way."

Multiple mosaics are marvelous from the standpoint of providing Millennials and other Canadians with an increasing range of options in virtually every area of life.

And as Millennials look to the future, the gloom and doom outlooks that some observers associate with them are largely missing. Millennials are exhibiting considerable resilience, optimism, and enthusiasm. Even if economic conditions might be tough and relationships far from lasting, most Millennials are anticipating positive personal futures in both cases, and in life as a whole.

There's not much of a downside, is there?

THE BAD

Hmm — are there really any "bad" things to report about today's Millennials?

The Complaint List

Interesting … if we listen to what adults in a wide array of settings are saying about Millennials — be they colleagues on university campuses, people in the media, parents, people writing letters to editors, and so on, lots of consternation is readily evident. Vision Critical, for example, in summing up U.S. sentiments toward Millennials, says: "If you believe what you read, the Millennial generation is responsible for all that ails the world."[12] Some common themes are readily apparent on both sides of the border. People are not lost for complaints.

- Millennials supposedly *have a sense of entitlement.* They want things handed to them. Many aren't inclined to want to work hard or put up with things they don't like. As a result, they aren't particularly conscientious or committed part-time workers or students and have limited patience and discipline when it comes to entry-level, full-time jobs. One restaurant owner told us he is getting out of the business, primarily because he has tired of trying to rely on young adult employees who simply have no commitment to his business.[13]
- Millennials are "know-it-alls." Technology, including their ever-present iPhones, has fuelled a prevalent sense among them that they know a lot about everything. They are not particularly teachable and treat adults as not particularly knowledgeable. Parents and grandparents, professors and employers, and adults who have casual contact with them are among those doing the lamenting. A common, caustic response from many observers to their alleged arrogance has been that, despite being armed with the Internet-plus, Millennials are actually "dumber" than previous generations — even dubbed "The Snowflake Generation."[14]
- Millennials are *focused on the here and now* and give little thought and have little understanding of the long-term consequences of their

decisions. One grandmother lamented that "they are into immediate gratification and have little appreciation for how today may affect tomorrow."

- Millennials *have no sense of history*. Ask them about almost anything that happened beyond three years ago and they draw a blank. Professors, for example, typically find that recognizable illustrative material has to be current.

- But wait a minute: we three can say with some authority that it also is not clear that Millennials have much *awareness of the present*. Make reference to something that happened in Canada or the world last week or yesterday or even earlier today and, as often as not, students admit they didn't know about "it." ... So much for the alleged information age.

- Millennials have *very short attention spans*. Having been reared on technology that focuses on sound bites and short clips, they have little patience with anything that takes very long — be it a job training seminar or a class presentation and, some say, even a Blue Jays baseball game. And surely those distracting fidget spinners that are enthralling young kids these days won't find their way into Millennial lives, will they?[15]

- A closely related problem is that Millennials *are primarily visual learners*. Raised on YouTube, Facebook, Instagram, and the Internet generally, they are used to videos and pictures. That in itself is not a fatal problem. But an important correlation is that many can't write ... or even read. Oh, and all that texting has not only decimated the ability to initiate or engage in a conversation with someone they don't know but has had a devastating effect on spelling!

- And while critics are on a roll, some undoubtedly would bring up the fact that Millennials are insular social media addicts, sharing the intimate details of their lives via their smartphones yet woefully inept at face-to-face conversations.[16]

- Moreover, Millennials' *obsession with technology and devices* — led by smartphones — *is often downright irritating*. Phones seem to always be on, whether Millennials are in the middle of a conversation or a crosswalk, in a hallway or on a highway. Communication between people

who don't know each other has become almost extinct, due to the fact Millennials carry out non-stop, non-verbal conversations with their thumbs ... or are focused on the sounds coming through the ear buds.
- Speaking of those thumbs, the health-conscious point out that Millennials may experience tendinitis ... and then there are the dangers of bad posture, eyes and ears failing, and, maybe worst of all, even cancer.

We could go on. But these illustrations provide a peek at some of the entries on "The Millennial Complaint List." We ourselves have a fair amount of contact with Millennials. Joel and Monetta are not very far removed age-wise from the Millennial cohort and, along with Reg, teach university students who are predominantly Millennials. We, like most readers, also have extensive informal contact with Millennials in a range of settings, families among them.

Our take on "The Complaint List"? We think the first thing that is needed is a bit of historical perspective. When we look at the laments, it's readily apparent that many are age-old. These were the kinds of criticisms that we all heard when we ourselves were moving into our 20s. It brings to mind our illustrations that we used at the beginning of the book: Canadians for many decades have been calling for youth curfews because "the kids" were so bad — and even that old line of Socrates about the young people of his time "gobbling their food and terrorizing their teachers."

Allegations about entitlement, young people thinking they know everything, being into immediate gratification, having no sense of history, being ignorant of the present, having short attention spans, preferring the visual, and being irritating — they've all been said of every new generation since the beginning of time. If we want to emphasize the negatives, we can do that with any age cohort. In reviewing literature, we were a bit taken back, for example, by this succinct assessment that veteran journalist Peter Stockland — himself a Boomer — offered of that allegedly famous generation: "The first wave of Baby Boomers left home and began behaving like cohabiting rabbits with Benzedrine in their water bottles. It would be unfair and untrue to say the era was a complete disaster. It was an incomplete disaster. In fairness, good things did come of the 1960s. They ended, for starters. That's a very good thing. Let's see ... what else? Hmph."

Is Millennial Entitlement a Myth?

James Cairns of Wilfrid Laurier University notes in his 2017 book, *The Myth of the Age of Entitlement*, that over the past decade a powerful myth about Millennials has taken shape and spread with many mouthpieces — including politicians, professors, reporters, bosses, TV producers, co-workers, and families. Young people today, allegedly more than at any point in history, expect to have a good life handed to them without having to do anything in return. The myth includes the assumption that young people have never had it so good. Yet, they still whine. Such excessive narcissism is seen as a serious threat to economic and social life.

Cairns maintains it is deeply problematic to suggest the main problem with young people today is that they expect too much. The fact of the matter is that they are entitled to much better than they are getting. Millions of Millennials have actually been *disentitled* on numerous fronts: employment, wages, job benefits, the cost of living, the cost of post-secondary education, and even a less livable Earth. The myth of entitlement also ignores important inequalities along lines of race, class, and gender that are far more powerful in shaping life than shared generational membership.

To define Millennials as an entitled generation, says Cairns, isn't just to say that they have high expectations; it's to say their expectations are too high and that young people ought to settle for less. The struggles over so-called youth entitlement tell us about broad societal struggles. Young people, he argues, need to reclaim their democratic entitlements to a decent and secure life — entitlements that they deserve. "It's in the interests of everyone and the planet itself that young people begin to expect more," he writes, "creating new visions and new systems for providing everything for everybody."

(Source: Cairns 2017: 152)

Those kinds of generational critiques aside, we think that, in assessing Millennials, it is critically important to differentiate between *major and minor issues* — and not "major on the minors."

Many if not all of these so-called new things and new tendencies fit into the "minors" category. Most are characteristic of life cycle and, as such, will dissipate and disappear in a relatively short time.

Technology Addiction?

"Steeped in digital technology and social media, they treat their multi-tasking hand-held gadgets almost like a body part." This is one observation from the 2010 Pew Research Center study on Millennials. Phones are the last things people look at before they close their eyes at the end of the day, and the first things people reach for when opening their eyes in the morning. Phones sit face-up in work meetings, dinner conversations with friends and family are interrupted by dingles and immediate responses by those around the table, and sacred settings like religious services, weddings, or funerals are interrupted by ringing cell phones.

While Millennials may be on the front edge of this phenomenon, it would be a mistake to isolate this demographic group. It seems that over time people across generations are complicit in these behaviours. And we cannot forget who is providing children at a young age with iPads, cell phones, and televisions for unending viewing pleasure: parents.

More and more research is coming out these days pointing to technology as an addiction, like addictions to alcohol, drugs, or sex. Dopamine, the brain chemical linked to pleasure, runs high when our phones dingle and we see the red circle pop up with a text message or "like" on any of our social media outlets. People feel lost without their phones and the thought of going "unplugged" for 24 hours is unimaginable. As Simon Sinek notes, "This is the equivalent of opening up the liquor cabinet and saying to our teenagers, 'Hey by the way, if this adolescence thing gets you down' ... but that is basically what is happening ... you have an entire generation that has access to an addictive, numbing chemical called dopamine through social media and cell phones as they are going through the high stress of adolescence." It would not surprise us if one day, in the not too distant future, technology addiction appears on the *Diagnostic and Statistical Manual of Mental Disorders*.

(Source: Sinek 2016)

Even "irritating" features of technological innovation might pass. Millennials and everyone else are still in the early stages of using digital technology and digital products. Once smartphones, for example, have been around for a few more years, the norms for using them will continue to be defined in the direction of safety and civility. Already their use is being regulated when people are driving cars. "No cell" signs are increasingly common in public places. There even have been discussions about regulating their use on Canadian public streets! Don't laugh. A 2016 poll found 66 percent of Canadians were in favour of "distracted walking" legislation, and politicians in places like Toronto and Vancouver have been mulling over introducing laws.[17] Canada would not be first. In October of 2017, Honolulu became the first major U.S. city to ban so-called distracted walking. Pedestrians can be fined between $35 and $99 for staring at their phones while crossing a street.[18]

Monetta throws in the parenthetical comment that among the redeeming features of cell phones is the fact that, ironically, they may be contributing to traits like politeness and civility more generally. After all, this is an era of scrutiny, when Millennials and the rest of us know well that our every move and every word can be monitored. They also are contributing to greater openness. Almost anything is acceptable to say online or via text, especially if one adds a smiley emoji!

We as profs are not particularly stodgy about laptops and iPads and other similar devices being used in the classroom. In some course instances, we encourage their use. But all three of us draw the line at overt texting (what goes on below desk surfaces is beyond our control). And so, as in the past, norms eventually catch up with technological advances, overcoming what sociologists long ago dubbed as "cultural lag."[19]

Older readers undoubtedly remember earlier times when young adults were carrying around those "annoying" transistor radios of the 1950s,[20] or when, in the 1980s their heads were in other places because they were hooked up to their Walkmans.[21]

As for setbacks with reading and writing? Yes, there's no doubt that Millennials have been top-heavy with sight and sound input as they have gone through their teens and entered their early 20s. But there's no reason to believe that any permanent reading and writing atrophy will result. On the contrary, to the extent that Millennials find themselves with barriers because of possible reading and writing limitations, they can be expected to readily make up any deficits — if, in fact, they find that it's necessary to do so. Reg is dogmatic about this; Joel is not so sure; Monetta is somewhere in the middle. What's needed are ongoing empirical readings.

But we are unanimous in believing that, when it comes to major issues — things like values, interpersonal relations, social concerns, social compassion, and hopes and expectations — Millennials are excelling. As we have suggested, their levels of acceptance and social compassion may, overall, be a noteworthy improvement on older age cohorts.

Their aspirations concerning the future are well-rounded, encompassing family, career, material comfort, and people in general. They have great hopes and high expectations and recognize that education, training, a considerable amount of hard work — and even a bit of luck — will be required if things are going to turn out the way that they would like.

In short, when it comes to "the majors" of life, Millennials are in excellent shape.

Not bad so far.

That said, we want to draw attention to two important possible glitches in the Millennials' "pluralism software" that require significant "fixes."[22] And, yes, they involve "major" issues.

The Need to Tap Our Diversity

First, given the extent to which they are embracing pluralism, there is a need for Millennials to address the blunt question, "What's so great about diversity?" On special days and weeks when we focus on cultural diversity, complete with food and festivals, we hear the common rhetorical refrain from any number of community leaders: "Diversity is a great thing for Canada." Just before he participated in Toronto's annual Pride Parade in 2017, Prime Minister Justin Trudeau told reporters, "It's all about how we celebrate the multiple layers of our identities that makes Canada extraordinary and strong."[23] Interesting, predictable. Our audacious question: "Does diversity really make Canada extraordinary and strong?"

A simple Google check reminds us that diversity just means "multiplicity," "variations," "a mixture." In and of itself, diversity is not much of anything. It certainly does not automatically translate into societal positives. On the contrary, as all of us know well, variations in any number of social settings sometimes contributes to a lot of conflict and not a lot of joy.

In Canada and anywhere else, if our emphasis on our differences becomes an end in itself, our focus and energies can be given to sheer co-existence. Imagine the focal objective of our relationship we have with someone we love simply being to "get along" and not upset each other. When it comes to interpersonal life in Canada, living out the mosaic can translate into minimal interaction, where people simply tolerate or try not to offend one another. As one Ottawa government bureaucrat facetiously but poignantly suggested to Reg a few decades ago, "Multiculturalism sometimes amounts to little more than staying out of the way of each other."[24]

Co-existence is better than conflict. But it certainly doesn't necessarily bring us together and translate into a social plus. In fact, when we actually think about it, if all we have in common is our diversity, we don't really have anything in common at all.[25]

What makes diversity a social asset is the fact it provides us with a rich range of cultural and social resources for viewing life and living it out. It can broaden the possibilities for how we can think and what we can do and thereby enhance our individual and collective lives.

That was the third point that Pierre Trudeau made on that historical occasion in 1971 when he introduced the multiculturalism policy in the Commons. Having emphasized that the implementation of multiculturalism would ensure that diverse people could participate fully in Canadian life, complete with those parts of their cultures that they wanted to retain, the former prime minister emphasized that the sharing of varied cultures would have a critically important result: "a richer life for us all."

The central point we want to make? Millennials and the rest of us need to ensure that we don't simply emphasize and applaud diversity as an end in itself. Diversity *is* a great thing for Canada. But what makes it great is when it not only exists but can be consciously tapped so that it contributes to our collective well-being.

There's absolutely no question that ensuring everyone is able to fully participate in Canadian life is what frees them up to bring their diverse resources to "the table." Women, young people, immigrants, Indigenous people, people of colour, the LGBTQ community, atheists, and any number of other marginalized people interact with men, older adults, the Canadian-born, white people, straight people, theists, and everyone else. What *an incredible mixture*! But what *incredible potential* that mixture has to elevate the lives of everyone involved. The individual parts are able to contribute much to the Canadian totality.

A simple illustration. Critics — and we purposely took a playful jab a few paragraphs back — have sometimes panned multiculturalism as little more than "food and festivals," with the latter in recent years including Pride parades. But maybe "food and festivals and parades" provide illustrative microcosms of what is possible. Food, for example, is something which is readily adopted across cultures — where the best from everywhere is enthusiastically consumed. We have no difficulty borrowing from one another when it comes to food, fashion, and music. We routinely recognize that variations readily transcend the blandness of sameness.

That's true of cultural and social diversity more generally.

Peaceful co-existence is an important start. Moving beyond tolerating each other to talking to each other gets us a junior high certificate. Enjoying each other and learning from each other results in a high school diploma. Incorporating into our lives the best features of our respective cultures and lifestyles — along with feelings of inclusion, belong, engagement, and citizenship[26] — get us a university degree.

That kind of life-enriching interaction is what makes diversity worth celebrating for Millennials and everyone else. The Millennials are emerging at a time when such interpersonal and intergroup initiatives are on the ascent. That needs to continue.

The Need to Make Good Choices

This brings us to pluralism's second potential glitch. As we have emphasized throughout, pluralism is providing Millennials and others with unprecedented options in every area of life. We've been reminded of the rich range of choices as we have looked at values, sources of enjoyment, education, career, residence, leisure, sexualities, family, and spirituality.

Let's be clear: choices are wonderful. That solid majority of people across the country who highly value freedom have to be euphoric about the incredible range of choices that Millennials and others have at this point in our history. Those choices obviously include being able to pursue ideas and think for oneself. The emphasis on the personal quest for truth has been an important corrective to the authoritarian imparting of ideas that tended to characterize the pre-1960s. Intellectual liberation has been a breath of fresh air for many.[27]

But the extensive number of options raises an extremely important issue for Millennials and the rest of us: the need to make good choices. As we highlighted last chapter, too much choice can be a problematic element for a person's psychological and social well-being, leaving individuals more likely to fret over and regret their decisions. Precisely because we encourage choices, we need to champion the critical concept of discernment. Millennials and everyone else need to learn how to choose.

One dominant response that many observers have had to the expanding number of life choices is to simply declare that "everything's relative" — implying that one choice is pretty much as good as another. Indeed, that two-word cliché has been solidly endorsed by Canadians. Reg's surveys have found that since the 1990s, around 70 percent of Canadians, young and old, have agreed with the two-word statement. As we saw earlier, a closely related item has generated a similar response. Dating back to the 1990s, teens and adults have been asked to respond to the statement, "What's right or wrong is a matter of personal opinion." The youth agreement level has been around 65 percent, the adult level about 50 percent.

However, just because people think things are relative and a matter of personal opinion doesn't make it so. Upon reflection, few people actually believe that "everything's relative." We all know that some options are better than others, that some choices bring pleasure and others bring pain. Like physical and social scientists, we are free to hypothesize anything. But that is hardly to say that every hypothesis has equal merit.[28]

Likewise, when it comes to morality — our sense of right and wrong — we have considerable consensus around some basic norms. As we have seen, the vast majority of Millennials and the rest of us place high value on traits like honesty, trust, compassion, decency, and respect for life. Conversely, think of how we respond to things like dishonesty, abuse, exploitation, theft, and physical and emotional pain. What is right and wrong is *not* just a matter of personal opinion. Morality may be decided by a vote. But not all issues receive the same number of positive and negative votes. If they did, social life would not be possible.

In short, the fact we have choices can lead to the claim that "everything's relative" and the idea that morality is a matter of personal opinion. But those abstract claims simply don't hold up in real life.

Some choices add more to our lives than others. That's why from the time Millennials and the rest of us were little kids, parents and teachers and others were encouraging us to "do this" and "not do that." From the earliest days of our lives, we found ourselves defining some things as "good" and others as "not so good," some choices as "better" and others as "best," some things as bringing us joy, others as bringing us pain.

The fact that Millennials have an unprecedented number of choices in every area of their lives if anything heightens the need for them to be able to distinguish between good options and not-so-good options — to understand the obvious reality: some choices lead to better consequences than others.

In the late 1980s, a University of Chicago philosopher surprised himself and his academic colleagues by writing a book that quickly became popular well beyond academic settings. In *The Closing of the American Mind*, Allan Bloom — who had taught briefly at the University of Toronto — argued that university students increasingly believed that truth is relative and that openness is consequently a moral virtue. Relativism, Bloom wrote, "has extinguished the real motive of education, the search for a good life."[29] … History and the study of cultures do not teach or prove that values or cultures are relative," said Bloom. "The fact that there have been different opinions about good and bad in different times and places in no way proves that [no claim] is true or [that no claim is] superior to others."[30] He called for a willingness to pursue truth, drawing on history and the wide array of available cultures.[31]

More recently, the need for being reflective about choices has been emphasized by best-selling American author Sam Harris. In addition to his well-known works on atheism, he has written a provocative book on morality entitled *The Moral Landscape: How Science Can Determine Human Values.*[32]

Diversity and Free Speech

As much as Canadians trumpet diversity as a good and beneficial aspect of social life, the topic is not without controversy at home or abroad. In universities across North America, conservative voices — be they faculty, students, or invited lecturers — are being shunned for speaking out on a range of "inclusive" subjects dominating public discourse. Our earlier example of Jordan Peterson, the psychologist at the University of Toronto, who has been publicly vilified for his views on gender identity, is just one example. Several conservative speakers have been "uninvited" of late at many U.S. universities as well. Ironically, the university is allegedly one institution where people openly and freely debate and exchange ideas, both liberal and conservative. This is a reminder that even the most inclusive narratives surrounding diversity can in fact be rather exclusive and intolerant — "we are an inclusive nation that values all people and perspectives, unless your views are too exclusive or intolerant for the majority's liking." And this perspective extends well beyond universities.

In recent years, considerable media attention was given to the heated exchanges between President Donald Trump and professional athletes over their right to kneel in protest during the singing of the American national anthem. In Germany, the Alternative for Germany party secured Parliament seats on an anti-immigration platform that some say harkens back to Nazi ideology. These and other events remind us that diversity is a highly contentious issue. Entire societies are grappling with how best to navigate diverse perspectives — including Canada.

Harris acknowledges that the pervasive idea exists that questions of meaning, morality, and purpose are outside the limits of science. In sharp contrast to such thinking, he maintains that science alone can uncover the facts that are needed to enable humans to flourish and to understand right and wrong in universal terms.

He recognizes that bringing science to bear on morality is not an easy task. "In 1947," he says, "when the United Nations was attempting to formulate a universal declaration of human rights, the American

Anthropological Association stepped forward and said it can't be done. Any notion of human rights is the product of culture. This was the best our social sciences could do with the crematory of Auschwitz still smoking."[33]

Harris challenges such a relativistic assumption, arguing that the point of moral consensus is well-being: "The concept of 'well-being' captures everything we can care about in the moral sphere."[34]

He is convinced that there are right and wrong answers to questions of human flourishing. Consequently, he feels that science needs to give top priority to exploring and developing a universal conception of human values.

In a stimulating TED Talk in 2010, Harris summed up his thoughts this way:

> The separation between science and human values is an illusion — and actually quite a dangerous one at this point in human history. There are truths to be known about how human communities flourish. In talking about morality, we are talking about facts. If questions affect human well-being then they do have answers. How have we convinced ourselves that in the moral sphere there is no such thing as moral expertise? How have we convinced ourselves that every opinion has to count ... that every culture has a point of view on these subjects worth considering? What the world needs now is people like ourselves to admit that there are right and wrong answers to questions of human flourishing. It is possible for individuals, and even whole cultures, to care about the wrong things. It seems patently obvious that we can no more respect and tolerate vast differences in notions of human well-being than we can respect or tolerate vast differences in the notions about how disease spread, or in the safety standards of buildings and airplanes. [35]

Canada's Millennials have a rich mosaic of ideas and behaviour from which they can choose. But the resource pool calls for much more than mindless relativism or uninformed personal opinion.

Millennials are faced with the tough task of thinking hard about what ideas are accurate and determining what behaviour leads to the outcomes they want. Not easy tasks — but essential to experiencing the best in life that is possible.

American sociologist Christian Smith, in his book *Lost in Transition*, similarly maintains that young adults could use some help beyond pervasive moral individualism and relativism in making moral decisions — beyond what makes them happy. Smith says that other adults have frequently dropped the ball in providing some direction.[36] They need to step up.

THE WILDCARDS

In case people don't know it, allow the three of us to break the news: sociologists — and social scientists more generally, for that matter — have not been particularly good at predicting the future. It's not that people haven't tried.

Way back in 1902, in a stimulating and radical lecture entitled "The Discovery of the Future," 36-year-old H.G. Wells told the Royal Institution in London that he believed the future could be scientifically known. "I believe that the time is drawing near," he said, "when it will be possible to suggest a systematic exploration of the future."[37] Projections about the future, he maintained, are possible to make using historical and trend data. Wells readily acknowledged that "the knowledge of the future that we may hope to gain will be general and not individual."[38] Broad social patterns could possibly be uncovered, but predictions specific to individuals would elude science. His belief in the ability of science to identity broad social trends was not a fleeting whim. Three decades later in a 1932 BBC broadcast, a 66-year-old Wells called for the creation of "Departments and Professors of Foresight."[39]

Sociologists routinely tell our students that the three classic goals of research are to (1) describe, (2) explain, and (3) predict. To date, we have been doing a good job of describing and a reasonable job of explaining. But we have had limited success in predicting. The only consolation is that most other social scientists have not fared any better.

The Gift that Keeps on Giving: Mentoring

I (Joel) remember the countless adult influences in my life as a child, teenager, and young adult. Guys in their early 20s from our church would take me to Chuck E. Cheese's, to concerts, to sporting events, and include me in games of street hockey, ice hockey, and football. When I started university, a few individuals in their 30s and 40s met me once or twice a month to mentor me on topics ranging from relationships to leadership to family to career. They often paid for my food too, telling me that one day in the future when I'd be in their position, I should "pay it back" to the next generation — in time, wisdom, expertise, and actual dollars!

As someone finding my way in sociology, a few scholars in particular took me under their wings intellectually. They pushed my thinking, introduced me to the giants of the field at academic conferences, and paved the way to explore publishing and presenting opportunities. This included Reg, who I met when I was 20 years old and first read his work. To think we would now collaborate on this project, after our many "intellectual exchanges" in print and person over the last 15 years! And now after teaching at Ambrose University for 10 years, I continue to be shaped and influenced by colleagues and others who have more life and professional experience.

These experiences inform how I, in turn, view the next generation. I have very close friends whose children, now teenagers, I have known since they were born. I see my role in their lives in much the same way as those who looked out for me in my earlier years. The same applies with my students in the classroom, my younger colleagues, and young people I meet in various social settings. Reiterating a common sociological thread throughout this book, my views and experiences with those younger than me is a reflection of the way I was raised and socialized to think about intergenerational ties.

In recent years, a specialty field known as futures studies has been emerging. Given the need to be comprehensive in considering factors that influence what lies ahead, futures studies is seen as having to be heavily interdisciplinary. Recognizing — as H.G. Wells did — that it is virtually impossible to come up with highly specific predictions, the field increasingly emphasizes what some refer to as "3 Ps and a W."[40] People speak of futures that are possible, probable, and preferable, in sharp contrast to trying to "predict" the future.[41]

Of particular importance for our purposes is the "W." Any of us — let alone futures specialists — knows that anticipating the future means having to allow for the unexpected — for "wildcards." They are viewed as low probability, high impact events or innovations. Who, for example, could have "predicted" in the 1950s or '60s that a thing known as "the Internet" would come into being that would quickly transform life around the world?

We've been maintaining that the bottom-line picture of Canada's Millennials is an extremely positive one. As they move into their 30s and 40s, they are going to increasingly occupy positions of leadership throughout Canadian life. And as their power and influence grows, we have every reason to believe that they will move life forward for Canadians. We will know increasing levels of personal and social well-being, equality, and social compassion.

So, what are some possible wildcards that might have an impact on the seemingly positive direction that life in Canada is headed? We want to briefly suggest six.

1. **Technology.** You may recall from the outset of this book that when Canadian Millennials were asked to identify what makes their generation unique, "digital literacy/social media/Internet" was far and away the leading descriptor that they used. In our read of Canadian Millennials, we have drawn attention to the many ways that technology intersects with nearly all facets of their experience and worldview. This includes, as outlined earlier in this chapter, a range of possible social concerns — imagined or otherwise — associated with the technological revolution sweeping social life. In some ways, technology has contributed to new realities that Millennials today confront, not experienced by previous cohorts of young people. In other ways, technological advances merely run parallel to common experiences of young people across generations, having negligible impact on the major social scripts for this stage of life.

The impact of technology on Millennials and vice versa, and the larger implications for Canada and the world, are very much yet to be determined in the short- and long-term future. Arguably all of the following items contained in our list of wildcards are in large measure interconnected with technological advances associated with the Internet, cell phones, and social media.

We would do well as scholars and citizens to pay close attention to how this narrative unfolds; to consider the personal and social benefits and drawbacks of technology. And importantly, drawing on the wisdom of social scientists, we should ground our assessments in concrete empirical data of the whole rather than isolated anecdotal stories of what "we think" technology is doing, for better or worse, in society.

2. **Immigration.** Reliable Statistics Canada population projections tell us that immigration levels will increase in the foreseeable future.[42] The reason, as most readers know well, is simple. Since about 2010, our national population has not been able to sustain itself through natural increase (births offsetting deaths). If Canada's population is to remain at its current level, let alone grow, immigration is essential. Consequently, increasing numbers of immigrants will be coming to Canada over at least the next several decades. The majority — as presently is the case — will be coming from Asian countries. If current trends continue, they will be almost equally divided between people who are Catholic, Muslim, and those who have no religion. Typically Catholic immigrants are more conservative than those born in Canada in their theological and social beliefs. Together with Muslims, they can be expected to add to the social conservative voice.

The common assumption is that newcomers to Canada will welcome, embrace, endorse, and perpetuate the pluralistic ideal. Maybe they will; a wildcard is that significant numbers may not. For example, many Catholics and Muslims do not approve of the availability of legal abortion, homosexuality, and either sex or parenting outside of marriage. It also is not clear that immigrants are necessarily sympathetic with the history of Indigenous Peoples and the need to pursue ameliorative responses, at least when they first arrive in Canada.

In short, immigration could be "a wildcard" that alters the current trends that are friendly to pluralism.

3. **The Economy.** Clearly a healthy and robust economy makes a significant positive contribution to personal and social well-being. When things are going well for the majority of people in a society, their inclinations to be generous and compassionate toward others can be expected to increase.

For some time now, Canadians have collectively shared in a country that has one of the highest standards of living in the world and routinely is rated as one of the top countries to live. The prosperity has contributed to a spirit of receptivity to diversity and, generally speaking, receptivity to immigrants.

Given the economy's pivotal role, it is possible that tough economic times, especially over a prolonged period of time, could severely threaten the current spirit of acceptance of different people and different cultures. It also could have a significant impact on the willingness to respond to the needs and expectations of any number of organizations and groups, including Indigenous Peoples. The issue is pretty basic: when resources are plentiful everyone can literally afford to be generous. When resources are tight, expenditures — in this case not only financial but also social — become restricted. That's why the economy is another potential wildcard that can be expected to impact the future.

4. **Backlash.** Social progress and social compassion are not always linear. History is replete with examples of societies where people have reacted to trends they don't like by initiating or becoming involved in movements to turn things around.

In Canada, such reversals have been reflected in switches in support of federal and provincial parties, some fairly dramatic. In the 1993 federal election, the ruling Conservative Party was reduced from 156 seats to a mere two. In Alberta, after 44 years of Conservative Party rule, the NDP seemingly came out of nowhere in 2015 to form a majority government for the first time in the province's history. Similarly, Quebec voters elected an unprecedented number of 59 NDP candidates in 2011 — up from one in 2008. In 2015, the number went back down to only 16 seats. Many believe the NDP's reign in Alberta will likewise be short-lived.

Majority governments come and go in large part because the electorate decides that it is time for a change. The possibility exists that immigration and faltering economies may contribute to a desire to curb what some might define as the excesses of pluralism. Lest some say, "It will never happen," we need only look stateside to see how someone like Donald Trump — playing up many of the alleged problems of excessive pluralism — could shock much of the nation by actually becoming president in 2016.

Backlash to perceived problems with pluralism, focusing on immigration, alleged threats to family life, the allegedly excessive demands of Indigenous Peoples, and so on is another "wildcard" that could have impact on the direction that Canada is going.

The best safeguard against severe backlash? A prosperous economy.

5. **Global Warfare.** We have not had a major world war since 1945 — a war that followed the First World War that ended in 1918. Hopefully we will never have to deal with such a reality, particularly in view of the widespread belief that technological advances in nuclear weaponry could result in the destruction or the near-destruction of the entire planet. Public rhetoric and tension between nuclear-power heavyweights like the United States, North Korea, Iran, and Russia do not help to allay our fears. Who knows what may yet transpire on this front, even between the time we write these words and you read them?

Suffice it to say that severe conflict on a global scale would alter pretty much everything, including our inclinations and abilities to deal with global diversity in our own country.

It's a wildcard that we hope we never have to consider.

6. **TBA.** Lest we end this chapter on such a morbid note, we want to rush to say that what we all need to keep an eye on are important wildcard possibilities that currently are unknown. There may or may not be something on the horizon of Internet-like proportions that will have a profound impact on where Canadian life is headed. Like the wise weather forecaster, we need to be alert to some unexpected

variables that seemingly are going to come out of nowhere — "low probability, high impact events or innovations." We need to stay alert and keep our cameras on.

FINAL THOUGHTS

In this book, we have turned to empirical data and sociological theory and concepts to help us better understand Canadian Millennial perceptions and realities. For us, and we hope others, comparative empirical data across cohorts and time is critically important to give us a current and accurate read of Millennials. As helpful as data are on their own, we also think that we need concepts and language to help us make sense of that data. Along the way, we have singled out *five significant and interrelated realities* that characterize Canada's young people.

The first is that, in many ways, *Millennials are not very different from previous generations.* The things that matter to them, their values and sources of enjoyment, hopes and fears, expectations, and so forth are not that dissimilar from their parents or grandparents. Moreover, interpersonally, this emerging generation of Canadian young adults is not only the most diverse we have ever known; they also are exhibiting greater levels of social compassion than adults who have gone before them. The empirical data and analysis presented throughout reminds us all that the sky is not falling with Millennials. Here again we can say with a high level of confidence that "the kids *will* be alright."

Second, *social environment influences how we think and behave in the world.* Millennials do not suddenly take on certain perspectives in a vacuum. The reason Millennials are more similar than not to other cohorts is because they are regularly and heavily socialized by influences in those cohorts — family, teachers, media, and so on. Take technology, for example. Millennials are commonly critiqued for always being on their phones, paying little attention to those physically around them. The three of us cannot help but notice when we are in different social settings where parents and children are together, be it in their homes, at schools, or in shopping malls, that many parents are just as likely to be on their phones as their children.

Could it be that Millennials are often simply mirroring the behaviours of adults around them? A 2015 international study of more than 6,000 families, including those in Canada, found that over 50 percent of 8- to 13-year-olds believed their parents checked their phones too often, and over one-third believed their parents were too easily distracted by their phones while having conversations with others. As a result, 32 percent of children said they felt unimportant to their parents in these social settings.[43] Our point is simply that Millennials are shaped by their social contexts. Before one wishes to rush to judgment on Millennials, it may be wise to consider the role of adult influence. At the same time, Millennials are not passive recipients of the culture around them. They embrace their potential to think and behave differently and, as we saw in the final two chapters, strongly believe that they have control over their lives and will determine their futures.

Third, *pluralism is central to the Millennial experience*. Millennials have grown up in the most diverse social context in history, and their response on the whole is to embrace pluralism, equality, and a just society. They especially stand out from their parents and grandparents in these areas when we deal with topics such as sexuality, gender, and ethnicity.

Fourth, *individualism and choice are cornerstone features to the modern Western world*. Millennials are on the cutting edge of embracing these values, and they expect others to do the same. On topics surrounding family, religion, sexuality, or politics, Millennials seem to readily exceed previous generations in the choices they have. In the process of navigating the choices before them, Millennials are adamant that they want to choose what seems right to them. They are not about to have others' thinking imposed on them. Such an outlook is resulting in many traditional social scripts — such as finishing high school, going to university, getting a job, getting married, buying a house, having children — becoming far less firm or predictable, despite the fact that they frequently and even typically are valued.

Last, for Millennials, *technology is what they believe sets their generation apart from others* — notably phones, computers, and social media. We are not here to pronounce whether technological use is good or bad for individuals, groups, or societies. Rather, hopefully, we have offered some useful data and insights surrounding some of the complexities concerning technology. For instance, the information age has accelerated the speed and volume of the information we can access. This in turn has multiplied the choices available and the need for resources to help people make wise decisions. Unfettered access to information has the potential to broaden and deepen our knowledge base, worldviews, and relationships, which can be tremendously positive. Alternatively, technology exposes us to any number of risks and dangers, as seen in things like endless scams, sexting, and cyberbullying. Statistics Canada says that 15 percent of youth aged 15 to 24 were cyberbullied or cyberstalked in the past five years.[44]

So, what now? Many young people and a good number of adults speak of the newest generations of adults "taking over," as if when the incoming generation comes of age, the other age cohorts will pass into oblivion.

Of course, that's not the way the world works. The fact of the matter is that Millennials will increasingly be living out life with people of all ages. Some workplaces today consist of four generations of people working side by side. Millennials alone will hardly control the Canada of tomorrow.

In reality, a more accurate analogy is to think of the hockey team where the rookies join the players who are in their second, third, and fourth years and together line up with the veterans who have been there even longer. It's a given in the sports world that teams benefit enormously from having a combination of players who are younger, older, and in-between.[45]

In the spring of 2017, Joel had the privilege of visiting Oslo, Norway. He spent some time in Vigeland Park — the world's largest sculpture park by a single artist, Gustav Vigeland. The focal sculpture among the more than 200 statues is called *The Monolith*. Its name comes from the fact it was carved from one single granite block. The statue is five metres high (17 feet) and includes 121 figures that document the cycle of life. The youngest are on the top, the oldest are at the bottom. There are two common interpretations. The first is that, in social life, youth are valued while seniors are diminished. The second? Older people are esteemed because they are the pillars holding up the highly valued young.

In this book, we obviously have given considerable attention to "the young." But it's in living and working in tandem that our Millennials and our older generations will move Canada and Canadians forward.

The Millennials have much to offer. But the same is true of Gen Xers, Boomers, and Pre-Boomers.

It's time to break down the organization of social life along lines of age and create more opportunities for intergenerational ties to be encouraged, fostered, and celebrated. Those with more life experience and wisdom can play an instrumental role in coming alongside Millennials in this process — not to coddle Millennials but to both encourage and say the difficult things that need to be said; to help Millennials distill the cacophony of noise and options around them and make wise decisions along the way. And, yes, people in those older cohorts need to "listen and learn" as well. In the end, we all benefit.

In combination, different generations can bring out the best in each other. In combination, they collectively have much to bring to Canada. As the old cliché puts it, "We are all in this together." And it's together that Millennials and the rest of us can maximize life for us all.

This brings us back to where we began.

When we started to pen the Introduction, we were well aware of the age-old consternation that adults have had about young people. That was our starting place for saying that the mystique surrounding technology has only heightened the consternation about the tech-savvy, emerging Millennial generation.

What we underestimated is another feature — the high level of derision and even hostility with which some Boomers, Pre-Boomers, and Gen Xers seem to be greeting Millennials. Perhaps significantly, the energetic negativism seems to be particularly pronounced south of the border, rather than in Canada. "Up here," public ridicule of Millennials — calling them "dumb" and "Snowflakes", and the like — is, well, not "the Canadian way."

Our data and that of others viewing Canadian Millennials allow us to paint a far more positive picture. Thanks to being equipped with technology and having greater access to higher education than any age cohort before them, they can be expected to evolve into the most informed generation in Canadian history. That hardly adds up to "dumb."

They also are not going to be permanently "squeezed" out of money and careers. The immediate economic and career concerns can be expected to decline for two very good reasons. First, as ever-growing numbers of Boomers and Gen Xers leave the paid workforce, increasing numbers of positions in a wide array of sectors will need to be filled. Second, contrary to the naive stereotype that wealthy, self-absorbed Boomers and Xers have been gobbling up resources strictly for themselves, those same aging adults, in accelerating numbers, are going to be leaving some of those resources behind. It is estimated that in the U.S., Millennials will inherit more than $30 trillion from their Boomer parents.[46] In Canada, with our much smaller population, the numbers are understandably much lower but still not too shabby. CIBC estimates that over the next decade alone, Canadians can expect a $750 billion windfall from their aging relatives in what it calls "the largest intergenerational wealth transfer in Canadian history." What's more, CIBC says that the amount will grow even larger in subsequent decades.[47] That Zoomer expert David Cravit says that any alleged "age rage" involving Millennials and their Gen X and Boomer parents is already dissipating. "The picture is clear," he writes. In both Canada and the United States, Boomers and Pre-Boomers "are providing significant financial help to the adult children," sometimes "on top of providing some financial support to aging parents."[48]

When it comes to brains and bucks, "the kids *will* be alright."

And why all the incivility on the part of older adults re: the lack of civility on the part of Millennials? As we've been emphasizing, our findings — along with those of others, notably Environics — are pretty conclusive: interpersonally, this emerging generation of Canadian young adults is not only the most diverse we have ever known, they also are exhibiting greater levels of social compassion than adults who have gone before them. Pluralism, as we've said now many times, is in their genes. Interpersonally, we can have high hopes for how they are going to treat one another. They are the Millennial mosaic. Here again we can say with a high level of confidence that "the kids *will* be alright."

All of this speaks well of the future of Canada.

Let us conclude with clarity. We are not on the edge of a utopia — not even close.

Our data conclusively corroborate realities with which Canadians are well aware. There are many young people struggling on the margins of

Canadian life. They include large numbers of hard-working immigrants, members of racialized groups, Indigenous Peoples, and those who are LGBTQ. Those are among the most vulnerable categories of young adults.

But in addition, younger Canadians as a whole need ongoing help as they pursue optimum lives and optimum living. To the extent that astute observers such as Paul Kershaw and James Cairns are correct in seeing Millennials as being "squeezed" out of their fair share of government resources and not being accorded access to the things in life to which they are rightfully entitled, significant adjustments are needed. Here we are not for one moment suggesting that "young adults on the margins" should not be given attention. On the contrary, what we are saying is that *all* young adults need to be given our attention.

There is much to celebrate about Canada. Our examination of Millennials leads us to the conclusion that the dream of the nation builders of the 1960s, led by Pierre Trudeau, of a society where we would recognize the value of our diversity and tap that diversity to create "a richer life for us all," is a dream in positive progress.

If today's diverse, pluralistically minded Millennials can experience that richer life and in turn pass those gains on to their children and those children to their children for at least another generation or three, who knows what is possible for Canada?

APPENDIX

THE TWO PIVOTAL NATIONAL SURVEYS

As indicated in the Introduction, the primary analyses for the book are based on two national surveys carried out in partnership with Angus Reid in 2015 and 2016. Both were conducted online, the first in March of 2015 with a highly representative sample of 3,040 Canadians, 18 and over; the second in October 2016 with a similar representative sample of 3,214 adults (see Table A1).

The use of the two samples allowed us to repeat a very large number of items — some 400 — that were previously used in Reg's Project Canada surveys of both adults (every five years from 1975 through 2005) and teens (1984, 1992, 2000, 2008). The adult surveys had samples of approximately 1,500 people each, the youth surveys samples of about 3,600 each. Full methodological details for both the Reid and Project Canada surveys are readily available elsewhere.[1] The two new surveys produced invaluable cross-sectional

Table A1 **Canadian Population and Sample Characteristics**

		Canada 2016	Sample 2015	Sample 2016
Millennials	(18–29)	19%	18	18
Xers	(30–49)	33	34	34
Boomers	(50–69)	34	37	36
Pre-Boomers	(70-plus)	14	11	12
British Columbia		13	13	13
Alberta		12	11	11
Saskatchewan–Manitoba		7	7	7
Ontario		38	37	37
Quebec		23	25	24
Atlantic		7	7	8
Female		51	51	50
Male		49	49	50
Religious identity		76*	79	78
No religious identity		24*	21	22

(Canada source: 2016 Census)
*Religion: 2011 National Household Survey

trend data. The sample sizes for the primary generational cohorts we are examining are approximately as follows in each of the two surveys: Millennials 600, Gen Xers and Baby Boomers 1,100 each, Pre-Boomers 400.

Those numbers for probability samples would translate into accuracy levels of about 4 percentage points either way 19 times in 20 for Millennials, about 2 points either way for Xers and Boomers, and around 5 percentage points either way 19 times in 20 for Pre-Boomers.

THE YOUTH TREND AND COHORT DATA

In making youth trend comparisons spanning 1984 through 2016, we have indicated in several places in the book that we are forced to compare 15- to 19-year-olds in the Project Teen Canada surveys with what we think are roughly comparable 18- to 23-year-old cohorts in our two latest surveys.

That's simply because of the difficulty of generating a representative, online sample of young people under the age of 18 — for whom parental consent is necessary. So we have done the next things possible. Our Project Teen Canada samples are very large (about 3,500 each). Of necessity, our 18- to 23-year-old cohorts are fairly modest — about 300 for each of the two new surveys. Yet, even with an error range of perhaps +/- 6 points 19 times in 20, the samples at minimum provide some preliminary trend data that other researchers can verify or refute.

We mention in the Introduction that the design of the two new surveys also made it possible to produce unique age cohort data for a large number of variables. Individuals who were 15- to 19-year-olds in the first Project Teen Canada survey in 1984 reappear in 2016 — 32 years later — as 47- to 51-year-olds in each of our latest large-scale national surveys. Similarly, we can "simulate" the changes over time for teen cohorts in 1992, 2000, and 2008, looking at them, respectively, 24, 16, and 8 years later. Very few researchers have such a data analysis luxury for such a large number of variables.

Here, while the design has the potential to generate fairly spectacular data, we readily acknowledge that the sample sizes are modest. Similar to the two 18- to 23-year-old samples, they come in at close to 300 people for each of the two surveys. Again, we wish the samples were larger. But one can only do what one can do with good but not unlimited resources. And to simulate each of those teen cohorts with some 300 individuals as of 2016 still provides some intriguing, heuristic data on how people in the cohorts have been changing or not changing over time. Moreover, sample limitations acknowledged, the data remain highly unique.

SAMPLE SIZES IN THE SUMMARY "MAGNIFIED MOSAIC" TABLES

At least once in each of the chapters prior to the Conclusion, we attempt to highlight the nature of Canada's youth mosaic by looking at the findings as they appear in a large number of the "individual tiles" — variables such as region, community size, gender, education, religion, country of birth, race, and sexual orientation.

Given total sample realities — where we are working with approximately 600 Millennials, this material is obviously only illustrative and the findings need to be corroborated with much larger samples and complementary research. Nonetheless, we think the data are worth sharing and we offer the analyses, believing that, at minimum, they are of heuristic, thought-provoking value — with the emphatic caveat that corroboration is required.

To repeat the well-worn adage, we haven't been able to do everything. But, wow, we have been able to do a lot and are in a position to make — we think — a highly significant contribution to both the cross-sectional, trend, and cohort data that are available on Canadians of all ages.

The numbers vary slightly for 2015 versus 2016, but the sample sizes are as follows in Table A2 on the following page.

Table A2 Sample Sizes of Magnified Mosaic Tables

	2015	2016		2015	2016
Totals	553	590	Religious Affiliation		
Region			Catholic	175	155
British Columbia	71	84	Mainline Protestant	51	49
Alberta	60	72	Evangelical	58	56
Saskatchewan–Manitoba	42	46	Other Christian	45	66
Ontario	207	224	Other world faith	70	79
Quebec	134	118	No religion	154	185
Atlantic	39	46	Service Attendance		
Outside Quebec	419	472	Monthly-plus	147	175
Quebec	134	118	Less than monthly	406	415
Community Size			Country of Birth		
Urban	490	503	Canada	481	471
Rural	63	87	Elsewhere	72	119
Gender			Race		
Male	253	295	Visible minority	170	147
Female	300	295	Caucasian	383	443
Income			Indigenous*		
<$50,000	213	224	Yes	93	95
$50–99,000	129	147	No	1486	1594
$100,000+	79	79			
Education			Sexual Orientation*		
Degree-plus	129	237	LGBTQ	76	163
Some post-secondary	148	171	Heterosexual	432	1527
HS or less	276	182			

*Millennials and Gen Xers combined because of small sample sizes.

ACKNOWLEDGEMENTS

Our primary focus is obviously young people. But in order to understand today's latest emerging generation, it's essential that we be able to put them into perspective by comparing them with older Canadians — not only how older adults are now but also what they were like when they were younger. We are able to do that because we have access to some unique Project Canada adult data that neophyte Reg began to generate in the mid-'70s, and some equally unique Project Teen Canada data Reg began gathering in the mid-'80s with the late Don Posterski. Those invaluable data sets include two vitally important surveys carried out in 2015 and 2016 in partnership with Angus Reid. Our debt to Angus is simply enormous; we are very grateful to him.

We want to thank people who played key roles in the production of this book. They include freelance copy editor Karri Yano, graphics specialist Jeff Bingley, production manager Rudi Garcia, associate publisher Kathryn Lane, and managing editor Elena Radic.

* * *

JOEL: I'd like to thank Reg for inviting me into this project. Our paths have crossed in many ways over the past 15-plus years, and it was good to have a mentor, friend, and colleague to collaborate with on this project. Ambrose University graciously provided me with a six-month sabbatical, which afforded me the space and time to help bring this project (and a few others!) to conclusion. And I'd like to acknowledge my good friends' three teenage children — they know who they are — for the continual fun and meaningful times together, helping in the process to ground my sociological thinking in the realities and experiences of "real" young people, who we try to better understand and describe.

* * *

MONETTA: I am incredibly grateful to Reg and Joel for inviting me to accompany them on this ride. It has been great to participate in this process. I am also thankful for my colleagues at Ambrose University and elsewhere who have always provided me with the space and opportunity to grow. Finally, thank you to my incredibly supportive family and friends, whose faith in my abilities has always exceeded my own. In particular, thank you to my nephew, who unbeknownst to him, allowed me to test out some of the ideas presented in the book on him. While he is not quite old enough to be considered a Millennial, his feedback on these ideas has been helpful. I trust that this information will be helpful to those who have young people in their lives.

* * *

REG: The University of Lethbridge has again been a great resource. It has been enjoyable to work with Joel and Monetta. I am particularly grateful to Lita and Sahara, whose patience with my love of ideas and writing has been an ongoing gift.

* * *

And thanks to you — yes, you — for taking a look at our book! Here's to a great conversation.

NOTES

Introduction. The Worrying Continues ... and Is Getting Worse

1. Kerr, *Youth of Europe*, 168.
2. Cited in Bibby and Posterski, *Teen trends*, 13.
3. Bibby, *Canada's teens*, 1.
4. Bump, "Here is when each generation begins and ends…"
5. Environics, *Canadian millennials*.
6. Vision Critical, *The everything guide to millennials*, 5.
7. Mills, *The sociological imagination*.
8. For an overview of sociological theoretical traditions, see, for example, Brym, *New society*, 12–26.
9. See, for example, Giroux, *Disposable youth* and *Youth in revolt*.
10. See, for example, Cote and Allahar, *Generation on hold* and *Critical youth studies*.

11. See, for example, pluralism as laid out in "The Pluralism Project" at Harvard University.
12. Environics, *Canadian millennials*; Pew Research Center, "Millennials, a portrait of generation next."
13. Cairns, *The myth of the age of entitlement*, 9.
14. Cairns, *The myth of the age of entitlement*, 28.
15. Cooley, *Human nature and the social order*.
16. Naisbitt interview, 2008.

Chapter 1. What Matters: Values/Enjoyment

1. Tannenbaum, "*Playboy* interview."
2. Varied, including Celebrity Net Worth 2017.
3. Tannenbaum, "*Playboy* interview."
4. Rokeach, *The nature of human values*.
5. For research on what is referred to as "the dependency paradox," see Feeney, "The dependency paradox in close relationships."
6. Adams, *Sex in the Snow*, 144.
7. Sinha, "Canadian identity, 2013"; the General Social Survey 2013.
8. Bibby, *The emerging millennials*, 34–35.
9. Valtchanov and Parry, "I like my peeps."
10. For extensive data, including survey data, see Sheldon et al., "Canadian online retail forecasts, 2014 to 2019"; CIRA 2016; and Opstart, "13 Stats and facts about online shopping in Canada."
11. Smith and Anderson, "Online shopping and e-commerce"; Faraldo, "5 Statistics that prove a growing love for online shopping."
12. Conference Board of Canada 2016.
13. Smith, Christoffersen, Davison, and Herzog, *Lost in transition*, 146.
14. Smith, Christoffersen, Davison, and Herzog, *Lost in transition*, 108.
15. McDaniel, "Born at the right time?"
16. See, for example, Bibby and Posterski, *Teen trends*, 137ff; Bibby, *Canada's teens*, 11ff; Bibby, *The emerging millennials*, 24ff.
17. Here again, the debt to Milton Rokeach is immense.
18. Cited in Narayan, "The Dalai Lama says female leaders are more compassionate … Hmmm."

19. See, for example, Seppala, "Are women really more compassionate?"
20. Bibby and Posterski, *Teen trends*, 141ff.
21. Bibby and Posterski, *Teen trends*, 143.
22. Environics, *Canadian millennials*.
23. Canadian Animal Health Institute 2017.
24. Vision Critical, *The everything guide to millennials*, 12.
25. Statistics Canada 2018.
26. Howe, "Millennials: A generation of page-turners."
27. Geiger, "Americans are the most likely generation of Americans to use public libraries."
28. Vision Critical, *The everything guide to millennials*, 18.
29. Statistics Canada 2017l.
30. Pew Research Center, "Millennials, a portrait of generation next," 25–37.
31. Twenge, "Have smartphones destroyed a generation?"
32. Ruksana, "Immigration journey"; Holtmann, "Tracking the emotional cost of immigration."
33. See, for example, Lauletta, "NFL TV ratings fall for second-straight year," and Thompson, "Why NFL ratings are plummeting."
34. Environics, *Canadian millennials*, 3.
35. Adkins, "What Millennials want from work and life."
36. See, for example, pluralism as laid out "The Pluralism Project" at Harvard University.

Chapter 2. Their Concerns: Personal/Social

1. McMahon, "A happiness historian explains why even happy lives involve pain."
2. Princeton's Robert Wuthnow (2007), writing a decade ago, identified seven changing realities for young adults compared with previous generations: delayed marriage, having fewer children and having them later in life, uncertainties of work and money, increased pressure for higher education, loosening relationships, globalization, and the information explosion. His findings pertaining primarily to Gen Xers reflect many characteristics of today's Millennials as well, both in the U.S. and Canada, particularly the four items at the top of the concern

list of young Canadians, noted by 60% or more: the *future*, lack of *money*, lack of *time*, and the feeling that they should be getting *more out of life*.

3. D. Thompson, "The unluckiest generation: What will become of Millennials?"

4. https://www.canada.ca/en/health-canada/corporate/about-health-canada/activities-responsibilities/partner-health-canadians.html.

5. For an overview of the guide and controversy surrounding it, see, for example, Hui, "The new Canada's Food Guide explained."

6. CBC News 2013, 2017; Statistics Canada 2015e.

7. https://www.participaction.com/en-ca/programs.

8. http://www.fcpc.ca/Priorities-Policy/Supporting-Canadians-Health-Wellness/Nutrition-Facts-Education-Campaign.

9. http://www.heartandstroke.ca/get-healthy.

10. Dowbiggin, "CBC's integrity brought into question by Cherry once again."

11. Vision Critical, *The everything guide to millennials*, 22.

12. Statistics Canada 2017h.

13. CIGNA 2018.

14. BBC News, "Minister of loneliness appointed to continue Jo Cox's work." January 17, 2018. https://www.bbc.com/news/uk-42708507. Retrieved July 2018.

15. Chai, "Why more Canadian millennials than ever are at 'high risk' of mental health issues."

16. Zick, "The shifting balance of adolescent time use."

17. Widely cited, including on IMDb: http://m.imdb.com/name/nm0000032/quotes.

18. Burnett, *Undiscovered Gyrl*, 2009.

19. Hirschi, *Causes of delinquency*.

20. See Bibby and Posterski, *The emerging generation* and *Teen trends*.

21. Statistics Canada 2016b, 2016d.

22. Statistics Canada 2018.

23. Statistics Canada 2018. See also Norris 2016.

24. Statistics Canada 2017k.

25. Government of Canada, March 27, 2018a.

26. Statistics Canada 2018.

27. Pakula, Shoveller, Ratner, and Carpiano, "Prevalence and co-occurrence of heavy drinking and anxiety and mood disorders among gay, lesbian, bisexual, and heterosexual Canadians."

28. Amos, "Lesbian, gay, bisexual Canadians report higher rates of mental health issues."

29. Environics, *Canadian millennials*, 3.

30. Ubelacker, "The inside history of Canada's opioid crisis"; Wells, "Can Ottawa stop Canada's deadly opioid crisis?"

31. Howlett et al., "How Canada got addicted to fentanyl."

32. See, for example, Russell, "Fentanyl overdoses killed hundreds of Canadians this year"; Ubelacker, "The inside history of Canada's opioid crisis."

33. Howlett et al., "How Canada got addicted to fentanyl."

34. Special Advisory Committee on the Epidemic of Opioid Overdoses 2018; Government of Canada 2018b.

35. Potkins, "On the Blood reserve, progress in the fight against opioid addiction and deaths."

36. For an overview, see Justin Trudeau 2015.

37. Mauss, *Social problems as social movements*.

38. From Reg's personal files. He worked extensively on a survey of the Archdiocese in 1985.

39. For an excellent exposition of this thesis, see Mauss, *Social problems as social movements*, 38–71.

40. IMDb, http://www.imdb.com/title/tt0085404. Retrieved May 6, 2017.

41. Cohen, *Folk devils and moral panics*.

42. Nettler, *Social concerns*, 10.

Chapter 3. How They See Life: Individuals/Institutions

1. Aristotle, *Politics*.

2. Dehaas, "Queen says Canada's 150th an opportunity 'to remind the world' of the country's values."

3. Ray, "Billions world-wide help others in need."

4. Ray, "Billions world-wide help others in need," 1.

5. Environics, *Canadian millennials*, 6. Both donations and volunteering increase with education.

6. See for example, Marano, "The dangers of loneliness"; Robert and Gilkinson, "Mental health and well-being of recent immigrants to Canada"; Shulevitz, "The lethality of loneliness"; Forbes, "Loneliness might be a bigger health risk than smoking or obesity."

7. Bibby, *The emerging millennials*, 72.

8. Taylor and Peter, *Every class in every school.*

9. See Martin, "Canadian schools 'unsafe' for LGBTQ students, U of W researcher says."

10. Vancouver, "Being and feeling safe and included."

11. Drake, "6 new findings about millennials."

12. Perreault, "Criminal victimization in Canada, 2014"; Statistics Canada 2016c.

13. Environics, *Canadian millennials*, 3.

14. Canadian Institute of Public Opinion 1950.

15. Canadian Institute of Public Opinion 1955.

16. Smith and Turner, *The radical transformation of diversity and inclusion*, 5.

17. Environics, "Canadian public opinion on Aboriginal Peoples."

18. See, for example, Bitonti, "Strain of racist sentiment remains, some Chinese Canadians believe."

19. Findlay and Kohler, "Too Asian?"

20. Maynard, *Policing Black lives.*

21. Global News 2017.

22. *Toronto Star* 2017.

23. Fleras, *Inequality matters*, 300.

24. Economic Innovation Group 2016.

25. Cao, "Visible minorities and confidence in the police"; and Sprott and Doob, "Confidence in the police."

26. Bibby, *The Bibby report*, 111.

27. Bibby, *The Bibby report*, 121.

28. Canadian Institute of Public Opinion 1945.

29. For a detailed exposition of Canadians' decline in deference, see Bibby, *The boomer factor*, 45ff.

30. Hustinx, Meijs, Handy, and Cnaan, "Monitorial citizens or civic omnivores? Repertoires of civic participation among university students."
31. Environics, *Canadian millennials*, 46.
32. Environics, *Canadian millennials*, 37–49.
33. Malatest, "Survey of electors following the 42nd general election"; Environics, *Canadian millennials*.
34. Malatest, "Survey of electors following the 42nd general election"; Nielsen Consumer Insights, "2015 national youth survey"; Samara Canada, "Can you hear me now?"
35. Malatest, "Survey of electors following the 42nd general election."
36. Samara Canada, "Can you hear me now?"
37. Statistics Canada 2018.
38. Environics, *Canadian millennials*.
39. Nielsen Consumer Insights, "2015 national youth survey."
40. Statistics Canada 2016a.
41. Elections Canada 2016.
42. Turcotte, "Civic engagement and political participation in Canada"; Statistics Canada 2016f.
43. CBC News 2016.
44. Vision Critical, *The everything guide to millennials*, 4.
45. Vision Critical, *The everything guide to millennials*, 8.

Chapter 4. Sexualities: Sex/Equality Issues

1. Paulsen, "Pat Paulsen's 1960s' television editorials."
2. Bibby, *The future families project.*
3. Cited by Holliday, "Transgender in Canada: Canadians say accept, accommodate, and move on."
4. See, for example, Terry and Hogg, *Attitudes, behavior, and social context*; Ajzen, *Attitudes, personality, and behavior.*
5. The Canadian Institute of Public Opinion (Gallup) did ask about premarital sexual attitudes in a poll released April 11, 1970. The item simply asked, "Do you think it is wrong for a man and a woman to have sex relations before marriage or not?" The sample consisted of Canadians 21 and older. Its value is limited, because of the biased

item and the fact adults 18–20 were not part of the sample. Some 57% indicated "wrong," 31% "wrong," and 12% were "undecided." Just five years later, with an 18-plus sample, Gallup reported that the "wrong" figure had "changed dramatically," falling to 36%.

6. Canadian Institute of Public Opinion, March 29, 1975.
7. For data, see Bibby and Posterski, *The emerging generation,* 82; Bibby, *The Bibby report,* 65.
8. Fulbright, "Defining sexual freedom."
9. Huffpost, "Celebrity cheating: What stars have to say about infidelity."
10. Twenge, Sherman, and Wells, "Changes in American adults' sexual behavior and attitudes, 1972–2012." For a summary, see Price, "Millennials less sexually active than Gen-X peers."
11. Ubelacker, "The inside history of Canada's opioid crisis."
12. For details, see, for example, *The Economist* 2016.
13. For details, see, for example, Long in *The Canadian Encyclopedia* 2016.
14. Examples of such initiatives among evangelicals and Catholics are offered by Boesveld 2015.
15. Employment and Social Development Canada 2018.
16. Connolly, "Anti-abortion efforts out of sync with Canadian society."
17. Fortney, "Police uniform ban at Calgary Pride Parade met with cheers, jeers."
18. According to Statistics Canada data for 2014 (2015a), 3% of Canadians indicated that they were either gay or lesbian (1.7%) or bisexual (1.3%).
19. Pew Research Center, "Millennials, a portrait of generation next," 61.
20. The correlation between the responses for same-sex marriage and same-sex adoption is 0.816.
21. Pew Research Center, *Changing attitudes on gay marriage.*
22. GLAAD 2017.
23. *New York Post* 2016.
24. Statistics Canada 2015a and 2017c.
25. Andersen and Fetner, "Cohort differences in tolerance of homosexuality."
26. In Figure 4.9, the item wording for 1984 and 2000 was "Sexual relations between two people of the same sex is sometimes alright"; in 2016, the wording was "Two persons of the same sex having sex-

ual relations" with the percentage reported referring to "Not wrong at all."

27. Troster, "The Canadian war on queer workers"; for a detailed examination of difficulties of gays in the workplace, see Kinsman and Gentile, *The Canadian war on queers.*

28. Alberta Education 2017.

29. See, for example, Fetner and Elafros 2015; Fetner et al. 2012.

30. CBC News Edmonton, May 15, 2015a and 2015b.

31. For a further summary of the Edmonton situation, see, for example, French, "Edmonton Catholic schools' latest policy to include students and staff is 'meaningless,' advocates say."

32. Department of Education, January 2016.

33. Egale Canada 2015.

34. https://www.merriam-webster.com/dictionary/gender. Retrieved May 26, 2017.

35. https://www.merriam-webster.com/dictionary/sex. Retrieved May 26, 2017.

36. American Psychological Association 2017.

37. For an excellent, stimulating article on the complexities of gender, see Henig, "How science is helping us understand gender."

38. McDaniel, "Born at the right time?"

39. A collection of her work, *On Intersectionality*, is scheduled to be released in 2019. For a recent presentation on intersectionality, see Crenshaw, "WOW Lecture on intersectionality." An excellent journalist's overview of Crenshaw and intersectionality is offered by Adewunmi, "Kimberlé Crenshaw on intersectionality."

40. For details, see Tait, "Two-spirit is a different conversation" and Mc-Linden, "The divide over pride: Calgary Pride's 'uniform ban' incites clash of opinions."

41. Government of Canada 2017.

42. Flores, Brown, and Park, *Public support for transgender rights.*

43. This survey was carried out by the Angus Reid Institute in August of 2016. Details can be found at Holliday, "Transgender in Canada: Canadians say accept, accommodate, and move on."

44. Angus Reid Institute 2017.

45. See, for example, the Canadian Conference of Catholic Bishops 2017 and Jones, "Gender identity given human rights status in Canada (Bill C-16)."

46. Quoted in VandenBeukel, "Jordan Peterson: The man who reignited Canada's culture war." Details on Peterson can be found via his website: jordanbpeterson.com.

47. See, for example, Bibby, *Resilient Gods*, 70ff.

48. Cooke, *National Post*/Canadian Press 2018.

Chapter 5. Families: Salience/Attitudes/Aspirations

1. Landis, *Sociology: concepts and characteristics*, 11.

2. Anich, "Why do soccer players walk out with kids?"

3. Ibid.

4. See, for example, Bibby's national survey for the Vanier Institute of the Family, 2004.

5. Environics, *Canadian millennials*, 11.

6. Environics, *Canadian millennials*, 11, 20.

7. Milan, *Marital status*.

8. Ibid.

9. Statistics Canada 2017e.

10. Milan, *Marital status*.

11. Drake, "6 new findings about millennials."

12. See, for example, Laucius, "Millennials and the 'Canadian dream': What's the plan?"; Barkho, "Why are millennials putting off marriage? Let me count the ways."

13. Milan, *Marital status*.

14. Statistics Canada 2015b.

15. For a clear overview of why, see Grant, "Statistics Canada to stop tracking marriage and divorce rates."

16. Arocho and Kamp Dush, "Like Mother, Like Child."

17. Siegel, "Why the choice to be childless is bad for America."

18. Bhatti, "Millennials are picking pets over people."

19. Siegel, "Why the choice to be childless is bad for America."

20. If one expands this discussion to couples without children, it is true that this demographic is growing faster than those couples with children (see Statistics Canada 2017d). But this finding should be interpreted very carefully. A major explanation is due to Baby Boomers becoming empty nesters, not because Millennials are staying clear of having children themselves.

21. Cravit, *Beyond age rage*, 64.

22. Statistics Canada 2017d.

23. See, for example, Clark, *Delayed transitions of young adults*; Statistics Canada 2017d.

24. Arnett, "Emerging adulthood."

25. See for example, Twenge, *Generation me*.

26. Lee, "Here's the science behind the fidget spinner craze."

27. See, for example, Bibby, *The future families project*, 42ff; Companies Committed to Kids 2015.

28. Cited in Bibby, *The Bibby report*, 103.

29. Cited in Bibby, *The Bibby report*, 104.

30. Pickhardt, "Adolescence and parental approval."

31. For a detailed review of literature, see Fortuna, "Male aggression: Why are men more violent?"

32. For an overview, focusing on anger, see Dittmann, "Anger across the gender divide."

33. Adams, "What a difference 50 years make."

34. Statistics Canada 2016d, 2016e.

35. Statistics Canada 2011.

36. For an overview of trends in racial intermarriage attitudes in the U.S., see Livingston and Brown, "Intermarriage in the U.S. 50 years after Loving v. Virginia."

37. Drake, "6 new findings about millennials"; Gao 2016.

38. Fry, "5 facts about Millennial households."

39. The sample size for the 1992 cohort as of 2016 is 263. Obviously, this is only large enough to offer some tentative, heuristic comparisons and would carry an error range of about +/- 6 percentage points, 18 times in 20.

Chapter 6. The Gods: Religion/Spirituality

1. See, for example, Kurt Warner in Ward, "Former Super Bowl MVP Kurt Warner talks about faith, football and reality TV show."

2. See, for example, Dueck, "Come together, pray together: The Blue Jays have us all on bended knee."

3. McNichol, "God and baseball."

4. Hoffman, foreword in Parry, Robinson, Watson, and Nesti, *Sport and spirituality*. See also Miller, "Sport and spirituality: A comparative perspective."

5. Cited widely, for example, https://twitter.com/golfdigest/status/471963218571571201.

6. Jhaveri, "Superstitious Sydney Crosby won't see mom and sister on game days."

7. MacGregor, "The writings on the stall."

8. See, for example, Lipka, "Millennials increasingly are driving growth of 'nones'"; Masci, "Q & A: Why millennials are less religious than older Americans."

9. See, for example, Bibby, *Restless gods*, 12, 73, 85.

10. Bibby and Reid, *Canada's Catholics*.

11. For extensive recent data on belief and spirituality, see Bibby, *Resilient Gods*.

12. See Clydesdale, *The first year out*; Smith and Denton, *Soul Searching*.

13. Bibby and Reid, *Canada's Catholics*, 53.

14. See also Reimer and Hiemstra, "The gains/losses of Canadian religious groups from immigration: Immigration flows, attendance and switching."

15. For current and projected sources, see, for example, Statistics Canada 2010: Catalogue 91-551-x.

16. Environics, "Survey of Muslims in Canada 2016: Final report."

17. See Bengtson, Putney, and Harris, *Families and faith*; Schwadel, "Period and cohort effects on religious non-affiliation and religious disaffiliation."

18. See Statistics Canada 2015d; also Bibby, *Restless gods*, 65, for intermarriage patterns for "nones."

19. Bibby, *Resilient Gods*, 37.

20. Todd, "Three of 10 Canadian bestsellers cover spirituality."

21. See, for example, Bibby, *Resilient Gods*, 145.

22. Thiessen, *The meaning of Sunday.*

23. Bibby, *Resilient Gods.*

24. Durkheim, *The elementary forms of the religious life*, 475.

25. Details concerning the movement are offered by Mari and Ganiel 2014.

26. Moody and Reed, "Emerging Christianity and religious identity," 35.

27. See, for example, Bibby and Reid, *Canada's Catholics*, 57ff.

28. Murphy, "Lesbian, gay and bisexual Americans differ from general public in their religious affiliations."

29. Beyer and Ramji, *Growing up Canadian.*

30. See, for example, American work by Wuthnow 2007:135; Smith and Denton, *Soul Searching*, 173; and Minganti's research ("Islamic revival and young women's negotiations on gender and racism," 21) on young Muslim women in Sweden.

31. Bengtson, Putney, and Harris, *Families and faith.*

Chapter 7. The Future: The Paradox/So Far/Great Expectations

1. Pew Research Center, "Millennials, a portrait of generation next," 39; see also Fry and Patten, "How Millennials today compare with their grandparents 50 years ago."

2. Carrick, "Gen Y on its work woes."

3. Quoted in Carrick.

4. Worth, "Who we are at work."

5. See, for example, Simon and Way "Why the gap?"; Statistics Canada 2017b.

6. Vision Critical, *The everything guide to millennials,*10.

7. Drake, "6 new findings about millennials."

8. University Affairs 2014.

9. Statistics Canada 2018.

10. Ibid.

11. For a succinct overview, see, for example, Blackwell, "Remember when? What have we learned from the 1980s and that 21% interest rate?"

12. See for example, Thiessen, "The outlook for the Canadian economy and the conduct of monetary policy."

13. Environics, *Canadian millennials*, 25.

14. See Lyengar and Kamenica, "Choice, proliferation, simplicity seeking, and asset allocation"; Schwartz, *The paradox of choice — Why more is less.*

15. Pew Research Center, "Millennials, a portrait of generation next," 48–49.

16. For details, see www.airnb.ca.

17. Vision Critical, *The everything guide to millennials*, 35, 37.

18. Pew Research Center, "Millennials, a portrait of generation next," 43.

19. Pew Research Center, "Millennials, a portrait of generation next," 40.

20. Drake, "6 new findings about millennials."

21. Cravit, *Beyond age rage*, 5.

22. Environics, *Canadian millennials*, 3.

23. Environics, *Canadian millennials*, 3.

Chapter 8. Conclusion: The Good, the Bad, and the Wildcards

1. Environics, *Canadian millennials*, 3.

2. North Studio 2014.

3. Trudeau, cited in Bibby, *Mosaic madness*, 49.

4. Tasker, "Governor General apologizes for saying Indigenous people were immigrants."

5. Brockbank and Xing, "Video shows woman demands a 'white doctor' treat son at Mississauga, Ont., clinic."

6. Tucker, "Lethbridge's pride rainbow crosswalk smeared with manure, rust paint."

7. See, for example, Bennett, "Ticats back down on hiring of disgraced coach Art Briles after fan backlash"; CFL.com 2017.

8. Vision Critical, *The everything guide to millennials*, 31, 33.

9. Bibby, *Mosaic madness*, 9.

10. Vision Critical, *The everything guide to millennials*, 41.

11. Joseph, "Religion increasingly seen as doing more harm than good in Canada."

12. Vision Critical, *The everything guide to millennials*, 6.

13. For an excellent illustrative overview of the entitlement position, see Cairns, *The myth of the age of entitlement*, 4–8.

14. See, for example, Bauerlein, *The dumbest generation*; C. Thompson, "The dumbest generation? No, Twitter is making kids smarter"; Stein, "Millennials: The me me me generation"; Howe, "Generation Snowflake: Really?"; a provocative defence is offered by Zakaria, "The try-hard generation."

15. For some takes on the nature of the current fidget spinner craze, see, for example, Best, "The fidget spinner fad: Adults don't get it and that's the point"; Cha, "America's love-hate relationship with the fidget spinner"; and Lee, "Here's the science behind the fidget spinner craze."

16. Vision Critical, *The everything guide to millennials*, 6.

17. See, for example, Brown, "Two-thirds of Canadians would welcome distracted-walking laws."

18. Thorbecke, "Honolulu passes law that makes texting while crossing the street illegal."

19. Ogburn, *Social change*.

20. A helpful overview of transistor radios is offered by Krakow, "Transistor radios play on."

21. For an excellent overview of the Walkman, see Haire, "A brief history of the Walkman."

22. The two issues were among a number raised by Reg in his provocative, best-selling book, *Mosaic madness: Pluralism without a cause* that was published some three decades ago at the height of Canada's so-called unity crisis.

23. Kappler, "'Happy pride!': Trudeau attends Toronto parade absent of police floats."

24. Cited in Bibby, *Mosaic madness*.

25. Bibby, *Mosaic madness*.

26. Such themes are emphasized by many, including Ravanera et al. "Youth integration and social capital"; Khanlou, "Psychosocial integration of second and third generation racialized youth in Canada"; DeVance et al. "Working with African American clients using narrative therapy"; Kazemipur, *The Muslim question in Canada*.

27. Bibby, *Mosaic madness*, 98.

28. Ibid.

29. Bloom, *The closing of the American mind*, 34.

30. Bloom, *The closing of the American mind*, 39.

31. Bibby, *Mosaic madness*, 99.

32. Harris, *The moral landscape*.

33. Harris in Edge 2010.

34. Ibid.

35. Harris, "Science can answer moral questions."

36. Smith, Christoffersen, Davison, and Herzog, *Lost in transition*.

37. Wells, *The discovery of the future (1913)*, 33.

38. Wells, *The discovery of the future (1913)*, 46.

39. Wells 1932.

40. See, for example, Conway, "Foresight: An introduction."

41. See, for example, Bell 1997a, 1997b, 2012.

42. See, for example, Statistics Canada 2017a.

43. Matthews, "Turn off that smartphone, mom and dad!"

44. Statistics Canada 2018.

45. This analogy was previously offered by Bibby, *Canada's teens*, 5.

46. Robaton, "Preparing for the $30 trillion great wealth transfer."

47. Marr, "'Bequest Boom': Canadian parents will pass on $750 billion to kids over next decade."

48. Cravit, *Beyond age rage*, 172.

Appendix

1. For methodological details on how Angus Reid and the Angus Reid Institute conduct surveys, see Reid 2017. Details on how the Project Canada adult surveys have been conducted can be found at Bibby 2006:225; detailed information on the Project Teen Canada youth surveys is available in Bibby 2009:216–217. An overview of the Project Canada Research Series is also available at www.reginaldbibby.com.

REFERENCES

Aaker, Jennifer, and Emily Esfahani Smith. 2014. "Not everyone wants to be happy." *Scientific American*. October 28. https://www .scientificamerican.com/article/not-everyone-wants-to-be-happy. Retrieved August 20, 2017.

Abrutyn, Seth, and Anna Mueller. 2014. "Are suicidal behaviours contagious in adolescence? Using longitudinal data to examine suicide suggestion." *American Sociological Review* 79(2):211–227.

Adams, Michael. 2003. *Fire and ice*. Toronto: Viking/Penguin.

Adams, Michael. 2006. *Sex in the snow: The surprising revolution in Canadian values*. Toronto: Penguin.

Adams, Michael. 2012. "What a difference 50 years make." *Globe and Mail*, September 6. https://www.theglobeandmail.com/opinion/what-a-difference-50-years-make/article1374288/?arc404=true. Retrieved September 11, 2017.

Adewunmi, Bim. 2014. "Kimberlé Crenshaw on intersectionality." *NewStatesman.com*, April 2. https://www.newstatesman.com/life-style/2014/04/kimberl-crenshaw-intersectionality-i-wanted-come-everyday-metaphor-anyone-could. Retrieved October 5, 2017.

Adkins, Amy. 2016. "What Millennials want from work and life." *Gallup Business Journal.* May 11. http://news.gallup.com/businessjournal/191435/millennials-work-life.aspx. Retrieved October 2, 2017.

Ajzen, Icek. 2005. *Attitudes, personality, and behavior.* Berkshire, England: Open University/McGraw-Hill.

Alberta Department of Education. 2016. *Guidelines for best practices.* https://education.alberta.ca/media/1626737/91383-attachment-1-guidelines-final.pdf.

Alberta Department of Education. 2017. *Gay-straight alliances.* https://education.alberta.ca/gay-straight-alliances/?searchMode=3. Retrieved May 27, 2017.

American Psychological Association. 2017. "Answers to your questions about individuals with intersex conditions." https://www.apa.org/topics/lgbt/intersex.pdf. Retrieved August 10, 2017.

Amos, Heather. 2016. "Lesbian, gay, bisexual Canadians report higher rates of mental health issues." *UBC News.* March 18. https://news.ubc.ca/2016/03/18/lesbian-gay-bisexual-canadians-report-higher-rates-of-mental-health-issues. Retrieved June 19, 2018.

Andersen, Robert, and Tina Fetner. 2008. "Cohort differences in tolerance of homosexuality: Attitudinal change in Canada and the United States, 1981:2000. *Public Opinion Quarterly* 72:311–330.

Angus Reid Institute. 2016. "What makes us Canadian? A study of values, beliefs, priorities and identity." http://angusreid.org/canada-values. Retrieved October 11, 2017.

Angus Reid Institute. 2017. "Gender-Neutral birth certificates." July 7. http://angusreid.org/gender-neutral-birth-certificates. Retrieved September 3, 2017.

Anich, Ivan. 2015. "Why do soccer players walk out with kids?" *The 18.com.* http://the18.com/news/why-do-soccer-players-walk-out-kids. Retrieved September 6, 2017.

Aristotle. 2000. *Politics*. New York: Dover Publications. First published 350.

Arnett, Jeffrey Jensen. 2000. "Emerging adulthood." *American Psychologist*, May: 469–480.

Arocho, Rachel, and Kamp Dush, Claire M. 2017. "Like Mother, Like Child: Offspring Marital Timing Desires and Maternal Marriage Timing and Stability." *Journal of Family Psychology* 31(3): 261–272.

Barkho, Gabriela. 2016. "Why are millennials putting off marriage? Let me count the ways." *Washington Post*, June 6. https://www .washingtonpost.com/news/soloish/wp/2016/06/06/why-are-millennials-putting-off-marriage-let-me-count-the-ways/?utm_ term=.35c3e48ab0aa. Retrieved September 9, 2017.

Bauerlein, Mark. 2009. *The dumbest generation: How the digital age stupefies young Americans and jeopardizes our future*. New York: TarcherPerigree.

Beaton, Caroline. 2017a. "Why Millennials are lonely." *Forbes*, February 9. https://www.forbes.com/sites/carolinebeaton/2017/02/09/why-millennials-are-lonely/ #51b9dafc7c35. Retrieved August 22, 2017.

Beaton, Caroline. 2017b. "The solution to Millennial loneliness." *Forbes*, March 3. https://www.forbes.com/sites/carolinebeaton/2017/03/03/ the-solution-to-millennialloneliness/#1b8669356731. Retrieved August 22, 2017.

Bell, Wendell. 1997a. *Foundations of futures studies I: History, purposes, knowledge*. New York: Transaction Publishers.

Bell, Wendell. 1997b. *Foundations of futures studies II: Values, objectivity, and the good society*. New York: Transaction Publishers.

Bell, Wendell. 2012. *Memories of the future*. New York: Transaction Publishers.

Bengtson, Vern L., with Norella M. Putney and Susan Harris. 2013. *Families and faith: How religion is passed down across generations*. New York: Oxford University Press.

Bennett, Kelly. 2017. "Ticats back down on hiring of disgraced coach Art Briles after fan backlash." *CBC Hamilton*. August 29, 2017. http:// www.cbc.ca/news/canada/hamilton/ticats-back-down-on-hiring-of-disgraced-coach-art-briles-after-fan-backlash-1.4265785. Retrieved September 17, 2017.

Best, Joel. 2017. "The fidget spinner fad: Adults don't get it and that's the point." *CNN Health.* May 22. http://www.cnn.com/2017/05/17/health/fidget-spinner-fad-partner/index.html. Retrieved October 8, 2017.

Beyer, Peter, and Rubina Ramji, eds. 2013. *Growing up Canadian: Muslims, Hindus, Buddhists.* Montreal: McGill-Queen's University Press.

Bhatti, Abha. 2016. "Millennials are picking pets over people." *Washington Post*, September 13. https://www.washingtonpost.com/news/business/wp/2016/09/13/millennials-are-picking-pets-overpeople/?utm_term=.d9695a54b36c. Also picked up by papers including the *Hamilton Spectator*, September 13, 2016. https://www.thespec.com/news-story/6855525-millennials-are-picking-pets-over-people. Retrieved September 10, 2017.

Bibby, Reginald W. 1987. *Fragmented Gods: The poverty and potential of religion in Canada.* Toronto: Irwin.

Bibby, Reginald W. 1990. *Mosaic madness: Pluralism without a cause.* Toronto: Stoddart.

Bibby, Reginald W. 1995. *The Bibby report: Social trends Canadian style.* Toronto: Stoddart.

Bibby, Reginald W. 2001. *Canada's teens: Today, yesterday, and tomorrow.* Toronto: Stoddart.

Bibby, Reginald W. 2002. *Restless gods: The renaissance of religion in Canada.* Toronto: Stoddart.

Bibby, Reginald W. 2004. *The future families project: A survey of Canadian hopes and dreams.* Ottawa: The Vanier Institute of the Family.

Bibby, Reginald W. 2006. *The boomer factor: what Canada's most famous generation is leaving behind.* Toronto: Bastian Books.

Bibby, Reginald W. 2009. *The emerging millennials: How Canada's newest generation is responding to change and choice.* Lethbridge: Project Canada Books.

Bibby, Reginald W., 2017. *Resilient Gods: Being pro-religious, low religious, or no religious in Canada.* Vancouver: UBC Press.

Bibby, Reginald W. and James Penner. 2010. *10 things we all need to know about teens.* Lethbridge: Project Canada Books.

Bibby, Reginald W., and Donald C. Posterski. 1985. *The emerging generation: An inside look at Canada's teenagers.* Toronto: Irwin.

Bibby, Reginald W., and Donald C. Posterski. 1992. *Teen trends: A nation in motion.* Toronto: Stoddart.

Bibby, Reginald W., and Angus Reid. 2016. *Canada's Catholics: Vitality and hope in a new era.* Toronto: Novalis.

Bitonti, Daniel. 2013. "Strain of racist sentiment remains, some Chinese Canadians believe." *Globe and Mail,* February 8. https://beta. theglobeandmail.com/news/british-columbia/strain-of-racistsentiment-remains-some-chinese-canadians-believe/ article8420178/? Retrieved September 30, 2017.

Blackwell, Richard. 2017. "Remember when? What have we learned from the 1980s and that 21% interest rate?" *Globe and Mail,* June 5. https://www.theglobeandmail.com/real-estate/the-market/remember-when-what-have-we-learned-from-80s-interest-rates/article24398735. Retrieved October 20, 2018.

Bloom, Allan. 1987. *The closing of the American mind.* New York: Simon and Schuster.

Boesveld, Sarah. 2015. "New Canadian debate on abortion is about if it's time to have a real debate about abortion." *National Post,* January 2015. http://nationalpost.com/news/canada/new-canadian-debate-on-abortion-is-about-if-its-time-to-have-a-real-debate-about-abortion. Retrieved September 2, 2017.

Brockbank, Nicole, and Lisa Xing. "Video shows woman demands a 'white doctor' treat son at Mississauga, Ont., clinic." CBC News Toronto. http://www.cbc.ca/news/canada/toronto/white-doctorvideo-mississauga-1.4168199. Retrieved August 1, 2017.

Brooks, Meghan. 2008. "Imagining Canada, negotiating belonging: Understanding the experiences of racism in second generation Canadians of colour." *Canadian Diversity* 6 (2):75–78.

Brown, Scott. 2016. "Two-thirds of Canadians would welcome distracted-walking laws." *Vancouver Sun,* October 26. http://vancouversun.com/news/local-news/two-thirds-of-canadians-would-welcomedistracted-walking-laws. Retrieved June 18, 2018.

Brym, Robert. 2017. *New society.* 8th edition. Toronto: Nelson.

Bump, Philip. 2014. "Here is when each generation begins and ends, according to facts." *The Atlantic,* March 25. https://www.theatlantic

.com/national/archive/2014/03/here-is-when-each-generation-begins-and-ends-according-to-facts/359589. Retrieved September 8, 2017.

Burnett, Allison. 2009. *Undiscovered gyrl*. New York: Vintage.

Cairns, James. 2017. *The myth of the age of entitlement: Millennials, austerity, and hope.* Toronto: University of Toronto Press.

Canadian Animal Health Institute. 2017. "Latest Canadian pet population figures released." https://www.canadianveterinarians.net/documents/canadian-pet-population-figures-cahi-2017. Retrieved August 20, 2017.

Canadian Conference of Catholic Bishops. 2017. "CCCB statement on the passage of Bill C-16 regarding gender identity and gender expression." July 7. http://www.cccb.ca/site/eng/media-room/statements-a-letters/4765-cccb-statement-on-the-passage-of-bill-c-16-regarding-gender-identity-and-gender-expression. Retrieved September 4, 2017.

CBC News. 2013. "Canada's war on smoking turns 50." http://www.cbc.ca/news/health/canada-s-war-on-smoking-turns-50-1.1303483. June 16, 2013. Retrieved August 21, 2017.

CBC News Edmonton. 2015a. "Edmonton Catholic school transgender child, 7, from girls' washroom." May 14a. http://www.cbc.ca/news/canada/edmonton/edmonton-catholic-school-bans-transgender-child-7-from-girls-washroom-1.3073737. Retrieved May 6, 2017.

CBC News Edmonton. 2015b. "Catholic trustees wage war over transgender seven-year-old." May 14. http://www.cbc.ca/news/canada/edmonton/catholic-trustees-wage-war-over-transgender-seven-year-old1.3074578. Retrieved May 26, 2017.

CBC News Edmonton. 2016. "Edmonton Catholic trustees pass 'inclusive' policy for schools." March 15. http://www.cbc.ca/news/canada/edmonton/edmonton-catholic-trustees-pass-inclusive-policy-for-schools-1.3493257. Retrieved May 26, 2017.

CBC News Vancouver. 2016. "CBC-Angus Reid Institute poll: Canadian millennials hold off on their love of country. http://www.cbc.ca/news/canada/british-columbia/angus-reid-millennials-proudcanada1.3788713. Retrieved October 10, 2017.

Cao, Liqun. 2011. "Visible minorities and confidence in the police." *Canadian Journal of Criminology and Criminal Justice.* 53(1):1–26.

Carlozo, Lou. 2017. "Millennials are set to inherit record wealth — and the way they manage it will be unprecedented." *U.S. News & World Report,* August 10. http://www.businessinsider.com/millennials-inherit-record-wealth-manage-money-technology-2017-8. Retrieved October 18, 2017.

Carrick, Rob. 2017. "Gen Y on its work woes." *Globe and Mail,* May 4. https://beta.theglobeandmail.com/globe-investor/personal-finance/genymoney/geny-millennialemployment-jobs-canada/article34867183/?ref=http://www.theglobeandmail.com&. Retrieved October 2, 2017.

Celebrity Net Worth. 2017. "Chad Kroeger net worth." https://www.celebritynetworth.com/richest-celebrities/rock-stars/chad-kroeger-net-worth. Retrieved August 16, 2017.

CFL.com. 2017. "CFL, Tiger-Cats issue statements regarding Art Briles." August 28. https://www.cfl.ca/2017/08/28/cfl-tiger-cats-issue-joint-statement-regarding-art-briles. Retrieved September 18, 2017.

Cha, Ariana Eunjung. 2017. "America's love-hate relationship with the fidget spinner." *Washington Post,* May 19. https://www.washingtonpost.com/news/to-your-health/wp/2017/05/19/americas-love-hate-relationship-with-the-fidget-spinner-is-technology-to-blame-for-our-estlessness/?utm_term=.37988188cb7d. Retrieved October 8, 2017.

Chai, Carmen. 2017. "Why more Canadian millennials than ever are at 'high risk' of mental health issues." *Global News.* May 2. http://globalnews.ca/news/3417600/why-more-canadian-millennials-than-ever-are-at-high-risk-of-mental-health-issues. Retrieved September 8, 2017.

CIRA. 2016. "The state of e-commerce in Canada." March. https://cira.ca/sites/default/files/public/Ecommerce-Factbook-March-2016.pdf. Retrieved September 10, 2017.

Clark, Warren. 2014. *Delayed transitions of young adults. Canadian Social Trends.* April 23. http://www.statcan.gc.ca/pub/11-008-x/2007004/10311-eng.htm. Retrieved September 10, 2017.

Clydesdale, Tim. 2007. *The first year out: Understanding American teens after high school.* Chicago, IL: University of Chicago Press.

Cohen, Stanley. 1972. *Folk devils and moral panics: The creation of the mods and rockers*. London: MacGibbon and Kee.

Companies Committed to Kids. 2015. *Taking the pulse of Canada's Kids*. Toronto: CCK. August 18. http://stream1.newswire.ca/media/2015/08/18/20150818_C9486_DOC_EN_44146.pdf. Retrieved September 10. 2017.

Conference Board, Inc. 2016. "How Fortune 100 brands understand the people that matter most." April 6. Ottawa: The Conference Board of Canada.

Connolly, Amanda. 2018. "Anti-abortion efforts out of sync with Canadian society: Trudeau." *Global News*, January 10. https://globalnews.ca/news/3957069/anti-abortion-efforts-out-of-sync-with-canadian-society-trudeau. Retrieved June 17, 2018.

Conroy, Shana, and Adam Cotter. 2017. "Self-reported sexual assault in Canada, 2014." July 11. Ottawa: Statistics Canada. Catalogue 85-002-X. http://www.statcan.gc.ca/pub/85-002-x/2017001/article/14842-eng.htm. Retrieved October 12, 2017.

Conway, Maree. 2015. "Foresight: An introduction." Online publication. https://static1.squarespace.com/static/580c492820099e7e75b9c3b4/t/58bcccee59cc68b969703f1e/1488768258680/TFRefGuideForesight1.pdf. Retrieved August 1, 2017.

Cooke, Alex. "Two-spirit N.B. First Nation chief says his election points to progress." *National Post*/Canadian Press, 2018. http://nationalpost.com/pmn/news-pmn/canada-news-pmn/two-spirited-n-b-first-nation-chief-says-his-election-points-to-progress. Retrieved June 21, 2018.

Cooley, Charles Horton. 1964. *Human nature and the social order*. New York: Schocken Books.

Coontz, Stephanie. 2017. "Do millennial men want stay-at-home wives?" *New York Times*, March 31. https://www.nytimes.com/2017/03/31/opinion/sunday/do-millennial-men-want-stay-at-home- wives.html. Retrieved October 10, 2017.

Coren, Michael. 2016. "Bill C-16: A glorious transformation that went mostly unnoticed." *Toronto Star*, May 22. https://www.thestar.com/opinion/commentary/2016/05/22/bill-c-16-a-glorious-trans-formation-that-went-mostly-unnoticed.html. Retrieved September 4, 2017.

Cossman, Brenda, and Ido Katri. 2017. "Today, trans Canadians celebrate Bill C-16. Tomorrow, the work begins for us all." *Globe and Mail.* June 15. https://beta.theglobeandmail.com/opinion/today-trans-canadians-celebrate-bill-c-16-tomorrow-the-work-begins-forusall/article35324961/?ref=http://www.theglobeandmail.com&. Retrieved September 4, 2017.

Cote, James E., and Anton L. Allahar. 1994. *Generation on hold.* Toronto: Stoddart.

Cote, James E. and Anton L. Allahar. 2005. *Critical youth studies: A Canadian focus.* Toronto: Pearson.

Cravit, David. 2012. *Beyond age rage: How the boomers and seniors are solving the war of the generations.* Toronto: BPS Books.

Crenshaw, Kimberlé. 2016. "WOW Lecture on intersectionality." https://www.youtube.com/ watch?v=-DW4HLgYPlA. Retrieved October 5, 2017.

CTV News/Canadian Press. 2018. "Cheers erupt as federal court judge approves military gay purge settlement." June 18. https://www.ctvnews.ca/canada/cheers-erupt-as-federal-court-judge-approves-military-gay-purge-settlement-1.3978477. Retrieved June 21, 2018.

Dawson, Lorne, and Joel Thiessen. 2013. *The Sociology of religion: A Canadian perspective.* Toronto: Oxford University Press.

Dehaas, Josh. 2017. "Queen says Canada's 150th an opportunity 'to remind the world' of the country's values." CTVNews. http://www.ctvnews.ca/canada/queen-says-canada-s-150th-an-opportunity-to-remind-the-world-of-country-s-values-1.3223906. Retrieved August 27, 2017.

DeVance Taliaferro, Jocelyn, Willa Casstevens, and Jessica DeCuir Gunby. 2013. "Working with African American clients using narrative therapy: An operational citizenship and critical race theory framework." *International Journal of Narrative Therapy & Community Work* 1: 34–45.

Dittmann, Melissa. 2003. "Anger across the gender divide." *Monitor on Psychology, APA.* March 34, 3. http://www.apa.org/monitor/mar03/angeracross.aspx. Retrieved September 11, 2017.

Donnelly, Kristin, Jean M. Twenger, Malissa A. Clark, Sarnia K. Shaikh, Angela Beiler-May, and Nathan T. Carter. 2016. "Attitudes toward women's work and family roles in the United States, 1976–2013." *Psychology of Women Quarterly* 40(10), 41–54.

Dowbiggen, Bruce. 2013. "CBC's integrity brought into question by Cherry once again." *Globe and Mail*, February 25. https://www.theglobeandmail.com/sports/dowbiggin-cbcs-integrity-brought-in-to-question-by-cherry-once-again/article9018047. Retrieved August 21, 2017.

Drake, Bruce. 2014. "6 new findings about millennials." March 7. Washington, DC: Pew Research Center. http://www.pewresearch.org/fact-tank/2014/03/07/6-new-findings-about-millennials. Retrieved September 20, 2017.

Dueck, Lorna. 2015. "Come together, pray together: The Blue Jays have us all on bended knee." *Globe and Mail*, October 21. https://www.theglobeandmail.com/opinion/come-together-pray-together-the-blue-jays-have-us-all-on-bended-knee/article26890611/?arc404=true. Retrieved September 16, 2017.

Durkheim, Émile. 1965. *The elementary forms of the religious life*. 1965. New York: Free Press. Originally published in 1912.

Economic Innovation Group. 2016. *The millennial economy*. Washington, DC. http://eig.org/millennial#1473660719617-6a185bea-4da7. Retrieved August 29, 2017.

Economist. 2016. "How America's abortion laws have changed." March 2. https://www.economist.com/blogs/economist-explains/2016/03/economist-explains-0. Retrieved September 2, 2017.

Edge. 2010. *The New Science of Morality*. An Edge Conference. http://www.edge.org/3rd_culture/morality10/morality10_index.html.

Egale Canada. 2015. *Transgender people in Ontario, Canada*: Trans PULSE Project. Schulich School of Medicine and Dentistry. London, ON: Western University. http://transpulseproject.ca/wp-content/uploads/2015/06/Trans-PULSE-Statistics-Relevant-for-Human-Rights-Policy-June-2015.pdf. Retrieved May 26, 2017.

Elections Canada. 2016. "Turnout and reasons for not voting during the 42nd general election: Results from the labour force survey." May 5. http://www.elections.ca/res/rec/eval/pes2015/lfs/lfs_e.pdf. Retrieved June 7, 2018.

Employment and Social Development Canada. 2018. "2018 Canada

summer jobs application/Agreement." Ottawa. https://catalogue
.servicecanada.gc.ca/content/dam/eforms/en/ESDC-EMP5396A.pdf.
Retrieved June 18, 2018.

Enos, Tony. 2017. "8 Things you should know about two spirit people."
Indian Country Today. March 28. https://indiancountrymedianetwork
.com/culture/social-issues/8-misconceptions-things-know-two-
spirit-people. Retrieved October 4, 2017.

Environics. 2016a. "Survey of Muslims in Canada 2016: Final report." Toronto: The Environics Institute. http://www.environicsinstitute.org/up-
loads/institute-projectssurvey%20of%20muslims%20in%20canada%20
2016%20-%20final%20report.pdf. Retrieved September 28, 2017.

Environics. 2016b. "Canadian public opinion on Aboriginal Peoples."
Final report, June. Toronto: The Environics Institute. http://www
.environicsinstitute.org/uploads/instituteprojects/canadian%20
public%20opinion%20on%20aboriginal%20peoples%202016%20-
%20final%20report.pdf. Retrieved October 20, 2017.

Environics. 2017. *Canadian millennials: Social values study*. Toronto: The
Environics Institute. February. https://www.environicsinstitute.org/docs/
default-source/project-documents/canadian-millennial-social-
values-study/final-report.pdf?sfvrsn=394cf27a_2. Retrieved June 7, 2018.

Experian Marketing Services. 2015. *Millennials come of age*. New York:
Experian Information Solutions. http://mmzone.afoz3ftdj4euebxpnz
.maxcdn-edge.com/wp-content/uploads/2015/09/2015-
Millennials-Come-of-Age.pdf. Retrieved October 5, 2017.

Faraldo, Dan. 2017. "5 Statistics that prove a growing love for online
shopping." *Canadian Pos*, April 19. http://cdnpos.com/5-statistics-
that-prove-a-growing-love-for-online-shopping. Retrieved August 17.

Faughnder, Ryan. March 2016. "Faith-based films are building followings
at the box office." *Los Angeles Times*, March 25. http://www.latimes
.com/entertainment/envelope/cotown/la-et-ct-faith-based-movies-
20160325-story.html. Retrieved October 13, 2017.

Faw, Larissa. 2012. "Why are so many professional illennial women unable to find dateable men?" *Forbes*, December 5. https://www
.forbes.com/sites/larissafaw/2012/12/05/why-are-so-many-professional-

millennial-women-unable-to-find-dateable-men/#565f388f8486. Retrieved October 6, 2017.

Feeney, Brooke C. 2007. "The dependency paradox in close relationships: Accepting dependencepromotes independence." *Journal of Personality and Social Psychology* 92(2):268–85.

Ferguson, Rick. 2012. *Born this way: The Canadian millennial loyalty survey.* Aimia.com. https://www.aimia.com/content/dam/aimiawebsite/ CaseStudiesWhitepapersResearch/english/Aimia_GenYWhitepaper-Canada_Final.pdf. Retrieved October 16, 2017.

Fetner, Tina, 2016. "U.S. attitudes toward lesbian and gay people are better than ever." *Contexts* 15:20–27.

Fetner, Tina, Athena Elafros, Sandra Bortolin, and Coralee Drechsler. 2012. "Safe spaces: Gay-straight alliances in high school." *Canadian Review of Sociology* 49:188–207.

Fetner, Tina, and Athena Elafros. 2015. "The GSA difference: LGBTQ and ally experiences in high schools with and without gay-straight alliances." *Social Sciences* 4:563–581.

Findlay, Stephanie, and Nicholas Kohler. 2010. "Too Asian?" *Maclean's,* November 10.http://www.macleans.ca/news/canada/too-asian. Retrieved September 30, 2017.

First Nations Information Governance Centre. 2018. *National Report of the First Nations Regional Health Survey Phase 3: Volume One.* Ottawa. http://fnigc.ca/sites/default/files/docs/fnigc_rhs_phase_3_national_ report_vol_1_en_final_web.pdf Retrieved June 11, 2018.

Fleras, Augie. *Inequality matters: Diversity and exclusion in Canada.* 2017. Toronto: Oxford University Press.

Flores, Andrew R., Taylor N.T. Brown, and Andrew S. Park. 2016. *Public support for transgender rights: A twenty-three-country survey.* Los Angeles: The Williams Institute, UCLA School of Law. December. https:// williamsinstitute.law.ucla.edu/wp-content/uploads/23-Country-Survey.pdf.

Forbes. 2017. "Loneliness might be a bigger health risk than smoking or obesity." January 18. https://www.forbes.com/sites/quora/2017/01/18/ loneliness-might-be-a-bigger-health-risk-than-smoking-or-obesity/#-15c41aff25d1. Retrieved August 30, 2017.

Fortney, Valerie. 2017. "Police uniform ban at Calgary Pride Parade met with cheers, jeers." *Calgary Herald*, July 27. http://news.anotao.com/link/ca/calgaryherald.com/opinion/columnists/fortney-police-uniform-ban-at-calgary-pride-parade-met-with-cheers-jeers. Retrieved October 4, 2017.

Fortuna, Dorian. 2014. "Male aggression: Why are men more violent?" *Psychology Today*, September 22. https://www.psychologytoday.com/blog/homo-aggressivus/201409/male-aggression. Retrieved March 14, 2019.

French, Janet. 2016. "Edmonton Catholic schools' latest policy to include students and staff is 'meaningless,' advocates say." *Edmonton Journal*. March 15. http://edmontonjournal.com/news/local-news/edmonton-catholic-school-board-to-vote-on-meaningless-inclusiveness-policy-critics-say. Retrieved May 26, 2017.

Fry, Richard. 2017. "5 facts about Millennial households." September 6. Washington, DC: Pew Research Center. http://www.pewresearch.org/fact-tank/2017/09/06/5-facts-about-millennial-households. Retrieved September 20, 2017.

Fry, Richard, Ruth Igielnik, and Eileen Patten. 2018. "How Millennials today compare with their grandparents 50 years ago." March 16. Washington, DC: Pew Research Center. http://www.pewresearch.org/fact-tank/2018/03/16/how-millennials-compare-with-their-grandparents. Retrieved February 26, 2019.

Fulbright, Yvonne K. 2009. "Defining sexual freedom." FoxNews. March 12. http://www.foxnews.com/story/2009/03/12/foxsexpert-defining-sexual-freedom.html. Retrieved September 2, 2017.

Gao, George. 2016. "Biggest share of whites in U.S. are Boomers, but for minority groups it's Millennials or younger." July 7. Washington, DC: Pew Research Center. http://www.pewresearch.org/fact-tank/2016/07/07/biggest-share-of-whites-in-u-s-are-boomers-but-for-minority-groups-its-millennials-or-younger. Retrieved September 20, 2017.

Gardner, Simon. 2005. "RCMP uses 'fruit machine' to detect gays." CBC Digital Archives. May 12. http://www.cbc.ca/archives/entry/rcmp-uses-fruit-machine-to-detect-gays. Retrieved September 3, 2017.

Geiger, Abigail. 2016. "Support for marijuana legalization continues to rise." October 12. http://www.pewresearch.org/fact-tank/2016/10/12/

support-for-marijuana-legalization-continues-to-rise. Retrieved September 21, 2017.

Geiger, Abigail. 2017. "Americans are the most likely generation of Americans to use public libraries." June 21. Washington, DC: Pew Research Center. http://www.pewresearch.org/fact-tank/2017/06/21/millennials-are-the-most-likely-generation-of-americans-to-use-public-libraries. Retrieved September 2017.

Giroux, Henry A. 2012. *Disposable youth: Racialized memories and the culture of cruelty.* New York: Routledge.

Giroux, Henry A. 2013. *Youth in revolt: Reclaiming a democratic future.* Boulder, CO: Paradigm Publishers.

GLADD. "Accelerating Acceptance 2017. A Harris Poll survey of Americans' acceptance of LGBTQ people." New York: GLAAD. http://www.glaad.org/files/aa/2017_GLAAD_Accelerating_Acceptance.pdf. Retrieved April 10, 2018.

Global News. 2017. "B'nai Brith records highest number of anti-Semitics incidents in Canada in 2016." May 9. https://globalnews.ca/news/3437317/bnai-brith-anti-semitic-incidents-canada. Retrieved October 1, 2017.

Government of Canada. 2017a. "Legalizing and strictly regulating cannabis: The facts." May 30. https://www.canada.ca/en/services/health/campaigns/legalizing-strictly-regulating-cannabis-facts.html. Retrieved September 21, 2017.

Government of Canada. 2017b. "Minister Hussen announces major step forward in gender equality by making changes to passports and immigration documents." Ottawa. Immigration, Refugees and Citizenship Canada. August 24. https://www.canada.ca/en/immigration-refugees-citizenship/news/2017/08/minister_hussen_announcesmajorstepforwardingender equalitybymakin.htm. Retrieved September 2017.

Government of Canada. 2018a. "Suicide prevention." March 27. https://www.canada.ca/en/indigenous-services-canada/services/first-nations-inuit-health/health-promotion/suicide-prevention.html. Retrieved June 19, 2018.

Government of Canada. 2018b. "Overview of national data on opioid-related harms and deaths." December 12. https://www.canada.ca/en/health-canada/services/substance-use/problematic-prescription-drug-use/opioids/data-surveillance-research/harms-deaths.html. Retrieved March 2, 2019.

Grant, Tavia, 2011. "Statistics Canada to stop tracking marriage and divorce rates." *Globe and Mail*, July 20. https://beta.theglobeandmail.com/news/national/statistics-canada-to-stop-tracking-marriage- and-divorce-rates/article4192704/?ref=http://www.theglobeandmail.com&. Retrieved September 9, 2017.

Grant, Tavia. 2013. "Five little-known trends in Canadian living standards." *Globe and Mail*, June 4. https://www.theglobeandmail.com/report-on-business/economy/economy-lab/five-little-known-trends-in-canadian-living-standards/article12322877. Retrieved August 17, 2017.

Haire, Meaghan. 2009. "A brief history of the Walkman." *Time*. July 1. http://content.time.com/time/ nation/article/0,8599,1907884,00.html. Retrieved August 1, 2017.

Hamby, Sherry. 2015. "'Don't talk to strangers.' Worst advice ever?" *Psychology Today*. October 27. https://www.psychologytoday.com/blog/the-web-violence/201510/dont-talk-strangers-worst-advice-ever. Retrieved August 27, 2017.

Harrington, Brad, Fred Van Deusen, Jennifer Sabatini Fraone, and Jeremiah Morelock. 2015. "How millennials navigate their career: Young adult views on work, life and success." http://www.bc.edu/content/dam/files/centers/cwf/research/publications/researchreports/How%20Millennials%20Navigate%20their%20Careers. Retrieved August 28, 2017.

Harris, Sam. 2010a. *The moral landscape: How science can determine human values*. New York: Free Press.

Harris, Sam. 2010b. "Science can answer moral questions." TedTalks. YouTube. https://www.youtube.com/watch?v=Hj9oB4zpHww.

Hauen, Jack. 2017. "Canada 'poured thousands and thousands' into 'fruit machine' — a wildly unsuccessful attempt at gaydar." *National Post*, May 25. http://nationalpost.com/news/canada/the-fruit-machine. Retrieved September 3, 2017.

Henig, Robin Marantz. 2017. "How science is helping us understand gender." *National Geographic Magazine*, January/01. http://www. nationalgeographic.com/magazine/2017/01/how-science-helps-us-understand-gender-identity. Retrieved September 4, 2017.

Hirschi, Travis. 1969. *Causes of delinquency*. Berkeley: University of California Press.

Holliday, Ian. 2016. "Transgender in Canada: Canadians say accept, accommodate, and move on." Angus Reid Institute, September 7. http://angusreid.org/transgender-issues.

Holtmann, Cathy, and Lucia Tramonte. 2014. "Tracking the emotional cost of immigration: Ethno-religious differences and women's mental health." *Journal of International Migration and Integration*. 15 (4): 633–654.

Hooven, Carole, Karen A. Snedker and Elaine Adams Thompson. 2012. "Suicide risk at young adulthood: Continuities and discontinuities from adolescence." *Youth and Society* 44(4):524–547.

Howe, Neil. 2017. "Millennials: A generation of page-turners." *Forbes*. January 16. https://www.forbes.com/sites/neilhowe/2017/01/16/ millennials-a-generation-of-page-turners/2/#6dcebb2465a9. Retrieved August 20, 2017.

Howe, Neil. 2017. "Generation Snowflake: Really?" *Forbes*, April 27. https://www.forbes.com/sites/neilhowe/2017/04/27/generation-snow-flake-really-part-1-of-3/#194a3de02914. Retrieved October 16, 2018.

Howlett, Karen, Justin Giovannetti, Nathan Vanderklippe, and Les Perreaux. 2016. "How Canada got addicted to fentanyl." *Globe and Mail*, April 8. https://beta.theglobeandmail.com/news/investigations/a-killer-high-how-canada-got-addicted-tofentanyl/article29570025/? ref=http://www.theglobeandmail.com&. Retrieved October 14, 2018.

Hoye, Bryce. 2017. "Transgender athletes still face barriers to inclusion." CBC News Manitoba. February 1. http://www.cbc.ca/news/canada/manitoba/ transgender-athletes-canada-1.3962226. Retrieved May 26, 2017.

HuffPost. 2013. "Celebrity cheating: What stars have to say about infidelity." July 4. http://www.huffingtonpost.com/2013/07/04/celebrity-cheating_n_3519415.html. Retrieved September 1, 2017.

Hughes, Jodi. 2016. "Perception vs. reality: the breakdown on how safe Canadian cities really are." Global News, August 16. http://globalnews.ca/news/2886558/perception-vs-reality-the-break-down-on-how-safe-canadian-cities-really-are.

Hui, Ann. 2019. "The new Canada's Food Guide explained: Goodbye four food groups and serving sizes, hello hydration." *Globe and Mail*, January 22. https://www.theglobeandmail.com/canada/article-new-canadas-food-guide-explained. Retrieved February 22, 2019.

————. Human Resources Professionals Association. 2016. "HR & Millennials: Insights into your new human capital." https://www.hrpa.ca/Documents/Public/Thought-Leadership/HRPA-Millennials-Report-20161122.pdf. Retrieved August 28, 2017.

Hune-Brown, Nicholas. 2013. "Mixie Me." *Toronto Life*. February 12. https://torontolife.com/city/mixie-me. Retrieved September 11, 2017.

Hustinx, Lesley, Lucas C.P.M. Meijs, Femida Handy, and Ram A. Cnaan. 2012. "Monitorial citizens or civic omnivores? Repertoires of civic participation among university students." *Youth and Society* 44(1):95–117.

Jaimet, Kate. 2017. "The fentanyl crisis." *Canadian Nurse*. January/February. https://www.canadian-nurse.com/en/articles/issues/2017/january-february-2017/the-fentanyl-crisis. Retrieved October 14, 2017.

Jamieson, Don. 2015. "Top 10 Songs About Hell." *Loudwire.com*. April 23. http://loudwire.com/top-songs-about-hell. Retrieved September 17, 2017.

Jhaveri, Hemal. 2015. "Superstitious Sydney Crosby won't see mom and sister on game days." *USA Today*, July 29. http://ftw.usatoday.com/2015/07/sidney-crosby-wont-see-mom-and-sister-on-game-days. Retrieved September 16.

Jones, Robert, and Daniel Cox. 2015. "How Race and Religion Shape Millennial Attitudes on Sexuality and Reproductive Health." *Public Religion Research Institute*. https://www.prri.org/research/survey-how-race-and-religion-shape-millennial-attitudes-on-sexuality-and-reproductive-health. Retrieved October 9, 2017.

Jones, Steve. 2017. "Gender identity given human rights status in Canada (Bill C-16)." August 28. President's Blog. http://www.fellowship.ca/AWordFromSteve. Retrieved September 4, 2017.

Joseph, Rebecca. 2017. "Religion increasingly seen as doing more harm than good in Canada." Global News, June 13. http://globalnews.ca/ news/3522802/religion-is-increasingly-seen-as-doing- more-harm-than-good-in-canada-ipsos-poll. Retrieved August 1, 2017.

Kappler, Maija. 2017. "'Happy pride!': Trudeau attends Toronto parade absent of police floats." The Canadian Press. June 25. http://www .nationalnewswatch.com/2017/06/25/prime-minister-to-march-in-canadas-largest-pride-parade-today/#.WYE8UGxK2HI. Retrieved July 18, 2017.

Kazemipur, Abdie. 2014. *The Muslim question in Canada*. Vancouver: UBC Press.

Kerr, Anthony. 1964. *Youth of Europe*. Chester Springs, PA: Dufour Editions.

Kershaw, Paul. 2018a. "Biography." The University of British Columbia. http://spph.ubc.ca/person/paul-kershaw. Retrieved June 11, 2018.

Kershaw, Paul. 2018b. "Generation squeeze" website. http://www .gensqueeze.ca. Retrieved June 11, 2018.

Kershaw, Paul. 2018c. *International injustice in Canadian public finance*. Vancouver: UBC School of Population and Public Health.

Khanlou, Nazilla. 2008. "Psychosocial integration of second and third generation racialized youth in Canada." *Canadian Diversity*. 6(2):54–57.

Kinsman, Gary, and Patrizia Gentile. 2010. *The Canadian war on queers: National Security as sexual regulation*. Vancouver: UBC Press.

Krakow, Gary. 2004. "Transistor radios play on." October 20.NBC News. com. http://www.nbcnews.com/id/6288916/ns/technology_and_ science-tech_and_gadgets/t/transistor-radios-play.

Landis, Judson R. 1992. *Sociology: concepts and characteristics*. Belmont, CA: Wadsworth.

La Puma, Joe. 2015. "The deep end." *Complex*, October/November. http://www.complex.com/music/justin-bieber-interview-2015-cover-story. Retrieved September 23, 2017.

Laucius, Joanne. 2016. "Millennials and the 'Canadian dream': What's the plan?" *Ottawa Citizen*, July 1. http://ottawacitizen.com/news/ national/millennials-and-the-canadian-dream-whats-the-plan. Retrieved September 7, 2017.

Lauletta, Tyler. 2018. "NFL TV ratings fall for second-straight year, but still dominate prime time." *Business Insider*, January 4. http://www .businessinsider.com/nfl-ratings-fall-still-dominate-prime-time-2018-1. Retrieved June 16, 2018.

Layous, Kristin, Jamie Kurtz, Joseph Chancellor, and Sonja Lyubomirsky. 2017. "Reframing the ordinary: Imagining time as scarce increases well-being." *The Journal of Positive Psychology*: 1–8.

Lee, Bruce Y. 2017. "Here's the science behind the fidget spinner craze." *Forbes*, May 19. https://www.forbes.com/sites/brucelee/2017/05/19/ heres-the-science-behind-the-fidget-spinner-craze/#19e458473af0. Retrieved October 7, 2017.

Legatum Institute. 2017. "The Legatum prosperity index 2016." http:// www.prosperity.com/rankings. Retrieved August 18, 2017.

Lipka, Michael. "Millennials increasingly are driving growth of 'nones.'" May 12. Washington, DC: Pew Research Center. http://www .pewresearch.org/fact-tank/2015/05/12/millennials-increasingly- are-driving-growth-of-nones. Retrieved September 20, 2017.

Livingston, Gretchen, and Anna Brown. 2017. "Intermarriage in the U.S. 50 years after Loving v. Virginia." May 18. Washington, DC: Pew Research Center. http://www.pewsocialtrends.org/2017/05/18/ intermarriage-in-the-u-s-50-years-after-loving-v-virginia. Retrieved September 20, 2017.

Long, Linda, 2016. "Abortion in Canada." *The Canadian Encyclopedia*. http://www.thecanadianencyclopedia.ca/en/article/abortion. Retrieved September 2, 2017.

Luscombe, Belinda. 2017. "Fewer young people want gender equality at home." *Time*, March 31. http://time.com/4718281/young-people- gender-equality-home. Retrieved October 9, 2017.

Lynengar, Sheena S., and Emir Kamenica. 2010. "Choice, proliferation, simplicity seeking, and asset allocation." *Journal of Public Economics* 94:530–539.

MacGregor, Roy. 2007. "The writings on the stall." *Globe and Mail*, April 13. https://beta.theglobeandmail.com/sports/macgregor-the- writings-on-the stall/article20396277/?ref=http://www.theglobeandmail .com&. Retrieved September 16, 2017.

Maimon, David, and Danielle C. Kuhl. 2008. "Social control and youth suicidality: Situating Durkheim's ideas in a multilevel framework." *American Sociological Review* 73(6):921–943.

Malatest. 2016. "Survey of electors following the 42nd general election." Ottawa, February 20. http://www.elections.ca/res/rec/eval/pes2015/surv/surv_e.pdf. Retrieved June 7, 2018.

Marano, Hara Estroff. 2003. "The dangers of loneliness." *Psychology Today*, July 1. https://www.psychologytoday.com/articles/200307/the-dangers-loneliness. Retrieved August 30, 2017.

Marr, Garry. 2016. "'Bequest Boom': Canadian parents will pass on $750 billion to kids over next decade." *Financial Post*, June 6.

Martin, Nick. 2016. "Canadian schools 'unsafe' for LGBTQ students, U of W researcher says." *Winnipeg Free Press*, July 8. https://www.winnipegfreepress.com/breakingnews/most-schools-want-to-improve-conditions-for-lgbttq-students-survey-386019291.html.

Masci, David. 2016. "Q & A: Why millennials are less religious than older Americans." Washington, DC: Pew Research Center, January 8. http://www.pewresearch.org/fact-tank/2016/01/08/qa-why-millennials-are-less-religious-than-older-americans. Retrieved August 1, 2017.

Matthews, Dona. 2017. "Turn off that smartphone, mom and dad!" *Psychology Today*, November 23. https://www.psychologytoday.com/ca/blog/going-beyond-intelligence/201711/turn-smartphone-mom-and-dad. Retrieved June 13, 2018.

Maynard, Robyn. 2017. *Policing Black lives: State violence in Canada from slavery to the present.* Winnipeg: Fernwood Books.

Mauss, Armand. 1975. *Social problems as social movements.* Pp. 38–71. Philadelphia: Lippincott.

McDaniel, Susan A. 2001. "Born at the right time? Gendered Generations and Webs of Entitlement and Responsibility." *The Canadian Journal of Sociology* 26(2):193–214.

McLinden, Amber. 2017. "The divide over pride: Calgary Pride's 'uniform ban' incites clash of opinions." *Calgary Journal*, August 30. https://www.calgaryjournal.ca/index.php/news/3756-the-divide-over-pride-calgary-pride-s-niform-ban-incites-clash-of-opinions. Retrieved October 5, 2017.

McMahon, Darrin. 2017. "A happiness historian explains why even happy lives involve pain." *Purpose*, August 7. https://www.thriveglobal.com/stories/11052-a-happiness-historian-explains-why-even-happy-lives-involve-pain. Retrieved August 2, 2017.

McNichol, Tom. 2011. "God and baseball." Huffpost. May 25. http://www.huffingtonpost.com/tom-mcnichol/god-and-baseball_b_71753.html. Retrieved September 16.

Milan, Anne. 2015. *Marital status: Overview, 2011*. Ottawa: Statistics Canada. Catalogue 91-209-X. November 30. http://www.statcan.gc.ca/pub/91-209-x/2013001/article/11788-eng.htm.

Milkman, Ruth. 2016. "A new political generation: Millennials and the post-2008 wave of protest." *American Sociological Review* 82(1):1–31.

Miller, Therese. 2008. "Sport and spirituality: A comparative perspective." *The Sports Journal*, July 7. http://thesportjournal.org/article/sport-and-spirituality-a-comparative-perspective. Retrieved September 16, 2017.

Mills, C. Wright. 1959. *The sociological imagination*. New York: Oxford University Press.

Minganti, Pia Karlsson. 2010. "Islamic revival and young women's negotiations on gender and racism." Pp. 115–122 in *Religion and youth*, edited by Sylvia Collins-Mayo and Pink Dandelion. Burlington, VT: Ashgate.

Moody, Katharine Sarah and Randall W. Reed. 2017. "Emerging Christianity and religious identity." *Journal for the Scientific Study of Religion* 56:33–40.

Moyser, Melissa. 2017. *Women in Canada: A gender-based statistical report*. Catalogue 89-593-X. Ottawa: Statistics Canada. http://publications.gc.ca/Collection/Statcan/89-593-X/89-593-XIE2003001.pdf. Retrieved October 9, 2017.

Mueller, Anna, and Seth Abrutyn. 2016. "Adolescents under pressure: A new Durkheimian framework for understanding adolescent suicide in a cohesive community." *American Sociological Review* 81(5):877–899.

Murphy, Caryle. 2015. "Lesbian, gay and bisexual Americans differ from general public in their religious affiliations." Pew Research Center. May 26. http://www.pewresearch.org/fact-tank/2015/05/26/lesbian-gay-and-bisexual-americans-differ-from-general-public-in-their-religious-affiliations. Retrieved June 20, 2018.

Naisbitt, John. 2008. Interview on predicting the future. YouTube. https://www.youtube.com/watch?v=4QLFObhKoXI. Retrieved April 15, 2017.

Narayan, Shoba. 2013. "The Dalai Lama says female leaders are more compassionate … Hmmm." *The Atlantic*, June 13. https://www.theatlantic. com/sexes/archive/2013/06/the-dalai-lama-says-female-leaders-are-more-compassionate-hmm/276843. Retrieved August 20, 2017.

Nettler, Gwynn. 1976. *Social concerns*. Toronto: McGraw-Hill.

Nielsen Consumer Insights. 2016. "2015 national youth survey." http://inspirerlademocratie-inspiredemocracy.ca/rsch/yth/nysr15/nys-e .pdf. Retrieved June 7, 2018.

Norris, Doug. 2016. *Millennials: The newest, biggest and most diverse target market*. Presented at the 9th Annual User Conference. Toronto: Environics. http://www.environicsanalytics.ca/docs/default-source/ eauc2015-presentations/dougnorris- afternoonplenary.pdf? sfvrsn=6%20. Retrieved August 23, 2017.

North Studio. 2014. "5 Facts about Millennials every marketer should know." Blog, July 8. https://www.northstudio.com/blog/5-facts-about-millennials-every-marketer-should-know. Retrieved October 6, 2017.

Ogburn, William F. 1966. *Social change: With respect to cultural and original nature*. Oxford: Delta Books. Originally published in 1922.

Ontario Women's Justice Network. 2017. "Sexting and the law about haring intimate images." August 24. http://owjn.org/2016/08/sexting-and-the-law-about-sharing-intimate-images. Retrieved September 2, 2017.

Opstart. 2017. "13 Stats and facts about online shopping in Canada." https://www.opstart.ca/13-stats-facts-online-shopping-canada-2. Retrieved August 17, 2017.

Pakula, Basia, Jean Shoveller, Pamela A. Ratner, and Richard Carpiano. 2016. "Prevalence and co-occurrence of heavy drinking and anxiety and mood disorders among gay, lesbian, bisexual, and heterosexual Canadians." *American Journal of Public Health*, June.

Parry, Jim, Simon Robinson, Nick Watson, and Mark Nesti. 2007. *Sport and spirituality: An introduction*. London: Routledge.

Paulsen, Pat. 2017. "Pat Paulsen's 1960's television editorials." http:// www.paulsen.com/editorials.html. Retrieved September 1, 2017.

Penner, James, Rachel Harder, Erika Anderson, Bruno Désorcy, and Rick Hiemstra. 2011. *Hemorrhaging faith: Why and when Canadian young adults are leaving, staying and returning to church.* http://tgcfcanada .org/hemorrhagingfaith/. Retrieved September 20, 2012.

Perreault, Samuel. 2015. "Criminal victimization in Canada, 2014." Ottawa: Statistics Canada. http://www.statcan.gc.ca/pub/85-002-x/ 2015001/article/14241-eng.htm#n22-refa.

Pew Research Center. 2010. "Millennials, a portrait of generation next: Confident. Connected. Open to Change." February. http://assets .pewresearch.org/wp-content/uploads/sites/3/2010/10/millennials-confident-connected-open-to-change.pdf. Retrieved August 18, 2017.

Pew Research Center. 2015a. *The future of world religions: Population growth projections, 2010–2050.* April 2. http://www.pewforum .org/2015/04/02/religious-projections-2010-2050. Retrieved October 12, 2017.

Pew Research Center. 2015b. *The whys and hows of generation research.* September 3. http://www.people-press.org/2015/09/03/the-whys-and-hows-of-generations-research. Retrieved September 21, 2017.

Pew Research Center. 2017a. *Changing attitudes on gay marriage.* June 26. http://www.pewforum.org/fact-sheet/changing-attitudes-on-gay-marriage. Retrieved September 22, 2017.

Pew Research Center. 2017b. "More Americans now say they're spiritual but not religious." September 6. http://www.pewresearch.org/fact-tank/2017/09/06/more-americans-now-say-theyre-spiritual-but-not-religious. Retrieved September 16, 2017.

Pew Research Center. 2018. "Defining generations: Where Millennials end and post-Millennials begin." March 1. http://www.pewresearch .org/fact-tank/2018/03/01/defining-generations-where-millennials-end-and-post-millennials-begin. Retrieved June 13, 2018.

Pickhardt, Carl E. 2011. "Adolescence and parental approval." *Psychology Today*, March 14. https://www.psychologytoday.com/blog/surviving-your-childs-adolescence/201103/adolescence-and-parental-approval. Retrieved September 11, 2017.

Potkins, Meghan. 2017. "On the Blood reserve, progress in the fight against opioid addiction and deaths." *Calgary Herald*, May 24. http://

calgaryherald.com/news/local-news/provincial-and-federal-officials-get-update-on-blood-reserves-fentanyl-fight. Retrieved October 15, 2017.

Powell, Kara, Jake Mulder, and Brad Griffin. 2016. *Growing young: Six essential strategies to help young people discover and love your church.* Grand Rapids, MI: Baker Books.

Price, Michael. 2016. "Millennials less sexually active than Gen-X peers." SDSU NewsCenter. August 02, 2016. http://newscenter.sdsu.edu/sdsu_newscenter/news_story.aspx?sid=76257. Retrieved February 26, 2019.

Pullin, Zachary. 2014. "Two Spirit: The story of a movement unfolds." *Native Peoples*, May-June. http://www.nativepeoples.com/Native-Peoples/May-June-2014/Two-Spirit-The-Story-of-a-Movement-Unfolds. Retrieved October 4, 2017.

Ravanera, Zenaida, Fernando Rajulton, and Pierre Turcotte. 2003. "Youth integration and social capital: An analysis of the Canadian General Social Survey on time use." *Youth and Society* 35(2):158–182.

Ray, Julie. Gallup, 2016. "Billions world-wide help others in need." Gallup: Washington, DC. http://www.gallup.com/poll/195659/billions-world-wide-help-others-need.aspx. Retrieved August 27.

Reid, Angus. 2017. "How we poll." Vancouver: Angus Reid Institute. http://angusreid.org/how-we-poll-ari. Retrieved October 20.

Reimer, Sam, and Rick Hiemstra. 2018. "The gains/losses of Canadian religious groups from immigration: Immigration flows, attendance and switching." *Studies in Religion* 47, 3:327–344.

Reitz, Jeffrey, Rupa Banerjee, Mai Phan, and Jordan Thompson. 2009. "Race, religion, and the social ntegration of new immigrant minorities in Canada." *International Migration Review* 43(4):695–726.

Robaton, Anna. 2016. "Preparing for the $30 trillion great wealth transfer." CNBC, November 30. https://www.cnbc.com/2016/11/29/preparing-for-the-30-trillion-great-wealth-transfer.html. Retrieved October 18, 2017.

Robert, Anne-Marie, and Tara Gilkinson. 2012. "Mental health and well-being of recent immigrants to Canada." Ottawa: Department of

Citizenship and Immigration." http://www.cic.gc.ca/english/pdf/ research-stats/mental-health.pdf. Retrieved August 30, 2017.

Rokeach, Milton. 1973. *The nature of human values*. New York: Free Press.

Ruksana, Rashid, David Gregory, Abdie Kazemipur, and Lynn Scruby. 2013. "Immigration journey: a holistic exploration of pre- and post-migration life stories in a sample of Canadian immigrant women." *International Journal of Migration, Health & Social Care*. 9 (4): 189–202.

Russell, Andrew. 2016. "Fentanyl overdoses killed hundreds of Canadians this year." Global News, December 13, 2016. https://globalnews.ca/ news/3122510/fentanyl-overdoses-killed-hundreds-of-canadians-this-year-experts-say-2017-could-be-deadlier. Accessed October 15, 2017.

Samara Canada. 2016. "Can you hear me now? Young people and the 2015 federal election." October 19. https://www.samaracanada.com/research/ active-citizenship/can-you-hear-me-now. Retrieved June 7, 2018.

Satzewich, Vic. 2011. *Issues in Canada: Racism in Canada*. Don Mills, ON: Oxford University Press.

Schwadel, Philip. 2010. "Period and cohort effects on religious non-affiliation and religious disaffiliation." *Journal for the Scientific Study of Religion* 49(2), 311–319.

Schwartz, Barry. 2004. *The paradox of choice – Why more is less*. New York: Harper.

Semley, John. 2017. "Cleaning up the devil's playground: Contemporary Christian cinema comes to Canada." *Globe and Mail*, April 27. https:// beta.theglobeandmail.com/arts/film/cleaning-up-the-devils-playground-contemporary-christian-cinema-comes-tocanada/ article34828207/?ref=http://www.theglobeandmail.com&

Seppala, Emma M. 2013. "Are women really more compassionate?" *Psychology Today* blog, June 20. https://www.psychologytoday.com/blog/ feeling-it/201306/are-women-really-more-compassionate. Retrieved August 20, 2017.

Sheldon, Peter, with Zia Daniell Wigder, Jeff Wray, Lily Varon, and Rebecca Katz. 2014. "Canadian online retail forecasts, 2014 to 2019." Forrester. October 14. https://www.forrester.com/report/Canadian+

Online+Retail+Forecast+2014+To+2019/-/E-RES115497. Retrieved August 17, 2017.

Shulevitz, Judith. 2013. "The lethality of loneliness." *New Republic.* May 12. https://newrepublic.com/article/113176/science-loneliness-how-isolation-can-kill-you. Retrieved August 30, 2017.

Siegel, Harry. 2013. "Why the choice to be childless is bad for America." *Newsweek*, February 19. http://www.newsweek.com/why-choice-be-childless-bad-america-63335. Retrieved September 10, 2017.

Silva, Jennifer. 2014. "Slight expectations: Making sense of the 'Me Me Me' generation." *Sociology Compass* 8(12): 1388–1397.

Simon, Jessica K. and Megan McDonald Way. 2016. "Why the gap? Determinants of self-employment earnings differentials for male and female millennials in the US." *Journal of Family Economic Issues* 37 (2):297–312.

Sinek, Simon. 2016. "Millennials in the workplace." YouTube. https://www.youtube.com/watch?v=hER0Qp6QJNU. Retrieved April 12, 2017.

Sinha, Maire. 2015. "Canadian identity, 2013." Catalogue no. 89-652-X. Ottawa: Statistics Canada. https://www150.statcan.gc.ca/n1/pub/89-652-x/89-652-x2015005-eng.htm Retrieved June 18, 2018.

Slaughter, Anne-Marie. 2012. "Why Women Still Can't Have It All." *The Atlantic*, July/August. https://www.theatlantic.com/magazine/archive/2012/07/why-women-still-cant-have-it-all/309020. Retrieved October 10, 2017.

Smith, Aaron, and Monica Anderson. 2016. "Online shopping and e-commerce." Washington, DC: Pew Research Center. December 19. http://www.pewinternet.org/2016/12/19/online-shopping-and-e-commerce. Accessed August 17, 2017.

Smith, Christian, and Melina Lundquist Denton. 2005. *Soul Searching.* New York: Oxford University Press.

Smith, Christian, with Patricia Snell. 2009. *Souls in transition: The religious and spiritual lives of emerging adults.* New York: Oxford University Press.

Smith, Christian, with Kari Christoffersen, Hilary Davison, and Patricia Snell Herzog. 2011. *Lost in transition: The dark side of emerging adulthood.* New York: Oxford University Press.

Smith, Christie, and Stephanie Turner. 2015. *The radical transformation of diversity and inclusion: The millennial influence.* New York: Deloitte University Leadership Center for Inclusion. https://www2.deloitte.com/content/dam/Deloitte/us/Documents/about-deloitte/us-inclus-millennial-influence-120215.pdf. Retrieved September 9.

Sonnenblume, Kollibri Terre. 2016. CounterPunch.org. "Dear fellow GenXers: Let's step aside for the Millennials. October 21. https://www.counterpunch.org/2016/10/21/dear-fellow-gen-xers-lets-step-aside-for-the-millennials. Retrieved October 1, 2017.

Special Advisory Committee on the Epidemic of Opioid Overdoses. 2018. *National report: Apparent opioid-related deaths in Canada (January 2016 to December 2017) Web-based Report.* June. Ottawa: Public Health Agency of Canada. https://www.canada.ca/en/public-health/services/publications/healthy-living/national-report-apparent-opioid-related-deaths-released-june-2018.html. Retrieved June 21, 2018.

Sprott, Jane, and Anthony Doob. 2014. "Confidence in the police: Variation across groups classified as visible minorities." *Canadian Journal of Criminology and Criminal Justice.* 56(3):367–379.

Statistics Canada. 2011. "Mixed unions in Canada." Catalogue 99-010-X. June 17. https://www.statcan.gc.ca/daily-quotidien/140617/dq140617b-eng.htm. Retrieved September 23, 2017.

Statistics Canada. 2015a. "Same-sex couples and sexual orientation ... by the numbers." *The Daily.* June 25. http://www.statcan.gc.ca/eng/dai/smr08/2015/smr08_203_2015. Retrieved August 10, 2017.

Statistics Canada. 2015b. "Table 6. Crude marriage rate and crude divorce rate, Canada, 1926 to 2008." Catalogue 89-503-X. November 30. http://www.statcan.gc.ca/pub/89-503-x/2010001/article/11546/c-g/c-g006-eng.htm. Retrieved September 6, 2017.

Statistics Canada. 2015c. "Table 1. Generations in Canada, 2011." December 21. http://www12.statcan.gc.ca/census-recensement/2011/as-sa/98-311-x/2011003/tbl/tbl3_2-1-eng.cfm. Retrieved October 17, 2017.

Statistics Canada. 2015d. "Table 2. Percentage distribution of couples by various ethnocultural characteristics." December 22. http://www12.statcan.gc.ca/nhs-enm/2011/as-sa/99-010-x/2011003/tbl/tbl2-eng.cfm. Retrieved September 24, 2017.

Statistics Canada. 2015e. "Current smoking trends." Catalogue 82-624-X. Health at a Glance. November 27. https://www.statcan.gc.ca/pub/ 82-624-x/2012001/article/11676-eng.htm. Retrieved October 19, 2017.

Statistics Canada. 2015f. "Health. Chart 19." *Aboriginal statistics at a glance.* 2nd edition. December 24. http://www.statcan.gc.ca/pub/ 89-645-x/89-645-x2015001-eng.htm.

Statistics Canada. 2016a. "Reasons for not voting in the federal election, October 19, 2015." *The Daily*, February 22. https://www.statcan.gc.ca/ daily-quotidien/160222/dq160222a-eng.htm. Retrieved October 15, 2017.

Statistics Canada. 2016b. "150 years of immigration in Canada." *The Daily*, June 29. http://www.statcan.gc.ca/pub/11-630-x/11-630-x2016006-eng.htm. Retrieved August 23, 2017.

Statistics Canada. 2016c. "Police-reported crime statistics, 2015." *The Daily*. July 20. http://www.statcan.gc.ca/daily-quotidien/160720/ dq160720a-eng.htm. Retrieved August 28, 2017.

Statistics Canada. 2016d. "Immigration and ethnocultural diversity in Canada." Catalogue 99-010-X. September 25. http://www12.statcan .gc.ca/nhs-enm/2011/as-sa/99-010-x/99-010-x2011001-eng.cfm. Retrieved August 23, 2017.

Statistics Canada. 2016e. "Ethnic diversity and immigration." Catalogue 11-402-X. October 7. http://www.statcan.gc.ca/pub/11-402-x/ 2011000/chap/imm/imm-eng.htm. Retrieved August 14, 2017.

Statistics Canada. 2016f. "Understanding the increase in voting rates between the 2011 and 2015 federal elections." October 12. https:// www150.statcan.gc.ca/n1/en/pub/75-006-x/2016001/article/ 14669-eng.pdf?st=LxIPa5XY. Retrieved June 7, 2018.

Statistics Canada. 2017a. *Immigration and diversity: Population projections for Canada and its regions, 2011 to 2036.* January 25, 2017. http:// www.statcan.gc.ca/pub/91-551-x/91-551-x2017001-eng.htm. Re- trieved November 11, 2017.

Statistics Canada. 2017b. "Table 206-0052: Income of individuals by age group, sex and income source, Canada, provinces and selected cen- sus metropolitan areas." May 26. http://www5.statcan.gc.ca/cansim/ a26?lang=eng&id=2060052&p2=33. Retrieved October 9, 2017.

Statistics Canada. 2017c. "Same-sex couples in Canada in 2016." Census in Brief. August 2. http://www12.statcan.gc.ca/census-recensement/2016/as-sa/98-200-x/2016007/98-200-x2016007-eng.cfm. Retrieved November 11, 2017.

Statistics Canada. 2017d. "Young adults living with their parents in Canada in 2016." Ottawa: Statistics Canada. August 2. http://www12.statcan.gc.ca/census-recensement/2016/as-sa/98-200-x/2016008/98-200-x2016008-eng.cfm. Retrieved August 25, 2017.

Statistics Canada 2017e. "Families, households and marital status: Key results from the 2016 Census." August 2, 2017. http://www.statcan.gc.ca/daily-quotidien/170802/dq170802a-eng.pdf. Retrieved September 19, 2017.

Statistics Canada. 2017f. "Study: International students, immigration and earnings growth." The Daily, August 22. http://www.statcan.gc.ca/daily-quotidien/170822/dq170822c-eng.htm. Retrieved August 23, 2017.

Statistics Canada. 2017g. "Same-sex couples in Canada in 2016." Census in Brief. August 2. http://www12.statcan.gc.ca/census-recensement/2016/as-sa/98-200-x/2016007/98-200-x2016007-eng.cfm. Retrieved November 11, 2017.

Statistics Canada, 2017h. "Canadian Community Health Survey, 2016." The Daily, September 27. https://www150.statcan.gc.ca/n1/daily-quotidien/170927/dq170927a-eng.htm. Retrieved June 19, 2018.

Statistics Canada 2017i. "Aboriginal peoples in Canada: Key results from the 2016 census." The Daily, October 25. http://www.statcan.gc.ca/daily-quotidien/171025/dq171025a-eng.htm. Retrieved November 11, 2017.

Statistics Canada 2017j. "Diverse family characteristics of Aboriginal children aged 0-4." Census in Brief. October 25. http://www12.statcan.gc.ca/census-recensement/2016/as-sa/98-200-x/2016020/98-200-x2016020-eng.cfm. Retrieved November 11, 2017.

Statistics Canada 2017k. "The housing conditions of Aboriginal people in Canada." Census in Brief. October 25. http://www12.statcan.gc.ca/census-recensement/2016/as-sa/98-200-x/2016021/98-200-x2016021-eng.cfm. Retrieved November 11, 2017.

Statistics Canada, 2017l. "Life in the fast lane: How are Canadians managing? 2016." *The Daily.* November 14. www150.statcan.gc.ca/n1/en/daily-quotidien/171114/dq171114a-eng.pdf?st= C8UpcQ0z. Retrieved June 19, 2018.

Statistics Canada. 2018. *A portrait of Canadian youth.* February 7. Catalogue 11-631-X. https://www150.statcan.gc.ca/n1/pub/11-631-x/11-631-x2018001-eng.htm. Retrieved June 21, 2018.

Steeves, Valerie. 2014. "Young Canadians in a wired world, Phase III: Sexuality and romantic relationships in a digital age." Ottawa: MediaSmarts. http://mediasmarts.ca/sites/mediasmarts/files/pdfs/publication-report/full.pdf. Retrieved September 22, 2017.

Stein, Joel. 2013. "Millennials: The me me me generation." *Time,* May 20. http://time.com/247/millennials-the-me-me-me-generation. Retrieved October 16, 2017.

Stockland, Peter. 2017. "Start the revolution without me." *Convivium,* July 28. https://www.convivium.ca/articles/start-the-revolution-without-me? Retrieved October 2, 2017.

Strauss, William, and Neil Howe. 2009. *Millennials rising.* New York: Vintage.

Tait, Carrie. 2017. "Two-spirit is a different conversation." *Globe and Mail,* September 1. https://beta.theglobeandmail.com/news/alberta/calgary-pride-indigenous-lgbtq-two-spirit/article36154435/?ref=http://www.theglobeandmail.com&. Retrieved October 4, 2017.

Tannenbaum, Rob. 2012. "*Playboy* interview: Chad Kroeger. *Playboy.* March 7. http://www.playboy.com/articles/playboy-interview-chad-kroeger. Retrieved August 16, 2017.

Tasker, John Paul. 2017. "Governor General apologizes for saying Indigenous people were immigrants." CBC News, June 19. http://www.cbc.ca/news/politics/governor-general-apologizes-indigenous-immigrants-1.4167348. Retrieved August 1, 2017.

Taylor, Catherine, and Tracey Peter. 2011. *Every class in every school: Final report on the first national climate survey on homophobia, biphobia, and transphobia in Canadian Schools.* Toronto: Egale Canada Human Rights Trust. https://www.uwinnipeg.ca/rise/docs/climate-survey-exec-summary.pdf. Accessed October 11, 2017.

Terry, Deborah J., and Michael A. Hogg (eds.). 2000. *Attitudes, behavior, and social context: The role of norms and group membership.* Mahwah, NJ: Lawrence Erlbaum Associates.

Thiessen, Gordon. 2000. "The outlook for the Canadian economy and the conduct of monetary policy." Remarks of the Governor of the Bank of Canada to the Calgary Chamber of Commerce. September 14. http://www.bankofcanada.ca/wp-content/uploads/2010/01/sp00-5.pdf. Retrieved August 1, 2017.

Thiessen, Joel. 2015. *The meaning of Sunday: The practice of belief in a secular age.* Montreal: McGill-Queen's University Press.

Thompson, Clive. 2013. "The dumbest generation? No, Twitter is making kids smarter." *Globe and Mail*, September 13. https://beta.theglobeandmail.com/life/how-new-digital-tools-are-making-kids-smarter/article14321886/?ref=http://www.theglobeandmail.com&. Retrieved October 16, 2017.

Thompson, Derek. 2013. "The unluckiest generation: What will become of Millennials?" *The Atlantic*, April 26. https://www.theatlantic.com/business/archive/2013/04/The-unluckiest-generation-what-will-become-of-millennials/275336. Retrieved August 21, 2017.

Thompson, Derek. 2018. "Why NFL ratings are plummeting: A two-part theory." *The Atlantic*, February 1. https://www.theatlantic.com/business/archive/2018/02/super-bowl-nfl-ratings-decline/551861. Retrieved June 16, 2018.

Thorbecke, Catherine. 2017. "Honolulu passes law that makes texting while crossing the street illegal." ABC News, October 25. https://abcnews.go.com/US/honolulu-passes-law-makes-texting-crossing-street-illegal/story?id=50695394. Retrieved June 18, 2018.

Todd, Douglas. 2013. "Three of 10 Canadian bestsellers cover spirituality." *Vancouver Sun*, January 8. http://vancouversun.com/news/staff-blogs/three-of-top-10-bestselling-books-by-canadians-cover-spirituality. Retrieved September 16, 2017.

Todd, Douglas. 2017. "Exaggerating racism." *Vancouver Sun*, April 1. http://vancouversun.com/opinion/columnists/douglas-todd-exaggerating-extent-of-racism-is-all-too-easy. Retrieved October 1, 2017.

Toronto Star. 2017. "Justin Trudeau must match welcome UN remarks on Indigenous reconciliation with deeds: Editorial." September 22. https://www.thestar.com/opinion/editorials/2017/09/21/justin-trudeau-must-match-welcome-un-remarks-on-indigenous-reconciliation-with-deeds-editorial.html. Retrieved October 1, 2017.

Troster, Ariel. 2010. "The Canadian war on queer workers." *Our Times* 29.3, June-July. http://ourtimes.ca/Features/article_127.php. Retrieved September 3, 2017.

Trudeau, Justin. 2015. "Official response to the Final Report of the Truth and Reconciliation Commission of Canada." December 15. Ottawa: Prime Minister of Canada. http://www.pm.gc.ca/eng/news/2015/12/15/ final-report-truth-and-reconciliation-commission-Canada. Retrieved August 10, 2017.

Truth and Reconciliation Commission of Canada: Calls to Action. 2015. Winnipeg. http://www.trc.ca/websites/trcinstitution/File/2015/Findings/Calls_to_Action_English2.pdf.

Tucker, Erika. 2017. "Lethbridge's pride rainbow crosswalk smeared with manure, rust paint." Global News Lethbridge, June 15. http://globalnews.ca/news/3530845/lethbridges-pride-rainbow-crosswalk-smeared-with-manure-rust-paint. Retrieved August 1.

Turcotte, Martin. 2015. "Civic engagement and political participation in Canada." *Statistics Canada.* http://publications.gc.ca/site/eng/9.802523/publication.html. Retrieved October 15, 2017.

Twenge, Jean M. 2014. *Generation me: Why today's young Americans are more confident, assertive, entitled — and more miserable than ever before.* New York: Atria Paperback.

Twenge, Jean M., Ryne A. Sherman, and Brooke E. Wells. 2015. "Changes in American adults' sexual behavior and attitudes, 1972–2012." *Archives of Sexual Behavior* 44, 8:2273–2285.

Twenge, Jean M. 2017. "Have smartphones destroyed a generation?" *The Atlantic*, September. https://www.theatlantic.com/magazine/archive/2017/09/has-the-smartphone-destroyed-a-generation/534198/. Retrieved September 4, 2017.

Ubelacker, Sheryl. 2017. "The inside history of Canada's opioid crisis."

Maclean's, April 25. http://www.macleans.ca/society/inside-the-history-of-canadas-opioid-crisis. Retrieved October 14, 2017.

UNews. 2017. "Vasey's gender studies research featured in *National Geographic* magazine, documentary." University of Lethbridge, February 2. https://www.uleth.ca/unews/article/vasey%E2%80%99s-gender-studies-research-featured-national-geographic-magazine-documentary#.WazvCWxK2HJ. Retrieved September 4, 2017.

Valtchanov, Bronwen L., and Diana C. Parry. 2017. "I like my peeps: Diversifying the net generation's digital leisure." *Leisure Sciences* 39(4):336–354.

Vancouver, City of. 2017. "Being and feeling safe and included." http://vancouver.ca/people-programs/being-and-feeling-safe-and-included.aspx. Retrieved August 28, 2017.

VandenBeukel, Jason. 2016. "Jordan Peterson: The man who reignited Canada's culture war." December 1. *C2C Journal.* http://www.c2cjournal.ca/2016/12/jordan-peterson-the-man-who-reignited-canadas-culture-war/?. Retrieved September 4, 2017.

Vision Critical. 2016. *The everything guide to millennials.* Vancouver: Vision Critical Communications. https://www.visioncritical.com/wp-content/uploads/2016/07/The_Everything_Guide_To_Millennial_eBook.pdf. Retrieved September 4, 2017.

Ward, David. 2013. "Former Super Bowl MVP Kurt Warner talks about faith, football and reality TV show." Deseret News, February 2. https://www.deseretnews.com/article/865571825/Former-Super-Bowl-MVP-Kurt-Warner-talks-about-faith-football-and-reality-TV-show.html. Retrieved September 16.

Watts-Smith, Candis, and Sarah Mayorga-Gallo. 2017. "The new principle-policy gap: How diversity ideology subverts diversity initiatives." *Sociological Perspectives* 60(5): 889–911.

Wells, H.G. 2009. *The discovery of the future (1913).* Republished, Whitefish, MT: Kessinger Publishing.

Wells, Paul. 2017. "Can Ottawa stop Canada's deadly opioid crisis?" *Maclean's* November. http://www.macleans.ca/politics/ottawa/can-ottawa-stop-canadas-deadly-opioid-crisis. Retrieved October 19, 2017.

Williams, Malayna. 2017. "Confronting Canada's ugly record of anti-blackness." *Maclean's*, September 19. http://www.macleans.ca/news/canada/confronting-canadas-ugly-record-of-anti-blackness. Retrieved September 30.

Worth, Nancy. 2016. "Who we are at work: Millennial women, everyday inequalities and insecure work." *Gender, Place and Culture* 23(9):1302–1314.

Wortley, Scot, and Akwasi Owusu-Bempah. 2009. "Unequal before the law: Immigrant and racial minority perceptions of the Canadian criminal justice system." *Journal of International Migration & Integration* 10(4):447–473. http://publications.gc.ca/site/eng/9.802523/publication.html.

Wuthnow, Robert. 2007. After the baby boomers. Princeton: Princeton University Press.

Zacharek, Stephanie, Eliana Dockterman, and Haley Sweetland Edwards. 2017. "Person of the Year 2017." *Time*. December 18. http://time.com/time-person-of-the-year-2017-silence-breakers. Retrieved June 17, 2018.

Zakaria, Fareed. 2015. "The try-hard generation." *The Atlantic*, June 20. https://www.theatlantic.com/education/archive/2015/06/in-defense-of-a-try-hard-generation/394535. Retrieved October 15, 2017.

Zick, Cathleen D. 2010. "The shifting balance of adolescent time use." *Youth and Society* 41 (4): 569–596.

INDEX

Figures are in italics, Tables are in bold.

ABOUT THE AUTHORS

Reginald W. Bibby, O.C., Ph.D., is a professor of sociology at the University of Lethbridge. The author of some seventeen books, he has been monitoring adult and youth social trends in Canada for more than four decades.

Joel Thiessen, Ph.D., is a full professor in sociology at Ambrose University in Calgary. His specialties include religion, family, youth, and Canadian culture. His many publications include books with Oxford, McGill-Queen's, and New York University Press.

Monetta Bailey, Ph.D., is a recent graduate of the University of Calgary who worked for a time with troubled youth in Alberta. She is also at Ambrose University, where she is an assistant professor in sociology, specializing in racialized youth, immigration, gender, and crime.

Book Credits

Managing Editor: Elena Radic
Editorial Assistant: Melissa Kawaguchi
Copy Editor: Karri Yano
Proofreader: Crissy Calhoun
Indexer: Sergey Lobachev

Designer: Laura Boyle

Publicist: Elham Ali